THE FIRST COUNCIL OF THE VATICAN

THE FIRST COUNCIL OF THE VATICAN: THE AMERICAN EXPERIENCE

JAMES HENNESEY, S.J.

HERDER AND HERDER

1963
HERDER AND HERDER   New York
232 Madison Avenue, New York 16, N.Y.

Imprimi potest: John J. McGinty, S.J.
Provincial, New York Province
Nihil obstat: Edward J. Sutfin, Ph.D.
Censor librorum
Imprimatur: † Robert F. Joyce
Bishop of Burlington
June 22, 1963

Library of Congress Catalogue Card Number: 63–18150

23346

TO MY PARENTS
CHARLES GREGORY HENNESEY
AND
ANNA LUDLOW HENNESEY
AND IN MEMORY OF
LORETTA BEGGANS HENNESEY

CONTENTS

Foreword

"OF all the prelates at Rome, none have a finer opportunity, to none is a more crucial test now applied, than to those of the United States." Deeply depressed by the fear that the First Vatican Council would endorse the *Syllabus of Errors,* and by the more certain prospect that the fathers would define the pope's infallibility, it was as though William Ewart Gladstone were staking his final hope on the Americans to turn the tide when he addressed these words to Lord Acton in the early summer of 1870. Alas, the Americans did not measure up to Gladstone's test, for in the final vote on July 18 twenty-five bishops from the United States were counted in favor of papal infallibility, twenty-two either absented themselves from the closing session or had already left for home, and one, Edward Fitzgerald, Bishop of Little Rock, Arkansas, joined the Bishop of Cajazzo in southern Italy to provide the only two votes registered against the definition.

At a time when American interest has been quickened by the presence of more than 200 bishops from the United States who constitute the second largest national delegation in the Second Vatican Council, it is a decided advantage for the educated reading public to have at hand in Father Hennesey's work a lively and thoroughly documented account of American participation in the council of 1869–1870. True, the representatives of the United States (forty-eight bishops and one abbot) achieved no such prominence as that of some of their brother prelates from France and Germany, the traditional rank and theological heritage of whose churches were much older and richer than those of the American Catholics. Yet the American contribution to the stirring debates of that historic winter and spring was not negligible. In fact, the American contribution had begun more than a year before the opening of the council when James A. Corcoran, a priest of the Diocese of Charleston, arrived in Rome as the sole representative of the United States among the approximately 100 theologians, canon lawyers, and other ecclesiastical scholars whose task it was to prepare the various schemata for the use of the bishops.

Dr. Corcoran was both a keen observer and a conscientious reporter of the currents of thought in the preparatory commissions. Soon after his arrival he informed James Gibbons, the future cardinal, that he felt the subject matter being proposed would "create animated and prolonged discussion" in the council. And revealing a good prophetic sense, he added, "Theologians here may have considered them all cut and dry and simply ready for acceptance. But the Bishops, many of them at least, will think otherwise. . . . " Many of the American bishops did, indeed, think otherwise with their thoughts ranging all the way from the conservative Bishop William Henry Elder of Natchez who assured the Archbishop of Baltimore that if manifestations of nationalism should develop in the council, "I should not want to lessen by even one voice the weight of thorough Romanism— 'Ubi Petrus ibi Ecclesia' . . . " to what some considered the Gallicanism of a man like the Sulpician Augustin Vérot, Bishop of Savannah and later of Saint Augustine in Florida.

The reader of 1963 will find a number of interesting contrasts between the attitudes of 1869 and those of his own day, for example, on ecumenism. Whereas the representatives of the other Christian churches invited in a somewhat awkward and ill-considered manner to serve at the First Vatican Council either declined or ignored the invitation, in the present council forty or more observers have occupied a conspicuous position in Saint Peter's and have reported in a highly favorable way of the sessions. The abundant sources and printed literature for the First

Vatican Council, which Father Hennesey has examined with critical perception, offered in the earlier gathering no such prospect, either before or during the conciliar sessions, as the remarkable statement of Augustine Cardinal Bea advocating universal religious freedom delivered at the annual brotherhood dinner in Rome on January 13, 1963. On that occasion he made it known that man had a right to decide freely according to his own conscience regarding his own destiny. "From this freedom is born the right and duty of man," said the cardinal, "to follow his own conscience, and it is the duty of the individual and of society to respect this freedom and right that man has to decide for himself." Furthermore, Cardinal Bea made it known that this principle would be sponsored in the second session of Vatican Council II by Secretariat for Promoting Christian Unity of which he is president.

In another aspect of the problem notable changes will be found in the language and approach of the bishops of 1869 and those of 1963. For example, a writer in a leading Catholic journal like the *Dublin Review* in October, 1868, predicting what the coming council might or might not do on a number of points, confidently asserted: "There is one thing, however, which the world may be certain the Council will *not* do; it will put forth no declaration against either the principle or the expediency of union between Church and State." And the writer was correct, for the subject had not the faintest chance of winning conciliar approval in 1869–1870. Yet the Americans at that time were basically of the same mind as their successors in 1963, for in the earlier council they were on guard lest the European concept of Church-State relations should receive endorsement at their hands, and thus they were at pains to distinguish civil and external tolerance such as obtained in their own country from the technical theological term. Nor did bishops like Thaddeus Amat of Los Angeles, Michael Domenec of Pittsburgh, and Patrick Lynch of Charleston hesitate to remonstrate strongly against the use of the word "intolerance" to define the Church's

11

attitude toward non-Catholic groups. In that connection one of the most unequivocal pronouncements ever made on the subject was prepared at this time by John B. Purcell, Archbishop of Cincinnati. When he found that he would not have an opportunity to put his views before the council he summarized them at a reception held in his honor after his return to his see city. Referring to his statement on Church and State he said:

In it I took occasion to show that ours is, I believe, the best form of human government. . . . I said that our civil constitution grants perfect liberty to every denomination of Christians . . . and that I verily believe this was infinitely better for the Catholic religion, than were it the special object of the State's patronage and protection; that all we want is a free field and no favor. . . . Truth is mighty and will prevail. . . . If they approve our religion, they will embrace it; if not they will stay away from it. I believe this is the best theory.

As it turned out, the First Vatican Council became so absorbed by the issue of papal infallibility and kindred doctrinal questions that the pastoral approach which Pope John XXIII has so strongly urged on the present council was at a disadvantage in the earlier gathering. But that did not mean that it was forgotten. Peter Richard Kenrick, Archbishop of St. Louis, for one, reminded the council on March 22, 1870, of this fact when he said: "We must remember that we have been summoned to the council not to compose a course in theology, and still less to pass judgment on philosophical systems, but to protect the faith by explaining it and condemning errors opposed to it." Doubtless many of the fathers agreed with Kenrick, but the feeling for and against infallibility was so high that all other issues suffered in consequence. And on this all-important subject the Americans were clearly divided between the two opposing camps. The redoubtable Bishop of Rochester, Bernard J. McQuaid, for example, was an inopportunist from the outset, and he was distinctly annoyed at the Jesuits and others whom he thought were pushing the definition. A week before the council opened he told the rector of his cathedral back in Rochester that "if in

12

any way the harmony of the Council is disturbed it will be by the introduction of this most unnecessary question." The harmony of the council was, to be sure, disturbed by bringing on the infallibility question, and on the opposite extreme from McQuaid stood another American, August Martin, Bishop of Natchitoches, who was in such anguish of spirit at the tactics of the inopportunists that he told his New Orleans friend, Father Napoleon Perché: ". . . we have to wrestle with a turbulent and agitated opposition, which considers all means good. Freedom of discussion is unlimited, but unlimited also is the abuse that is made of it. Some are real revolutionaries, others servile creatures of power, others more or less avowed enemies of the Holy See, others those who from their youth have sucked the poison of heresy."

The Americans had their say, then, whenever they felt disposed to say it, and that whether on the major question of papal infallibility or on ecclesiastical discipline and other topics that came before the council. To these men from the far side of the Atlantic it must have been an extraordinary experience to be personal witnesses to the great drama as first Manning of Westminster, the whip of the majority party, and then Dupanloup of Orléans, his opposite number, moved forward, was temporarily halted, or perhaps thrown back. There were days of tedium as well as moments of high excitement, and there were occasions when one might say that both were combined as on the day in early January when the Bishop of Saint Gall made a speech that prompted Bishop William Ullathorne of Birmingham to comment: "We have got home from a meeting of the Council where we were almost stunned by a Swiss bishop, who spoke for an hour, and roared as if he were talking from one mountain to another against wind and thunder."

All of this—and much more—Father Hennesey has told with engaging candor and unfailing dignity, for he never loses sight of the sacred character of the issues upon which the bishops debated and at times differed with so much vehemence and sincerity. Father Hennesey's scholarship is beyond question, his literary style attractive and compelling, and his sense of history both real and reverent. Readers of this book will find a fascinating story of the American participation in the First Vatican Council that will enlighten them concerning the participation of the bishops of today in the Church's twenty-first ecumenical council. In fine, here is the unusual combination of a first rate subject treated in a superior fashion by one who understands that if the history of the Church is to be taken seriously it must conform to the canons of scientific research, and if it is to be read with lasting profit by the children of the Church, it must be handled with reverence and respect.

JOHN TRACY ELLIS

Abbreviations

AAB   Archives of the Archdiocese of Baltimore
AAC   Archives of the Archdiocese of Cincinnati
AAD   Archives of the Archdiocese of Dublin
AAHC   Archives of All Hallows College, Dublin
AAM   Archives of the Archdiocese of Malines-Brussels
AANO   Archives of the Archdiocese of New Orleans
AANY   Archives of the Archdiocese of New York
AAS   Archives of the Archdiocese of Seattle
AASF   Archives of the Archdiocese of San Francisco
AASP   Archives of the Abbey of St. Paul outside the Walls,
       Rome
ADC   Archives of the Diocese of Charleston
ADCL   Archives of the Diocese of Cleveland
ADSA   Archives of the Diocese of St. Augustine
AIC   Archives of the Irish College, Rome
ASMP   Du Boÿs Family Archives, St.-Martin de la Place
       (Maine et Loire)
ASS   General Archives of the Society of St.-Sulpice, Paris
ASV   Vatican Secret Archives, Vatican City

Collectio Lacensis   *Acta et Decreta Sacrorum Conciliorum Recentiorum.* 5 vols. Freiburg, 1870–1900.

Conzemius Transcripts   Manuscript collection of Acton-Döllinger correspondence loaned by the Reverend Victor Conzemius, Munich.

Mansi   Joannes D. Mansi. *Sacrorum Conciliorum Nova et Amplissima Collectio.* Vols. XLIX–LIII. Ed. L. Petit and J. B. Martin. Leipzig, 1923–27.

UND   Manuscript Collections, University of Notre Dame.

Introduction

ON December 6, 1864, Pope Pius IX intimated to the cardinals at Rome his hope of summoning an ecumenical council, the first such assembly since that of Trent, 300 years before. Two and one-half years later, on June 29, 1867, in the presence of nearly five hundred bishops who had come to Rome to commemorate the eighteenth centenary of the martyrdom of Saints Peter and Paul, the pope formally announced that a council would be held; and, exactly a year later, on June 29, 1868, the bull of convocation *Aeterni Patris* was promulgated. Pius IX presided at the solemn inauguration of the twentieth ecumenical council—the First Council of the Vatican—on December 8, 1869. Nine months later the Italian army of Victor Emmanuel II occupied the Eternal City, and, on October 20, 1870, the pope adjourned the council indefinitely by the bull *Postquam Dei munere.* Its sessions were never resumed.

The story of the First Council of the Vatican has been told several times over and in several languages, but scant attention has been paid to its history as seen from an American point of view.[1] There are reasons for this. In the eighty-nine general congregations which took place between December, 1869, and September, 1870, only eight of the forty-nine American prelates in attendance ventured to speak from the rostrum. The council was set in the context of a clash between liberal and conservative tendencies in the European Church, and the Church in the United States knew little of such doctrinaire controversies. Even

[1] The only previous general study of the subject is that of Raymond J. Clancy, C.S.C., "American Prelates in the Vatican Council," *Historical Records and Studies,* XXVIII (1937), 1–135.

the possible definition of papal infallibility, focal point of much of the European discussion, was not a burning issue in the American Church. Church-State relations and the question of religious toleration were problems shared by Europeans and Americans alike, but even in these areas they had differing frames of reference. The First Vatican Council was truly ecumenical. Nevertheless, its primary emphasis was European. The bishops from the United States were novices here, the council, an introduction to their episcopal function of responsibility for the whole Church. They brought with them as their contribution their own problems and some uniquely American solutions to those problems and to others. If their impact on the council was not as marked as it might have been, their very presence was extremely significant. For the first time in the eighteen-hundred-year history of ecumenical councils the New World was represented, and the bishops of the United States were part of its delegation. The following pages tell the story of their participation in the council, and, through their eyes, the story of the council itself.[2]

One of the more pleasant tasks which confronts a writer is to make due acknowledgment of the many generous collaborators who have assisted him in his work. In the present instance, thanks must go first and foremost to the Right Reverend John Tracy Ellis of the Catholic University of America. Without his enthusiasm, help, and encouragement this study could never have been brought to completion. I am grateful also to the Very Reverend Louis Arand, S.S., and to Dr. John K. Zeender, both of the Catholic University, for their careful reading of the manuscript.

A host of fellow Jesuits in the United States and in Europe contributed generously of their time, hospitality, and help while

[2] American participation in the council really began with the fall, 1868 arrival in Rome of Dr. James A. Corcoran, the United States hierarchy's representative in the work of preparing the conciliar agenda. See James J. Hennesey, S.J., "James A. Corcoran's Mission to Rome; 1868–1869," *Catholic Historical Review,* XLVIII (July, 1962), 157–81.

the work of research and writing was in progress. This corporative expression of thanks is all too small a recompense for their fraternal charity.

It is impossible to list all the diocesan and other officials who made various archival deposits available. I can only single out for special mention the Reverend J. Joseph Gallagher and Miss Elizabeth Bradley of Baltimore; the Reverend Thomas T. McAvoy, C.S.C., of the University of Notre Dame; the Right Reverend Jeremiah J. Brennan of New York; the Very Reverend Cornelius M. Power and the Reverend John McCorkle, S.S., of Seattle; the Very Reverend Joseph L. Bernardin of Charleston; the Right Reverend Charles J. Plauché of New Orleans; the Right Reverend Joseph J. Schneider and the staff of the archives of the Archdiocese of Cincinnati; and Sister Mary Paul Fitzgerald, S.C.L., of St. Mary College, Xavier, Kansas. The Most Reverend Paul J. Hallinan not only opened the archives of the Diocese of Charleston to inspection, but also supplied information from his own research in the archives of the Diocese of Cleveland.

In Rome, Cardinal Amleto Cicognani and the Right Reverend Martino Giusti made available pertinent documents in the Vatican Archives, and two Benedictines, the Very Reverend Lambert Dunne and the Reverend Oliver Kapsner, arranged for a visit to the archives of the Abbey of St. Paul outside the Walls. One of the most important collections used was the archives of the Society of St.-Sulpice in Paris, which were placed at my disposal by the Reverend Irenee Noyé, P.S.S., who also provided an introduction to M. Jacques Gadille of the University of Dijon. M. Gadille generously supplied transcripts of the Albert du Boÿs papers. Mr. Douglas Woodruff of the London *Tablet* allowed me to use the Acton papers in his possession. The Most Reverend John Charles McQuaid, C.S.Sp., the Right Reverend John M. O'Regan, and the Reverend Kevin Condon, C.M., of Dublin, and the Very Reverend Raphael Canon Tambuyser of Malines-Brussels facilitated access to manuscripts in their custody.

19

One of the most important single contributions to the story of the American bishops at the Vatican Council was made by the Reverend Victor Conzemius, a priest of the Diocese of Luxembourg. Under the auspices of the Bavarian Academy of Science, Father Conzemius is preparing for publication the collected correspondence of Johann Ignaz Döllinger and Lord Acton at the time of the council. He lent me his manuscript and gave full permission to quote passages from the Acton-Döllinger letters which pertained to the American hierarchy.

A number of fellow American historians have also assisted in various phases of the project. The names of the Reverend Oscar Hugh Lipscomb of Mobile, and of the Reverends Michael V. Gannon of St. Augustine and Damian McElrath, O.F.M., must stand for the rest. Finally, it is impossible to enumerate the many services rendered by Mr. Fritz Samson, Librarian of Woodstock College, and his assistant, Mr. Robert Matthews. To them and to all who have in any way assisted me in this work, this small expression of gratitude is wholly inadequate.

JAMES HENNESEY, S.J.

Fordham University
College of Philosophy and Letters
Shrub Oak, New York
April 20, 1963

THE FIRST COUNCIL OF THE VATICAN

I

The Bishops Go to Rome

As the year 1869 wore on, there were signs of quickening interest in the forthcoming Vatican Council among the bishops of the United States. Archbishops Martin J. Spalding of Baltimore and John McCloskey of New York were among the first to think about plans for the trip to Rome. On February 8, the Archbishop of Baltimore inquired how many bishops from the New York area would be going, adding that he hoped to sail from Baltimore about November 1.[1] McCloskey answered that, as far as he knew, all his suffragans planned to attend the council.

However, not all the bishops were anxious to leave their dioceses for an indefinite stay abroad. One of the first to make his excuses was John Baptist Miége, S.J., Vicar Apostolic of the Indian Territory East of the Rocky Mountains. Miége thought that the problem of clearing the $100,000 debt on his newly constructed cathedral at Leavenworth, Kansas, was more pressing than attendance at the council, and in September, 1868, he asked the Jesuit General if he could be excused. His request was refused.[2] Seventy-two-year-old Bishop Augustin Blanchet of Nesqually was ultimately successful in his petition for exemption, although he had to write twice to Cardinal Barnabò before his petition was approved.[3] At least two other bishops made the

[1] AANY, A-35, Spalding to McCloskey, Baltimore, February 8, 1869.
[2] Gilbert J. Garraghan, S.J., *The Jesuits of the Middle United States* (3 vols.; New York: 1938), III, 21–2.
[3] AAS, Historical Archives, V, A. M. Blanchet Register, April 23, 1869 and August 4, 1869.

journey to Rome after having sought or received permission to absent themselves. Augustus Martin of Natchitoches told Archbishop Odin of New Orleans, in April, that he had asked Barnabò if he might stay home, remarking that they were both old men ("vieillards") who could well leave representation of the Province of New Orleans to its other four bishops.[4] Whatever the answer Martin received from Cardinal Barnabò, both he and Odin were in Rome when the council opened. Financial reasons prompted Bishop Patrick Lynch of Charleston to ask that he be excused, but he was another who decided to make the trip, after he had received permission to be absent.[5] One last comment came from William Henry Elder, Bishop of Natchez. He had also considered asking exemption, but did not do so and wrote to Spalding: "In case there should be manifestations of nationalism, I should not want to lessen by even one voice the weight of thorough Romanism—'Ubi Petrus ibi Ecclesia'—and I shall try hard to overcome what obstacles are rising before me."[6]

The final results of American participation in the council were impressive. In 1869 there were fifty-five bishops active in the United States. Forty-eight of them and one abbot, Boniface Wimmer, O.S.B., of St. Vincent's Abbey in Pennsylvania, came to Rome for the sessions. Thomas A. Becker of Wilmington; Augustin Blanchet of Nesqually; Thomas L. Grace, O.P., of St. Paul; John H. Luers of Fort Wayne; Sylvester Rosecrans of Columbus and two vicars apostolic, Joseph Machebeuf of Colorado and Utah and John Baptist Salpointe of Arizona, all active American bishops, were excused. At least three of these named priests as procurators to represent them. Isaac Hecker, C.S.P. acted for Rosecrans, John Ireland for Grace, and Bartholomew Delorme for Augustin Blanchet. Five other American

---

[4] AANO, Odin Papers, Martin to Odin, Natchitoches, April 2, 1869.
[5] ADC, Lynch Papers, Spalding to Lynch, Baltimore, April 1, 1869, and Barnabò to Lynch, Rome, September 10, 1869.
[6] AAB, 36A-G-20, Elder to Spalding, Canton, Mississippi, July 17, 1869.

24

bishops were absent: Celestin de la Hailandière, formerly of Vincennes, and Frederick Résé, still technically Bishop of Detroit, were living in retirement in Europe; James Duggan of Chicago became mentally incompetent in the spring of 1869 and was confined to an asylum; James Whelan, O.P., former Bishop of Nashville, and Michael O'Connor, who had resigned the See of Pittsburgh to enter the Society of Jesus, were living in communities of their respective religious orders. None of the five bishops consecrated in the United States while the council was in session attended any of its meetings. These bishops were: Napoleon J. Perché, consecrated titular Bishop of Abdera on March 21, who became Archbishop of New Orleans on May 26; Peter Baltes of Alton; Caspar Borgess, titular Bishop of Calydon and Administrator of Detroit; Thomas Foley, titular Bishop of Pergamum and Administrator of Chicago; and Augustine Toebbe of Covington.

The mass movement of forty-nine prelates and their secretaries to Europe demanded a certain amount of logistic planning. Three immediate problems occasioned considerable correspondence in the spring and summer of 1869. The bishops wanted to know how they would get to Rome, where they would live when they got there, and what they would need in the way of robes and vestments. This last problem must have seemed minor to Spalding's European correspondents, but, he reminded Cardinal Barnabò that many of the Americans did not possess a complete episcopal outfit,[7] not even the Archbishop of New York.

Before leaving for Rome, most of the bishops addressed pastoral letters on the council to their respective dioceses. For the most part, these letters, and the sermons which were preached on them, stressed the need for prayers that the council's work might be successful. On May 22, Archbishop Spalding published the apostolic letter of Pope Pius IX, issued on April 11, which announced a jubilee indulgence on the occasion of the

[7] AAB, Spalding Letterbook, p. 583, Spalding to Barnabò, Baltimore, March 24, 1869.

opening of the council. Spalding instructed his clergy to add the prayer of the Holy Spirit to all Masses said between June 1, 1869 and the end of the council, and that the Mass of the Holy Spirit be celebrated every Thursday, in all parish churches and college and convent chapels, for the success of the council.[8] The pastoral of Bishop Whelan of Wheeling traced the history of the church councils from that of Jerusalem in apostolic times down to the present, asked prayers for the coming twentieth council, and explained the jubilee indulgence.[9] In proclaiming the jubilee, Bishop Bayley of Newark expressed his opinion that no new definitions on matters of faith would be proposed at the council, which he thought would concern itself principally with pastoral matters.[10] More practically, John McGill, the Bishop of Richmond, was careful to stress that the requirement of the Mass of the Holy Spirit was not obligatory in the United States. He pointed out that the very wording of the Roman decree made it clear that it referred to the ecclesiastical organization of Europe, where there were collegiate churches, canonical parishes, benefices, and so on.[11]

Some of the bishops used the occasion to comment on what they felt was the lamentable state of contemporary religious life. Archbishop Joseph Sadoc Alemany, O.P., of San Francisco, devoted the first eight pages of his pastoral to a detailed and documented exposé of depravity in the ancient world, from the time of the Egyptians and Babylonians to that of the Greeks and Romans. He then added nine more pages on the iniquities of modern secret societies and concluded with a request for prayers for the council.[12] Augustin Vérot, S.S., Bishop of Savannah, struck a more optimistic note. He asked prayers, praised Pius IX for his zeal, firmness, and prudence, and addressed him-

---

[8] *Catholic Mirror,* May 22 and 29, 1869.

[9] *Catholic Mirror,* June 5, 1869.

[10] *Freeman's Journal* (New York), June 19, 1869. Bayley's pastoral letter was dated May 26, 1869.

[11] *Catholic Mirror,* July 3, 1869.

[12] AASF, Alemany Papers, *Pastoral Letter,* September 15, 1869.

self to his Protestant neighbors, inviting them to compare the Catholic Church on the eve of ecumenical council with their own denominations, which, he claimed, were more often than not marked by religious apathy and indifference.[13] One American prelate who predicted with some accuracy the intentions of the Roman authorities for the council was Bishop Williams of Boston. In a sermon delivered in Holy Cross Cathedral two days before his departure for Europe, Williams referred to the prevalent errors of the day which had been condemned by Pius IX in the Syllabus of Errors of 1864. He told the congregation that the work of the Roman assembly would be "to place these errors before the world, again to make a protest against them, and to condemn them anew."[14] Another sermon is interesting as indicative of the American frame of mind on the eve of the council. This time the preacher was not a bishop, but the Superior-General of the Paulist Fathers Isaac Hecker. He laid great stress on the infallibility of the Church, and was optimistic in his hopes, as he said:

The Catholic faith teaches that the church founded on the rock of Peter is infallible. . . . In an oecumenical council, where the universal episcopate is gathered together under the presidency of its head, the successor of Peter, as Vicar of Christ, the Catholic Church is organized for deliberation and action in the most perfect way possible.

In the same sermon he emphasized the infallibility of conciliar decisions and cited his own experience as testimony that "there is no place where there is so much freedom of opinion and discussion as Rome." He also took issue with critics of the Syllabus of Errors.

One of the best travelogues of the mass migration of the bishops was kept by Archbishop Francis Norbert Blanchet of Oregon City.[15] It started with his sixteen-day, 2800-mile trip

<hr />

13 *Banner of the South* (Augusta, Georgia), September 8, 1869.
14 Robert H. Lord, John E. Sexton, and Edward T. Harrington, *History of the Archdiocese of Boston* (3 vols.; New York: 1944), III, 30–33.
15 AAS, "Journal de l'Archevêque d'Oregoncity á Rome pour le concile oecumenique, 1869," cited hereafter as F. N. Blanchet Journal.

from Portland, Oregon, to New York City, by ship, stagecoach, and railroad. At San Francisco, Thaddeus Amat, C.M., the Bishop of Monterey–Los Angeles, joined Blanchet's small party, and together they reached New York on October 21, booking passage on the *France* which sailed on the following day. The fare from New York to Liverpool was $80.00, and the archbishop shared a cabin with the two companions who had accompanied him from Oregon, a priest and a seminarian. Among the several other clergymen aboard was Father John Ireland, who was enroute to Rome as the representative of the Bishop of St. Paul. Transatlantic sailing time was twelve and one-half days, and Blanchet records frequent rough weather and seasickness.

A diary like that of Archbishop Blanchet re-creates something of the atmosphere of the time and points up the difficulties faced by the bishops going to Rome for the council. The trip to Rome also had another aspect. In many instances it brought American bishops face to face, for the first time, with the troubled ecclesiastical scene across the Atlantic. Even a relatively well-informed prelate like Archbishop Spalding had not appreciated all the ramifications of the quarrels that were the steady diet of churchmen in most of the countries of Europe. The Archbishop of Baltimore, perhaps with a bit of rhetorical exaggeration, later dated his change of heart on the need for a definition of papal infallibility from his days aboard the *Baltimore*. Just before embarkation someone had given him a copy of a "Letter from Munich," and in Paris he read Bishop Félix Dupanloup's November 11th letter to his clergy, which Butler has characterized as "the most public and clearest popular formulation of the case of the 'Inopportunists.'"[16] Spalding asserted that this

---

[16] Cuthbert Butler, O.S.B., *The Vatican Council: The Story Told From the Inside in Bishop Ullathorne's Letters* (New York: 1930). The "Letter from Munich" was probably one of the many pamphlets which appeared in Germany in the wake of Johann Döllinger's *Der Papst und das Konzil*, published at Leipzig in 1869 under the pseudonym of "Janus."

reading persuaded him that he had been wrong in believing that Gallicanism was dead in the Church.[17]

Even more important for the future history of the council were the contacts made enroute to Rome by Peter Richard Kenrick, Archbishop of St. Louis, and Isaac Hecker, procurator for the Bishop of Columbus. Kenrick visited Ireland and Paris, and in Paris he had a chance meeting in the Cathedral of Notre Dame with the Archbishop of Westminster, Henry Edward Manning, who invited him to dinner.

For the last leg of the journey, Kenrick joined Archbishop Thomas L. Connolly, O.F.M.Cap., of Halifax, and Father Hecker. After visiting Strasbourg and Munich, they crossed the Brenner Pass, stopped at Trent, where the last general council was held, and made their way to Rome by December 1.[18] It was during this trip that Kenrick made indirect contact with Johann von Döllinger, who had by that time established himself as the chief antipapal voice in Germany. The intermediary was Hecker.

On the way to Paris, Father Hecker and Archbishop Connolly had visited London, where they met Richard Simpson, the close friend and collaborator of Lord Acton, who was in turn Döllinger's favorite disciple and a leader of the liberal party among English Catholics. Acton was then in Rome. After the Connolly-Hecker visit, Simpson wrote to him:

I have taken the liberty of giving Father Hecker, the American Paulist of New York, a letter of introduction for you. You will be very glad to know a man of such energy of character. He has great

17 AAB, 39–N–10, Draft of a letter from Spalding to Dupanloup. The letter was probably written in April, 1870. Spalding's change of heart was not as sudden as he later claimed. On December 1, 1869, he told the Sulpician Superior-General, Henri Icard, that he had no doubts as to the doctrine itself, but had not yet decided whether a definition would be opportune. (ASS, H. Icard, "Journal de mon voyage et de mon séjour à Rome, 1869–1870." p. 14). This will be cited hereafter as Icard Journal.

18 John Rothensteiner, "Archbishop Peter Richard Kenrick and the Vatican Council," *Illinois Catholic Historical Review*, XI (1928), 9. Rothensteiner's source is a letter of Kenrick's secretary, Constantine P. Smith, originally addressed to the editor of the St. Louis *Globe-Democrat* and reprinted in the *Catholic Standard and Times* (Philadelphia), March 21, 1896.

influence with the Episcopate of the U.S. and Canada and he thinks that the former at least will go the right way and withstand to the last any innovation. He and the Archbishop of Halifax dined with me on Sunday. Renouf [the Egyptologist, Sir Peter Le Page Renouf] met them. He has every confidence in Hecker and much confidence in the Archbishop whose acknowledged ignorance might make him the dupe of men like Manning. But he has at present the grace to think Manning an imposter if not a hypocrite. The American U.S. Bishops want to hold earnest meetings at the American College and to secure some German Bishops as their spokesmen. Hecker asked me about it, and I said that I would rather trust the Archbishop of St. Louis than Hefele to stand stiff against the allurements and terrors of the Curia. . . . I think that the English and Irish Bishops should be acted on through the Americans who are perfectly misunderstood at Rome. They have the art of hiding an uncompromising resistance under the show of most hearty loyalty and so they are more listened to than we are, who if we resist, usually resist without that show. Hecker as a missionary to convert the semi-literary class in the U.S. puts this truth into the first place—that it is impossible to believe against evidence and not only impossible but wicked to attempt it. So he is toto coelo opposed to the Jesuit school whose triumph he thinks would be the greatest of calamities.[19]

A second letter to Acton contained more details. This time the writer was Döllinger, who reported:

Bishops are now passing through Munich daily, and one hears much about their frame of mind. The Bishop of Strasbourg asserted in conversation with me: The North American bishops are strong adherents and supporters of the infallibility doctrine, as are also a considerable part of the French.

But Döllinger had also had another guest, and this one disagreed with the Bishop of Strasbourg. Döllinger's letter continued:

Father Hecker from New York spoke to me yesterday for two hours about conditions in America and the prospects of the Catholic Church there; he is also on the way to Rome, along with some American bishops. According to his assurances, they are all opponents of the dogma of infallibility, but at the same time very devoted to the Pope

[19] Conzemius Transcripts, Simpson to Acton, Clapham, November 9, 1869.

personally. He has a letter from Simpson, and it is certainly advisable to cultivate his acquaintance. He seems profoundly convinced that the triumph of ultramontanism would be fatal to the Church in America. Hecker asserts, and from firsthand knowledge, since he has just been in Ireland, that the Irish bishops, especially MacHale of Tuam, are also opponents of the infallibility dogma. But unfortunately all of them, Germans, French, Americans, etc., choose to fight the battle on the unhappily chosen ground of inexpediency; there they are already half beaten before they start.[20]

A balanced judgment of Isaac Hecker's role at the Vatican Council must await the opening of the Paulist Archives on the subject. Hecker had been anxious to attend the council, and in April, 1869, he reported to Spalding that Archbishop Dechamps of Malines and Count Charles de Montalembert were encouraging him to come to Rome. He added that he wanted to be on hand as a member of a religious community, as a man active in the apostolate of the press, and as an American. He told Spalding that he had asked if he were not entitled to a seat as Superior-General of the Paulists, but had received a negative reply from Cardinal Barnabò. In May he noted with regret the news sent him by the Archbishop of Baltimore that bishops would not take theologians with them. Finally he was appointed in June as procurator for Bishop Rosecrans of Columbus. As will be seen, he played a prominent part in the preliminary activities of the council.[21]

The American bishops were received by the pope in groups, very few private audiences were given. Typical was the audience attended by Blanchet on November 27. The invitation was delivered by a mounted dragoon on November 26, and next day, at 11:00 A.M., sixteen Americans were received by the pope. The audience lasted twenty minutes, and Pius IX was most gracious. On leaving, many of the bishops lefts sums of silver or paper money on a table. Blanchet himself contributed 800

[20] Conzemius Transcripts, Döllinger to Acton, Munich, November 22, 1869.
[21] Hecker's Letters to Spalding are in AAB 36-A-K-5, 7, 8.

31

gold francs as an offering from the people of his archdiocese. Climbing the long staircases of the Vatican Palace, he came upon Archbishop Odin of New Orleans, who was out of breath and stopping every other moment.[22] Bishop Gibbons later wrote to his brother that the pope had subsequently ordered that Odin be carried to papal audiences in a sedan chair.[23] What must have been one of the more startling incidents in this series of audiences occurred when Bishop Eugene O'Connell of Grass Valley was received by the pope. It was reported that the bishop from the Gold Rush country brought with him ingots and nuggets of silver and gold as gifts from the people of northern California. One block of silver came from an Irish immigrant, Denis J. Oliver. It weighed 350 pounds, was valued at 1,000 pounds sterling and had to be carried into the audience chamber by half a dozen soldiers.[24] But despite all the novelty and pageantry, not all the Americans were happy in Rome. Bishop McQuaid was frankly bored, and he wrote to Father Early in Rochester: "If I had my own way, without having as yet seen the tenth part of Rome, I would soon start for home. I am quite tired of being away from my usual duties, whilst the curiosity to see sights and places is growing less."[25]

The first session of the council was a presynodal congregation held in the Sistine Chapel at 10:00 A.M. on December 2. The pope delivered an exhortation on unity to the four or five hundred prelates present, and then one of the cardinals read out the names of the officers of the council. Five presidents were appointed: Cardinals Karl von Reisach, Antonio de Luca, Giuseppe Bizzarri, Luigi Bilio, and Annibale Capalti. Josef Fessler, Bishop of Sankt Pölten in Austria, was named secretary, with

[22] AAS, F.N. Blanchet Journal, November 27, 1869.

[23] James Gibbons to John Gibbons, Rome, January 19, 1870, printed in the *Morning Star and Catholic Messenger* (New Orleans), February 20, 1870.

[24] *Morning Star and Catholic Messenger*, February 6, 1870.

[25] McQuaid to Early, Rome, December 16, 1869, in Henry J. Browne (ed.), "The Letters of Bishop McQuaid from the Vatican Council," *The Catholic Historical Review*, XLI (January, 1956), 413.

Monsignor Luigi Jacobini and Canons Camillo Santori and Angelo Jacobini to assist him. Of the forty-four other functionaries appointed, all were Italians except one of the vote-collectors and two of the ushers. Twenty-three stenographers also took the oath of office on December 7. They came from the various national colleges in Rome and included two Americans, Peter Geyer of Cincinnati and Theodore H. Metcalf of Boston, whose appointments Father Corcoran had announced to Archbishop McCloskey the preceding March.[26]

The main business of the presynodal congregation was promulgation of the apostolic letter *Multiplices inter,* the parliamentary handbook of the council. By this decree the right of proposing questions for deliberation was reserved to the pope. However, the pope would name a special congregation or committee of members of the council to which individual fathers might submit proposals. The apostolic letter provided for two types of meetings, the more common general congregations and the solemn public sessions. At general congregations the fathers were to discuss *schemata* previously prepared by the preliminary commissions. Anyone could speak; it was only necessary that they register their names with the cardinal presidents. If the *schemata* needed revision, this would be done by one of four deputations to be elected by the fathers. When the final draft of a constitution had been completed, decrees would be voted upon in public session, in the presence of the pope. At general congregations three types of votes were possible, namely: approval (*placet*), disapproval (*non placet*), and conditional approval (*placet juxta modum*). In public sessions conditional votes were not to be allowed. All voting was to be by roll call, but in general congregations written ballots were also acceptable. Finally, the apostolic letter reminded the fathers of their obligation to

[26] Theodor Granderath, S.J. *Histoire du Concile du Vatican* (3 vols.; Brussels: 1907–19), II, 1, 9–14. Cardinal Reisach died on December 29, and was succeeded by Cardinal Filippo de Angelis. For the work of the stenographers, see Leone Dehon, *Diario del Concilio Vaticano I* (Rome: 1962).

secrecy about the affairs of the council and informed them that they were not to quit Rome without explicit permission.[27]

The French statesman Émile Ollivier has made a comparative study of procedure at the Vatican Council and at that of Trent 300 years before. The most striking difference he found was the tendency to shift the initiative from the fathers to the pope. At Trent there was no previously prepared agenda, and no regulations were laid down ahead of time. Matters under consideration were first debated in a public assembly of theologians, often with as many as 2,000 spectators present. The theologians submitted topics to general congregations composed of those with a decisive vote and certain others who were permitted consultative voice. General congregations were private. Each father was asked his opinion, and absolute freedom of speech was guaranteed. Secrecy was ill-kept, and many of the speeches were long, but the papal legates never did more than exhort the council on these points. In public sessions the legates were unsuccessful in efforts to restrict the votes to *placet* or *non placet*. Deputations to revise and formulate decrees were not set up beforehand, but appointed by the fathers as the need arose. Ollivier concluded his analysis by singling out the following as the principal procedural differences between Trent and the Vatican: The preparatory commissions held their sessions before the Vatican Council convened, and their members were chosen solely by the Holy See. Debate in the general congregations was not preceded by a report from the theologians, but only by presentation of an already formulated *schema*. Committees to revise the *schemata* were not set up *ad hoc* by the fathers, but elected at the beginning of the council. Several questions which had continued in dispute, all during the Tridentine sessions, were resolved: Conditional ballots and written ballots from absent fathers were not allowed in public sessions; the right of proposing topics for discussion was reserved solely to the pope, with the concession that fathers might submit proposals to the

27 Mansi, L. 215*–22*.

special papal commission; and, finally, the secrecy which had been recommended at Trent was absolutely imposed at the Vatican.[28] Ollivier's comparison was made in terms of *Multiplices inter*. Further procedural revisions were made during the Vatican Council's sessions, but they did not alter substantially the points of contrast between the two councils.

One more minor problem had to be solved before the council started. On October 10, 1869, the ceremonial commission had decided that fathers should be seated in the council hall by rank and then, in the case of those in episcopal orders, according to date of election and not of consecration. The commission also recommended that primates be allowed precedence over other archbishops.[29] In December, 1869, there were fifty-five cardinals, eleven eastern and western patriarchs, and nine primates. The primatial See of Armagh was vacant, and several other such sees and the Patriarchate of Venice were held by cardinals. Although the Seventh Provincial Council of Baltimore had asked in 1849 that the Archbishop of Baltimore be declared primate of the United States, no action had ever been taken by the Holy See, and Archbishop Spalding had only the "prerogative of place" among the American archbishops which had been conceded to the occupant of the See of Baltimore in a letter of Cardinal Barnabò dated August 15, 1858.[30] Spalding entered a petition that he be allowed a seat among the primates, but Fessler, the Secretary of the council, informed him that his precedence was local to the United States, and did not entitle him to a special place in Rome.[31] The leader of the American hierarchy found himself seated ninety-third among the 124 primates and archbishops present at the first public session,

[28] Émile Ollivier, *L'Eglise et L'Etat au Concile du Vatican* (2 vols.; Paris: 1879), I, 466–501.

[29] Mansi, L. 187*–9*.

[30] Peter Guilday, *A History of the Councils of Baltimore, 1791–1884* (New York: 1932), pp. 157, 202.

[31] AAB, 36A-T-5, Fessler to Spalding, Rome, December 7, 1869. Those recognized as primates were the archbishops of: Antivari, Braga, Gniezno, Lyons, Malines, Salerno, Salzburg, São Salvador da Bahia, and Tarragona.

35

and only Archbishop McCloskey, among the American metropolitans, was placed below him.[32]

The bishops had to rise early on December 8. Archbishop Blanchet recorded the fact that he got up at 4:00 A.M., said Mass at five, took coffee at seven, and was on his way to St. Peter's by eight.[33] The day was a dismal one. Bishop Bayley wrote that "the opening was a grand affair, but unfortunately the weather was very bad. It rained on S. Bibiana's day [December 2] & has been raining ever since to fulfill the proverb."[34] According to an American journalist, the rain did not fall in torrents, but in "slow and measured showers." The scalpers were out in force, and it cost from one to two dollars for a half-mile carriage ride. St. Peter's Square was jammed with people and the soldiers were unable to budge the crowd.[35] Even Bishop McQuaid had difficulty getting into the church, and he wrote that he intended sending his chaplain home after the Christmas holidays because, as he said:

> Bishops' chaplains here at grand ceremonies should be valets. They were treated most shabbily at the opening of the Council. Even Father [Francis] McNeirny [Abp. McCloskey's secretary] was pushed to one side. . . . I had to do some rough work myself to pass through the crowd and reach the vestry room. I succeeded and made way for half a dozen more bishops.[36]

Archbishops and bishops put on white miters and copes in a room over the portico of St. Peter's, and at nine the procession started down the *Scala Regia* and moved across the porch of the basilica and into the central nave. Over 700 prelates took part. Papal Zouaves kept a narrow passage clear as the fathers walked down the center of the church, uncovered their heads before the Blessed Sacrament exposed on the papal altar under the cupola, and turned to the right into the north transept. The council hall had been prepared there, complete with Brussels

32 Mansi, L, 22–35.
33 AAS, F. N. Blanchet Journal, December 8, 1869.
34 AANY, C-2, Bayley to Corrigan, Rome, December 11, 1869.
35 The *Catholic* (Pittsburgh), January 8, 1870.
36 McQuaid to Early, Rome, December 16, 1870, in Browne, p. 413.

carpeting donated by the King of Prussia and with the fathers' places covered in red, purple, or green damask, according to their rank. Noble Guards and Knights of Malta stood at the main entrance, and the Swiss Guard was posted at the other doors. The processional hymn was the *Veni Creator Spiritus*. The pope, who had been carried to the main door of St. Peter's in the *sedia gestatoria,* walked the length of the nave on foot, intoned some prayers before the Blessed Sacrament, and entered the hall, where his throne was located at the far end, in front of the altar of Saints Processus and Martinian. Cardinals and patriarchs took their places in the apse, and the rest of the fathers were ranged in long rows of choir stalls, eight rows deep, which ran the length of the chapel.

The dean of the sacred college, Cardinal Constantino Patrizi, celebrated Mass at 10:00 A.M., a full hour after the start of the procession. Before the last gospel a sermon was preached by Archbishop Luigi Puecher Passavalli, O.F.M.Cap., a curial official. After the Mass each of the fathers made his obedience to the pope; cardinals kissing his hand, bishops of all ranks his knee, and abbots and religious superiors his foot. A series of prayers and litanies followed, and Pope Pius gave a brief exhortation. The session should then have been closed to the public, but the presence of a number of royal personages and ambassadors in the tribunes made this awkward, and so the hall was not cleared when Antonio Valenziani, Bishop of Fabriano and Matelica in the Papal States, read a formal decree declaring the council opened. The fathers gave unanimous approval to this by voice vote. A second decree announced that the next public session would be held on January 6. The *Te Deum* was then sung, and the meeting adjourned. It was approximately 4:00 P.M. The services had taken seven hours. Archbishop Blanchet closed his account of the day's events with some wry comments about the difficulties attendant on so long a stay in the hall.[37]

[37] Granderath, II, 1, 20–33; Butler, I, 162–5; AAS, F. N. Blanchet Journal, December 8, 1869; "The First Oecumenical Council of the Vatican," *Catholic World,* X (1870), 693–705.

According to official figures, 698 fathers attended the opening session. Of these, forty-five were from the United States. Bishop McQuaid's name is missing from the list, but he was most emphatically present. The same was true of Abbot Wimmer of St. Vincent's. The Rome correspondent of the Pittsburgh *Catholic* reported that the abbot was the first father to enter the council hall, and that could have been his place in the procession, since the abbots preceded the bishops and cardinals, while other religious superiors followed the pope.[38] The final count of Americans should probably be set at forty-seven.[39]

The first general congregation was held on December 10.[40] After an introductory address by Cardinal de Luca, the subsecretary Monsignor Jacobini read the names of those appointed by Pius IX to the congregation for receiving proposals. Among the twenty-six prelates designated was Archbishop Spalding,

[38] The official list is in Mansi, L, 22–35. See also the *Catholic*, January 8, 1870.

[39] The Americans present were: Archbishops Joseph Sadoc Alemany, O.P. (San Francisco); Francis N. Blanchet (Oregon City); Peter R. Kenrick (St. Louis); John McCloskey (New York); John B. Purcell (Cincinnati); and Martin J. Spalding (Baltimore); Bishops Thaddeus Amat, C.M. (Monterey-Los Angeles); David W. Bacon (Portland); James R. Bayley (Newark); John J. Conroy (Albany); Michael Domenec, C.M. (Pittsburgh); Claude M. Dubuis, C.M. (Galveston); William H. Elder (Natchez); Patrick Feehan (Nashville); Edward Fitzgerald (Little Rock); James Gibbons (North Carolina); Louis de Goesbriand (Burlington); Michael Heiss (La Crosse); John Hennessy (Dubuque); John M. Henni (Milwaukee); John J. Hogan (St. Joseph); John B. Lamy (Santa Fe); Louis Lootens (Idaho); John Loughlin (Brooklyn); Patrick N. Lynch (Charleston); Francis P. McFarland (Hartford); John McGill (Richmond); Bernard J. McQuaid (Rochester); Augustus M. Martin (Natchitoches); Joseph Melcher (Green Bay); John B. Miége, S.J. (Kansas); Ignatius Mrak (Sault-Ste.-Marie and Marquette); Tobias Mullen (Erie); Eugene O'Connell (Grass Valley); James O'Gorman, O.C.S.O. (Nebraska); William O'Hara (Scranton); Ignatius Persico, O.F.M. Cap. (titular of Gratianopolis); John Quinlan (Mobile); Amadeus Rappe (Cleveland); Stephen V. Ryan, C.M. (Buffalo); Maurice de St.-Palais (Vincennes); Jeremiah Shanahan (Harrisburg); Augustin Vérot, S.S. (Savannah); Richard V. Whelan (Wheeling); John J. Williams (Boston); James F. Wood (Philadelphia); and Abbot Boniface Wimmer, O.S.B. (St. Vincent's Abbey). Archbishop John M. Odin, C.M., of New Orleans was in Rome on December 8, but did not attend the public session.

[40] Mansi, L, 45–8.

38

who had received notice of his selection in a letter from the papal Secretary of State on December 7.[41] The next order of business was the election of two committees, one to grant leaves of absence and the second to handle controversies which might come up with regard to seating, precedence, and so on. Each father was first asked to write down the names of five members of the council whom he wanted as "judges of excuses." The votes were then to be collected and tabulated, and they would proceed to the choice of "judges of complaints and controversies." However, instead of filling out a ballot, Archbishop Kenrick sent a note to Cardinal Bilio, one of the presidents, suggesting that a totally different procedure be adopted. He asked that seven fathers be designated to retire from the hall and draw up a list of candidates for the committees from among those present. Those elected should be of different nationalities and languages. Kenrick also wanted the elections postponed to the next general congregation, when the fathers would vote for the suggested slate or for others of their own choosing. His proposal was ignored, and a request by Bishop Joseph Strossmayer of Diakovár—that the elections be held over until the fathers had had time to make one another's acquaintance—was also denied.[42] The elections continued as planned, and it was announced that the results would be made known at the congregation of December 14. Two documents were also distributed on December 10. One of them was the *schema* on Catholic doctrine, the other the bull *Cum Romanis pontificibus,* which automatically suspended the council in case the pope should die during its sessions and provided that the election of a successor should be carried out in the normal way by the College of Cardinals.[43]

The Strossmayer and Kenrick protests at the first congrega-

---

[41] AAB, 39-K-1, Antonelli to Spalding, December 7, 1869.

[42] Granderath, II, 1, 79–82.

[43] Ollivier, I, 463–6, puts this bull into historical context. Other popes had laid down similar provisions, but Pius IX made a rule for all time.

tion were not isolated phenomena. As early as mid-December forces were already at work which would ultimately divide the council on very basic issues. The surface manifestation of this division was a series of petitions directed to the pope or the presidents on a number of procedural points. Under the surface, a good deal of maneuvering went on, and two antithetic groups began to take shape. The first petition was sent to Pius IX and was granted. Thirteen fathers headed by Cardinal Prince Friedrich zu Schwarzenberg, Archbishop of Prague, asked that only the deputation on faith be elected at the December 14th congregation, with the remaining three deputations to be chosen at subsequent sessions. All the signers of this petition were Austrian, German, or Hungarian except the Archbishop of Paris Georges Darboy and Archbishop Purcell of Cincinnati.[44] Another letter along the same lines was addressed to the cardinal presidents by Archbishop Victor Dechamps, C.Ss.R., of Malines.[45]

A second petition struck more closely at some of the provisions of *Multiplices inter.* It was forwarded to the pope by nineteen bishops, most of them French, but including Strossmayer and two Americans, Kenrick and McQuaid. The petitioners were concerned that the liberty of the council be made apparent. They therefore suggested that the fathers be permitted to elect additional members to the appointed committee on proposals. They also wanted sessions of the deputations thrown open to all members of the council, and they asked that the deputations be polled frequently. Since the deputations were to play such an important role in the practical elaboration of decrees, they felt that it was imperative that their membership be drawn from the most capable fathers available, and not merely left to chance. Another suggestion was that nothing be presented to the council until it had been thoroughly considered in the appropriate deputation, so that the initiative in proposing topics

[44] Mansi, L, 40–41.
[45] Mansi, L, 41.

would seem to rest with the fathers. Finally the petitioners pointed out that it was customary in modern times to give publicity to parliamentary proceedings, and they asked that the rule of secrecy with regard to journalists be relaxed, so that unnecessary suspicion of the Church and of the council could be avoided.[46] This petition was rejected in a verbal communication from Fessler to one of the signers, Bishop Felix de Las Cases of Constantine and Hippo, on January 28. Fessler told Las Cases that the pope intended *Multiplices inter* to stand as written, although he would entertain requests for modifications as the occasion warranted.[47]

A third unsuccessful petition was obviously American in origin. It went to Cardinal de Luca on December 14, and was an appeal on behalf of the procurators sent to represent absent bishops. The signers asked that the procurators be allowed a consultative vote, as had been done in past councils, and that they be seated after the superiors-general of religious orders. All the American archbishops, except Spalding and Odin, and twenty-nine American bishops signed the request. Among the thirty other signatures, there was not one from a prominent European prelate.[48]

As December ended, petitions were still being handed in. Two Peruvian bishops asked that speeches delivered in the council be printed and distributed. They received no answer.[49] The German-Austrian-Hungarian group presented two more petitions on *Multiplices inter,* both on January 2, 1870. The first repeated the request for elected members of the congregation on proposals and asked free access to its meetings for all the fathers. Pius IX replied through Bishop Fessler that the apostolic letter prejudiced no episcopal rights, the requests had no foundation, and *Multiplices inter* would not be revised. Arch-

46 Mansi, L, 41–4.
47 Mansi, L, 44.
48 Mansi, L, 44–5.
49 Mansi, L, 51.

bishop Kenrick was the only signer of this petition from a country outside the central European bloc.[50]

The second petition of January 2 raised a number of practical difficulties. This time all the signers were from Germany and Austria-Hungary. They asked that the council be divided into smaller language groups, suggesting that each of these could then send two delegates to present their views at deputation meetings. They also spoke of the difficulty that many of the fathers, who were not accustomed to speaking Latin, had and intimated that, although the council hall was admirably situated near the tomb of St. Peter, it was not really suitable for genuine discussion. Another cause of complaint was that stenographic reports of the discussions had not been distributed as had been promised. In lieu of these, they requested permission for the fathers to have their speeches printed and circulated. Finally they asked to have the *schema* on discipline given out, so that it could be compared with the one on doctrine, which was then under consideration. Again Fessler answered in person. He said that it had never been customary to let the fathers of a council know all that they were to discuss, and he claimed that special reasons forbade it in the present instance. Private meetings were not forbidden, the secretary said, and delegates could be sent to speak at general congregations, but they had to speak in their own name and not as representatives of any group. Lastly, Fessler stated that there was no need to have the speeches printed, since the deputations took account of them in their revision of the *schemata*.[51]

The story behind these petitions is vital to an understanding of the subsequent history of the council. They represented the thought of those members of the hierarchy who felt that the council should approximate to some degree a parliamentary assembly. They were also among the first skirmishes in the great battle over a definition of papal infallibility. Bishop

50 Mansi, L, 52–4.
51 Mansi, L, 54–8.

Ullathorne explained this when he wrote on December 16: "We are now in the agony of electing the special deputation *de Fide*. Everybody feels that on the twenty-four [members of the deputation] much will depend when the *question* comes on."[52] The deputation elections, which will be considered next, and the petitions, which have just been seen, were all part of a pattern. They manifested a basic divergence of view between those who placed emphasis in church government on the monarchical role of the papacy and those who felt that somehow the stress should fall on co-operative rule by the pope *and* the bishops. It would be easy, but inaccurate to the point of falsification, to call one party—those who emphasized the papal role—"Ultramontanes," and the other "Gallicans." Neither is it necessary here to sort out all the varying shades of opinion within these two parties. This will be done for the American bishops when their role in the council is studied later, and this approach seems preferable to "typing" them beforehand. It is better, therefore, to adopt a purely pragmatic norm in the matter of nomenclature, and to speak simply of the majority and the minority. The petitioners of December and January belonged to the minority. By and large they remained in the minority on the question of the deputation elections and on the question of defining papal infallibility. Given a greater or lesser degree of "papal-episcopal" orientation in their thinking, in the broad sense already suggested, the consistency and inevitability of their position in the three controversies mentioned is obvious, just as the same is true, from the opposite standpoint, of those who opposed them and who, in point of numbers, constituted the majority of the fathers.

In his December 16 letter, Ullathorne mentioned that different national groups met in the early part of that month to select candidates for the all-important deputation on faith. He commented that the Irish, the English, and the Americans were

---

[52] Butler, I, 167.

co-operating, but he reported a split in the ranks of both the Germans and the French. As for the Spaniards, they "had put out a lithograph list, taken up by all the sheep tribe who follow at a gap."[53]

The "lithograph list" was not in fact a Spanish production. Archbishop Manning and Bishop Ignaz von Senestréy of Regensburg have written its history. Manning told how he, Senestréy, Dechamps, and the Bishops of Paderborn and Carcassonne "began meeting in order to watch and counteract the French and German bishops who were united in an International Committee." They met at first in Manning's apartment, then in the rooms of Senestréy and of Conrad Martin, the Bishop of Paderborn, and finally obtained permanent use of a room in the Redemptorist generalate, the Villa Caserta, near the Basilica of St. Mary Major.[54] Two more names should be added to those of the leaders of this group. They were Gaspard Mermillod, Auxiliary Bishop of Geneva, and Bishop Charles Plantier of Nîmes. Senestréy's diary described the purposes of the committee and its tactics. They approached the election to the deputation on faith as preliminary to what they envisioned as the major issue facing the council, definition of papal infallibility. More than forty bishops, including Michael Heiss of La Crosse, met at the Villa Caserta. They set it down as a fundamental rule that no one should be elected to the deputation who was known to oppose the definition. Candidates were then selected from various countries, and the names given to Manning, who prepared the final list of twenty-four names. This was submitted for approval to Cardinal Filippo de Angelis, the future first president of the council, and then Senestréy had it lithographed and distributed to the fathers.[55]

Granderath has tried to show that de Angelis played only

---

[53] Butler, I, 167.
[54] Edmund S. Purcell, *Life of Cardinal Manning, Archbishop of Westminster* (2 vols.; London: 1895), II 453–4; Butler, I, 171; Granderath, II, 1, 87.
[55] Mansi, LIII, 157–9.

a very secondary part in all these proceedings. Two letters from Mermillod indicate that the cardinal's role was important, perhaps as important as that of Archbishop Manning, who has generally been considered the prime mover in the Villa Caserta committee. The Auxiliary Bishop of Geneva wrote to Archbishop Dechamps as follows:

> I do not have any influence for the list. You must have the goodness to write to Cardinal de Angelis or to Monsignor Manning. Do it directly by a word to Cardinal de Angelis. I will do it for my part. It is important that it be soon. I am sad at the answer of the Bishop of Orléans to Monsignor Manning. It stirs up false-heartedness and instigates accusations against the Church.

In another letter to Dechamps, Mermillod wrote:

> I do not know if His Eminence Cardinal de Angelis has sent you the plans of the lists. I do not yet have them. It is important to distribute them as quickly as possible and to recommend to the Belgians, Dutch and others whom you see to support the lists *without any modification,* so as to prevent the partisans of a parliamentary church from slipping in through the links of misunderstanding.[56]

Of the twenty-four names on the majority list, only one later opposed the definition of papal infallibility. He was Archbishop Janos Simor of Esztergom, who had issued a pastoral in line with the majority viewpoint before leaving Hungary, but joined the minority party when he reached Rome.[57] Two American names were included, those of Archbishop Spalding and Archbishop Alemany.

The Villa Caserta committee was not the only one to offer a list of candidates. Opponents of a definition of papal infallibility had also organized their forces. Implementing a scheme

---

[56] AAM, Dechamps Papers, Mermillod to Dechamps, Rome, "Wednesday evening," and "5 Sunday of the year 1869." The election to the deputation on faith took place on Tuesday, December 14. The Wednesday in question is probably December 8, the day of the first public session, or it may have been earlier, although this is doubtful. The Sunday is probably December 5. In the original French, the dateline reads: "5 dimanche de l'année 1869."
[57] Butler, I, 175.

originated by Hungarian Archbishop Lajos Haynald of Kalocsa, they built upon national groups which sent delegates to an international co-ordinating committee.[58] By December 12, four major national groups were represented: the French headed by Cardinal Jacques Mathieu of Besançon and Archbishop Darboy of Paris, the Austro-Germans under Cardinals Schwarzenberg of Prague and Rauscher of Vienna, the Hungarians led by their primate, Archbishop Simor, and the North Americans, whose chief spokesmen were Archbishop Kenrick and the Canadian Archbishop Connolly of Halifax. There was also a scattering of representatives from other nations, including the Italian anti-infallibilists.[59] Information on the international committee is sketchy. Apparently the inner circle in the formative period was small. Besides those already mentioned, Bishops Dupanloup and Strossmayer played leading roles, with the former being looked upon as the leader of the group. Father Hecker also assisted in the work of the committee. On December 11, he brought the American list to Schwarzenberg,[60] and on January 4 Lord Acton made grateful mention of his help in a letter to Döllinger.[61] Acton himself was at the center of the anti-infallibilist activities. Albert du Boÿs, a confidant of Dupanloup, noted in his memoirs that some fifteen or twenty North American prelates, among them Kenrick and Connolly, frequented Acton's salon and met there with their German counterparts.[62]

Another bishop from the United States who interested himself in the composition of the deputation on faith was Augustin Vérot of Savannah. His activity indicated the comparative ignorance of the Americans about the personalities and issues in-

[58] F. Lagrange, *Vie de Mgr. Dupanloup, Evêque d'Orléans* (3 vols.; Paris: 1884), III, 156.

[59] Granderath, II, 1, 86. For the Italians, see the somewhat naïve study by Nicola Menna, *Vescovi Italiani anti-infallibilisti al Concilio Vaticano* (Naples, 1958). Eighteen Italian fathers opposed the definition, or seven per cent of the Italian episcopate.

[60] Cölestin Wolfsgruber, O.S.B., *Friedrich Kardinal Schwarzenberg* (3 vols.; Vienna: 1906–17), III, 231.

[61] Conzemius Transcripts, Acton to Döllinger, Rome, January 4, 1870.

[62] ASMP, Du Boÿs Papers, Memoirs of the Council, p. 5.

volved in the fundamentally European disputes with which they were confronted. Henri Icard, Superior-General of the Sulpicians, was in Rome as theologian to Archbishop Victor Bernardou of Sens. In his diary for December 9, Icard related that Vérot, a fellow Sulpician, had called to see him while he was out. Immediately upon learning of the visit, Icard went to the American College and found that Vérot wanted to inquire about the French lists for the deputation. The Bishop of Savannah was also interested in the nature of the disagreements within the French hierarchy, and he asked Icard what was meant by the term "Liberal bishops," and if it were true that they were of one mind on the expediency of defining papal infallibility. Icard told him that the lists were not yet ready, and explained that he thought the French bishops agreed on fundamentals, but differed in matters of practical policy. Then the Sulpician superior gave a rather Machiavellian interpretation of the mind of the liberals, saying that none of the French doubted that freedom of the press, of worship, and of assembly were evil in themselves, but that some of them felt that the Church should accommodate itself to these modern "aberrations" and even use them to its own profit, while others were more reserved in this regard. According to Icard, Vérot agreed with the liberal approach as he had described it, and claimed that these sentiments reflected the thinking of the American bishops. Icard also told the Bishop of Savannah that anyone who thought that the great majority of the French bishops believed a definition of infallibility expedient was ill-informed, although he conceded that circumstances might alter the complexion of things.[63]

The list of candidates for the deputation on faith prepared by the international committee represented a majority opposed to the definition, but at least seven proponents were included, among them two of the Villa Caserta nominees, Archbishop Manuel Garcia Gil, O.P., of Saragossa and Bishop Antonio

[63] ASS, Icard Journal, December 9, 1869.

Monescillo of Jaen. There were only twenty-one names. Besides Kenrick, three Canadians represented the North Americans: Connolly, Bishop John Lynch, C.M., of Toronto, and Coadjutor Bishop Louis La Flèche of Three Rivers.[64]

The election to the deputation was held at the second general congregation on December 14, and all those supported by the Villa Caserta committee were elected, including Archbishops Spalding and Alemany.[65] The results were announced at the third congregation on December 20, at which the election for a second deputation, that on ecclesiastical discipline, took place. Again there were competing lists, and again what was now clearly the majority party carried the day. Two Americans were chosen, Archbishop McCloskey and Bishop Heiss.[66] Heiss was of course associated with the majority, but McCloskey was not. His name appeared on both lists, and he led the poll.[67] The second and third choices, Ullathorne and MacHale, were also acceptable to the minority. Kenrick and Bishop Richard Whelan were nominated by the international committee, but failed of election.[68] A particularly pathetic figure among the minority candidates was the Armenian Archbishop of Antioch, Placide Casangian, who later made a melodramatic exit from Rome

[64] Butler, I, 174–5. The complete list of minority candidates is in Johann Friedrich, *Tagebuch während des Vatikanischen Concils* (Nördlingen, 1871), p. 27.

[65] Mansi, L, 47–8.

[66] Mansi, L, 28–50; 119–35.

[67] In his funeral eulogy of McCloskey, the then Archbishop James Gibbons spoke of his work on the deputation: "He was deemed worthy of being made a member of the Committee on Discipline, one of the most important in the Council, and Cardinal Capalti, who presided over the Committee, spoke in terms of highest admiration of the wisdom of the Archbishop of New York." (*Sunday Democrat* [New York], October 18, 1885.) On the same occasion Manning wrote to Archbishop Michael A. Corrigan: "We met in Rome during the Vatican Council in a way to make me know his worth, & I have always venerated him for his grace and gentle character." (AANY, C-2, Manning to Corrigan, Westminster, October 11, 1885.)

[68] Friedrich, p. 30. The minority had nominated Ullathorne for the discipline deputation, but not MacHale, although the latter had been put forward for that on faith.

during the council and became the leader of a schism in the Armenian Church.[69]

Two more deputations were subsequently elected, but without the excitement which had attended the selection of the deputations on faith and on ecclesiastical discipline. On January 3, the names of the deputation on religious orders were announced, Bishop Ryan of Buffalo representing the United States,[70] while Bishop de Goesbriand of Burlington became a member of the deputation for eastern churches and foreign missions.[71] The international committee made no effort to put up candidates in this last election. Archbishop Kenrick, however, let it be known that he had handed in a blank ballot in protest against the lithographed list distributed by Cardinal de Angelis.[72]

Kenrick's futile gesture in the final deputation election bespoke the feelings of a number of the fathers.[73] But not all the Americans shared the same view of the proceedings. Bishop William Henry Elder of Natchez was one who was considerably less disturbed. Writing to William Fortune, Rector of All Hallows College in Dublin, he scoffed at reports that there had

---

[69] Louis Veuillot, *Rome pendant le Concile* (2 vols.; Paris: 1872), II, 390, commented that on packing up to leave Rome he found the minority list among his papers. He continued: "I see there names on which time has projected an interesting light. Two among others, who were not yet well known, have been disastrously illuminated; one is Mgr. Kenrik [*sic*], Archbishop of St. Louis in the United States; the other is Mgr. Kazagian [*sic*], Bishop of Antioch of the Armenian rite, now an apostate."

[70] Mansi, L, 161.

[71] Mansi, L, 358; 397.

[72] Conzemius Transcripts, Acton to Döllinger, Rome, January 22, 1870; Johann Friedrich, *Geschichte des Vatikanischen Konzils* (3 vols.; Bonn: 1877–87), III, 1, 437.

[73] Granderath, II, 2, 95–6, gives several examples of protest ballots which were handed in during the different elections. On December 20, one father deposited a blank ballot with a note asking Cardinal de Angelis to fill in the names of those bishops who enjoyed his protection. Another complained at the third election that the distribution of lithographed lists had made a farce of the secret ballot. Two blank ballots were also handed in at this election, one of them torn in three pieces. In the final election, one of the fathers wrote a note saying that he was abstaining because no account was taken of the wishes of the minority.

49

been a scene in the council hall, and that Dupanloup and others had stalked out in disgust. Of the second congregation he stated: "The whole business was an election in which no words were uttered [except] by the officers asking for tickets—and we separated quietly & pleasantly—only with some good-natured grumbling that we were losing time by such short sessions.[74] Bishop Bernard McQuaid was not quite so tractable. In late December he wrote the rector of his cathedral:

We have not yet got through with the voting for committees. The voting, however, is all one way. One of the Italian Cardinals, Archbp. Manning and the Jesuits prepare and print a list of their candidates. The Italians, the Spaniards, South American Spaniards and others vote it. They have the whole thing in their own hands. Archbp. Manning picks out such American Bishops as he chooses, nearly always going against the expressed unanimous choice of the American Bishops. Although we, more than half of the French Bishops, nearly all the Germans, most of the Irish, English, English Colonial and Eastern Bishops vote one ticket, it has no chance against what is called the Jesuits' ticket. This is a difficulty, however, that cannot be remedied. The majority carries the day, and they have the majority. The English Bishops voted for Dr. Grant [Thomas Grant, Bishop of Southwark] as their representative but Dr. Manning was placed on the prepared ticket and of course elected.[75]

The complicated story of the deputation elections was bound to have repercussions within the American delegation, and it also brought at least some of the bishops into clearer focus for European observers. The visitors from across the sea had been something of an enigma when they first arrived in Rome. The correspondent of the *Times* of London, Thomas Mozley, made an inaccurate and superficial analysis in a letter dated November 26: "The British and American Bishops, it is said, will be as ultramontane as can be desired, for they will not thereby offend the intellect or the taste of their flocks.[76] A week later Mozley

[74] AAHC, Natchez File, Elder to Fortune, Rome, December 26, 1869.
[75] McQuaid to Early, Rome, December 28, 1869, in Browne, p. 416.
[76] Thomas Mozley, *Letters from Rome on the Occasion of the Oecumenical Council* (2 vols. London: 1891), I, 22–3.

wrote: "The English, Irish and American Bishops represent the reaction against Anglicanism and its manifold progeny of free sects. Of course they are most faithful."[77] Estimates like these were echoed by the New York *Herald* on December 12. Contrasting the bishops of the United States with the French and the Germans, the newspaper editorialized that it was "a strange spectacle for the world at large—the bishops from the land that is foremost in all that material progress which is thought to be leading the nations . . . accepting the utmost the Church can require, and leaving their brethren of the less progressive countries to assert the necessity for greater freedom of thought."[78]

A more careful and better informed observer, and one who was vitally interested in the true state of opinion among the Americans, was less sure of himself. On November 22, Lord Acton reported to Döllinger that there was growing apprehension in Rome. One reason for this was that the North Americans were not as devoted as had been expected.[79] Four weeks later Acton was still optimistic, as he reported that at least half the Americans and Canadians belonged to the minority party.[80] By the end of December there was some doubt. On December 21, Döllinger sent Acton a set of six questions about the situation in Rome. Number five asked: "Don't you know any details about the Americans and the Irish?"[81] Acton replied that he felt they could count provisionally on the Americans, but that no one knew how strong and firm they would be.[82] This hesitation over the American stand is reflected in the *Letters from Rome on the Council* which Döllinger published

---

[77] *Ibid.*, p. 48.
[78] New York *Herald*, December 19, 1869, quoted in J. Ryan Beiser, *American Secular Newspapers and the Vatican Council, 1869–1870* (Washington: 1942), p. 119.
[79] Conzemius Transcripts, Acton to Döllinger, Rome, November 22, 1869.
[80] *Ibid.*, Acton to Döllinger, Rome, December 18/19, 1869.
[81] *Ibid.*, Döllinger to Acton, Munich, December 21, 1869.
[82] *Ibid.*, Acton to Döllinger, Rome, December 24, 1869.

under the name "Quirinus," and which were based on information supplied by Acton, Johann Friedrich, and one anonymous correspondent. In the first Quirinus letter, Döllinger stated in one place that among those opposed to the infallibilists and to "that great ecclesiastical polypus, with its thousand feelers and arms, the Jesuit Order," are "all the French, American and Irish Bishops who possess any culture and knowledge," but earlier in the same letter he had said: "One knows least of the votes of the Italian and United States Bishops, who, like the Irish, will probably be divided."[83]

While Acton, Mozley, and others were attempting to chart the course of the Americans, the bishops of the United States had themselves taken steps to organize and orientate their forces. They inaugurated a series of meetings at the American College and also began talks looking to the establishment of a common policy on the part of all the English-speaking bishops, who, after the Italians, formed the largest single-language group at the council.[84] Only fragmentary minutes of the meetings of the American hierarchy have survived. Sessions were held frequently, often once or twice a week.[85] Archbishop Spalding served as chairman, and, at least in the beginning, Bishop Lynch of Charleston was secretary. The Blanchet diary mentions meetings on December 19 and 27.[86] The first set of minutes found was taken by Lynch on December 22.[87] Most of the sessions dealt with purely domestic issues, such as promulgation of the decrees of the Second Plenary Council of Baltimore, the hotly contested question of establishing canonical parishes in the United States, and certain formalities connected with the ordination of priests and their transfer from one diocese to another.

[83] Quirinus, *Letters from Rome on the Council* (New York: 1870), pp. 74; 66.

[84] Emilio Campana, *Il Concilio Vaticano* (2 vols.; Lugano; 1926), II, 749.

[85] *Freeman's Journal,* January 22, 1870.

[86] AAS, F. N. Blanchet Journal, December 9 and 27, 1869.

[87] ADC, Lynch Papers, Minutes of the Meeting of the American Bishops, December 22, 1869.

On January 24, Spalding explained the operation of the "initiatory committee," the congregation on proposals to which he had been appointed.[88]

The January 24 meeting also marked a change in the status of Father Hecker. The Paulist Superior-General had been closely associated with the minority party in the struggle over the deputation elections, and he had continued that association during the initial stages of discussion on the infallibility question proper. His name occurred for almost the last time in the Acton-Döllinger correspondence on January 22, after he had told Acton that not five of forty-five United States bishops would sign a petition asking that infallibility be defined.[89] On January 24 he was admitted to the deliberations of the American hierarchy as theologian to Archbishop Spalding, whose petition for an implicit definition had been submitted on January 3. Hecker had come to the council as procurator for the absent Bishop Rosecrans of Columbus, but the latter told Archbishop Purcell: "Contrary to your very natural supposition, Father Hecker does not keep me posted—in fact has never written a line to me since he reached Rome. On this account I did not care about his having a vote as he does not know me well enough to present my views without instructions."[90] Hecker wrote home after his selection:

The Archbishop of Baltimore has made me his theologian of his own accord. This gives me the privilege of reading all the documents of the Council, of knowing all that takes place in it, its discussions, etc. As his theologian I take part in the meetings and deliberations of the American hierarchy, which is, as it were, a permanent council concerning the interests of the Church in the United States, in which I feel a strong and special interest.[91]

88 *Ibid.*, January 24, 1870.
89 Conzemius Transcripts, Acton to Döllinger, Rome, January 22, 1870. Ten fathers from the United States had signed such a petition, which was submitted on January 3. (Mansi, LI, 650–57.) The Spalding petition was signed by five American bishops (*Ibid.*, LI, 663–4).
90 UND, Purcell Papers, Rosecrans to Purcell, Cincinnati, April 23, 1870.
91 Walter Elliott, *The Life of Father Hecker* (4th ed., New York: 1898), p. 362.

The action of the bishops in Hecker's case helped to relieve an embarrassing situation. The earlier petition of the American hierarchy and a petition of their own, addressed to the pope on January 11, had been ignored, and the procurators still had no access to general congregations.[92] The bishops also agreed to admit John Ireland to their deliberations as soon as some one of them should adopt him as theologian. Two other items from the American gatherings are of importance. Archbishop Purcell later reported that at a meeting attended by twenty bishops, Spalding had encouraged the framing of a petition opposing the definition of papal infallibility.[93] This was the document drawn up by Purcell and submitted on January 15 with the signatures of twenty-seven English-speaking fathers.[94] It will be seen in context in a later chapter. The second item was a report submitted at the January 24 meeting which told of efforts to promote concerted action with bishops from various territories of the British Empire.[95]

Butler has told the story of the proposed English-speaking co-operation from the letters of Bishop Ullathorne.[96] The initiative came from Cardinal Barnabò, who told Ullathorne in early December that he should get the English bishops to meet with the Americans and others and prepare a list of common proposals. Negotiations continued through the month. When the question of the deputations arose, the Irish, the English, and the Americans agreed to support each other's candidates. The Americans proved to be the most aggressive in presenting their wants. Ullathorne described how he had felt it his duty to temper their enthusiasm for united action, and he reported that some of the leading Irish bishops were "a little shy of the go-ahead Americans," although the Australians were more enthusi-

[92] Granderath, II, 1, 140–41, has the text of the January 11 petition, signed by Ireland and Hecker.

[93] *Catholic Telegraph,* August 25, 1870.

[94] Mansi, LI, 681–2.

[95] ADC, Lynch Papers, Minutes of the Meeting of the American Bishops, January 24, 1870.

[96] Butler, I, 160, 167–8, 177, 183, 192.

astic about them. Collaboration was organized more formally after December 22, when Archbishops Kenrick and McCloskey were deputed to represent the American interest. They met with Ullathorne on December 23 and drew up a plan according to which the bishops of the British Empire and of the United States would submit proposals to a conference of two delegates from each nation, which would meet at the American College. Manning and Ullathorne were selected to represent England. The first joint meeting took place on the last day of 1869. It lasted two hours, and another session was scheduled for January 4. Meetings apparently continued through January, but the American report of January 24 stated that a unified policy had thus far proved to be impracticable. Kenrick and McCloskey suggested that further attempts be made and that a committee be selected to draw up the American proposals. They were assigned the task, together with Archbishop Purcell and Bishops Amat, McFarland, and Quinlan.[97] No record has been found of subsequent meetings. By the end of January, divisions among the fathers which transcended national lines had become sharp, and the issues which faced the council did not lend themselves readily to action by particular language groups.

The first phases of the conciliar proceedings had proved to be a liberal education for the bishops from the United States. They had come a long way from the days when they worried about whether to buy copes at Lyons or Rome, or where they would find lodging. They learned a great deal about the Roman way of doing things, and many of them found the city an uncomfortable place to live. They also learned a great deal about the state of the European Church and its controversies, which were the primary concern of the council. By and large, the Americans made a quick adjustment to the situation, and, considering the fact that they were virtually unknown in November, several had achieved substantial prominence before the council

[97] ADC, Lynch Papers, Minutes of the Meeting of the American Bishops, January 24, 1870.

55

completed its first month. The spotlight fell particularly on two men, Spalding and Kenrick, whose influence was destined to grow in the course of the next few months.

It soon became clear that Peter Richard Kenrick was no more overawed by a council in Rome than he had been by one in Baltimore, where he had spoken his mind freely and forthrightly on what he thought were procedural irregularities. He was the first father of the Vatican Council to enter a protest during the sessions, with his note to Cardinal Bilio on December 10. During December Kenrick became the acknowledged leader of the sizable group of Americans who joined the minority, and he represented them on the international committee. But he had only begun to make his mark on the work of the council. His role grew as the months passed.

Archbishop Spalding's position was harder to define. He came to Rome as the recognized, if unofficial, head of the American Church. His guidance had been accepted in the appointment of James Corcoran as the hierarchy's representative on the preparatory commission, and he had been consulted about arrangements for the trip to Rome. He retained chairmanship of the bishop's conference during the council, and Bishop Lynch spontaneously affirmed his primary position when, in recording Father Hecker's nomination as theologian, he wrote that Hecker had been named theologian "to the Archbishop." There were six other metropolitans, but Spalding was "The Archbishop." Further recognition came to the Archbishop of Baltimore with his nomination to the congregation on proposals and his election to the deputation on faith, the two most important committees of the council. Nevertheless, as December came to an end, there were two very large question marks concerning "The Archbishop": had he lost effective leadership of the American hierarchy, and had he compromised his convictions for the sake of preference?

The first question can be answered adequately only after all the data are in, and the whole story of American participation in the council has been studied. For the present, it is sufficient to observe that it would be misleading to speak of the Americans as a bloc which could be led by anyone. When they came to Rome in 1869, the bishops of the United States frequently found themselves faced with problems which were not of their own making, and which had little reference to the actual situation of their dioceses. For the most part, they approached these problems as individuals, and there was never a discernible "American policy" in the council, even if at times individual bishops from the United States gave evidence of a distinctively American approach to particular items of conciliar business. Spalding was not the leader of the American bloc, because no such bloc existed. Neither he nor anyone else could have formed one.

The second question is much more serious. Its very asking demands an explanation. The charge came down to this, that the Archbishop of Baltimore had come to the council an "inopportunist," opposed to the definition of the pope's infallibility, and that he had abandoned that position in return for seats on the two committees. It is as bald and direct as that. On January 29, 1870, a correspondent of the New York *Daily Tribune* claimed that Spalding had been preferred over others either because he was an ultramontane, or because "he has not yet crucified the love of human favor."[98] In itself, the *Tribune*'s accusation is no more worthy of notice than most of the journalistic chaff that came out of Rome in those days, but its substance was repeated in the course of later controversy in a letter published over the signatures of Archbishops Kenrick and Purcell. Writing to Bishop Dupanloup in the name of "several" bishops of the United States, the two Midwestern metropolitans observed that Spalding had changed his mind about the expediency of a definition, and asserted that this had occurred "since the honorable prelate has found himself a member of two deputations of the Council."[99] Finally, a St. Louis Catholic newspaper, the

[98] New York *Daily Tribune*, January 29, 1870, quoted in Beiser, p. 53.
[99] The original of this letter is in the Sulpician archives in Paris. It will be studied in detail in a later chapter. A translation appeared in the *Freeman's Journal*, May 21, 1870.

Western Watchman, a zealous defender of Archbishop Kenrick, summarized the whole line of argument in an attack, made toward the close of the council, on an address which the clergy of Baltimore had presented to Spalding. The *Watchman's* editorial ran in part as follows:

These generous clergymen proclaim Archbishop Spalding as the first and greatest of American prelates. We fail to see the claims of this prelate to this high distinction. Will the clergy of Baltimore tell us whether it was on account of his having maneuvered so masterly a flanking movement on his colleagues, upon his assignment to the two deputations? If changing one's lifelong convictions in the short space of twenty-four hours be sufficient to make a man great, then is the distinction a positive mark of disgrace.[100]

These charges are not set down as an accurate portrayal of Archbishop Spalding's mind or of his motivation. The consistency of his position must be judged in the light of evidence which is yet to come. He himself dealt with imputations on his sincerity, and this will be seen in its proper place. For now, it is sufficient to know that accusations of this kind were made, and that they constituted, at least in certain quarters, part of his public image.[101] The harsh interpretation of his conduct, made even by fellow bishops, also indicated the depths of feeling aroused at the council. These emotional overtones are important for an understanding of the debates and of the extra-conciliar activities of the fathers. They are likewise testimony of a remarkable degree of involvement on the part of American bishops who, until the very eve of the council, had seemed for the most part unaware of the issues which would be discussed and on which they would be asked to sit in their capacity as "judges of the faith."

[100] *Western Watchman* (St. Louis), July 16, 1870.
[101] At least one outside observer thought he could detect hostility to Spalding on the part of the latter's colleagues. Albert du Boÿs wrote in his memoirs of the council that the Archbishop of Baltimore was "not very popular in his own country, as far as one can see." (ASMP, Du Boÿs Papers, Memoirs of the Council, pp. 14–5). The remark was made in connection with Spalding's efforts during January to enlist support for his compromise solution on the infallibility question. This will be considered at length in Chapter III.

II

The First Phase

On December 26, Bishop Bayley wrote to Father Michael Corrigan: "We have done little or nothing here yet. Though 'hornets-nests' await me at Newark, yet I would rather be home."[1] The net accomplishment of the three weeks since the council's grand opening had been the election of two deputations and two minor committees. Comparative idleness fanned the flames of speculation and anticipation. All had not gone smoothly with the deputation elections, and it was clear that parties were forming among the fathers. Back in the United States, most of the Catholic newspapers contented themselves with more or less general accounts of events in Rome or ran explanations of some of the issues—like the Syllabus and papal infallibility—which were likely to come before the council. James A. McMaster, editor of the New York *Freeman's Journal,* was a notable exception.[2] McMaster's general thesis was that the

---

[1] AANY, C-2, Bayley to Corrigan, Rome, December 26, 1869.

[2] John Talbot Smith, *The Catholic Church in New York* (2 vols.; New York: 1905), II, 395–7, summed up McMaster and the *Journal* as follows: "It was a noisy and pompous sheet, very poorly edited, offensive in its orthodoxy, and half the time on the wrong side. . . . His [McMaster's] service to the development of sound thought on public questions was vitiated by his bitter attacks on all opponents. Whoso did not agree with him was heretical and foredamned. On this method he conducted his journal for over thirty years. He had a certain following, because many have a taste for unscrupulous denunciation. His pomposity provoked laughter. . . . The secret of his method was that he admired Louis Veuillot, the noted editor of the violent, hateful, and popular *L'Univers* of France, a capable and poetic writer, who thought society and the Church could not be saved except through his methods.

bishops had been summoned to Rome to learn a new lesson in faith.[3] He conceded that the "few noisy talkers" among them would be heard out, and he spoke scornfully of "rancid Gallicans" and "the little handful of frivolous men in episcopal position who want to make a fuss," but he could not bring himself to believe that anyone would actually oppose the *schemata* in what he called the "general sessions" of the council. However, the first debate on the proposed constitution on Catholic doctrine belied his prediction.

This *schema* on Catholic doctrine had been distributed to the fathers on December 10. It contained eighteen chapters, the first eleven of which dealt with more general aspects of Catholic teaching and the errors opposed to it. Among the topics covered were materialism, rationalism, pantheism, divine revelation, mysteries, the nature of faith and the motives for belief, and the interrelation of faith and natural science. The final seven chapters discussed specific doctrines, namely, the mystery of the Holy Trinity, creation, the Incarnation and Redemption, the origin of the human race from Adam and the state of original justice, original sin, eternal punishment, and grace.[4] Butler has remarked that "it may be surmised that the average elderly bishop, whose recollection of theological niceties had grown dim in the work of the pastorate, must have perused this very stiff bit of theology for the subject matter of debate with feelings akin to consternation."[5] This may well be true, but it did not prevent thirty-five prelates from addressing the six general congregations which were held between December 28 and January 10. Two of these were from the United States, Archbishop Peter Richard Kenrick of St. Louis and Bishop Augustin Vérot of Savannah.

The debate opened at the fourth general congregation with a speech by the Archbishop of Vienna Cardinal Rauscher which

[3] *Freeman's Journal,* January 29, 1870.
[4] Mansi, L, 59–74.
[5] Butler, I, 187.

set the tone for most of the subsequent discussion of the *schema*. Rauscher's approach was practical and pastoral and displayed an awareness of the actual contemporary religious situation. He pointed out that it was not heresy with which the modern Church had principally to contend, but the much more fundamental denial of God's role in human affairs. What was wanted, said the cardinal, was a vigorous and pointed reaffirmation of the Church's stand, and not a theology textbook in the guise of a doctrinal decree. Succeeding speakers made the same points and added others. There was general dissatisfaction with the treatise-form of the constitution, which was thought to depart from the more traditional conciliar practice of first enunciating Catholic doctrine positively and only then mentioning opposite errors. In addition some fathers complained that there was no need to re-enunciate already defined dogmas, while others felt that too much emphasis was placed on forgotten errors and that there was a tendency to demand too uniform an acceptance of positions which had hitherto been freely disputed among Catholics. Opposition was by no means unanimous. Seven Italian fathers and several others praised the *schema*, while asking slight modifications, but the opponents were in the majority, and they were outspoken, even if all did not go quite as far as Archbishop Connolly of Halifax, who suggested that the best thing that could be done with the constitution was "to bury it with honor."[6] Among those who had strong reservations were the two American speakers.

Bishop Gibbons later recalled that Archbishop Kenrick spoke Latin "with admirable ease and eloquence" and without the aid of notes.[7] Kenrick's speech on the opening day was the shortest one delivered at that session. He found the proposed constitution impossibly long and remarked that it attempted to cover the whole gamut of revealed truth. In itself, he had no objection to

[6] Granderath, II, 1, pp. 109–62, summarizes the debate.
[7] James Cardinal Gibbons. A Retrospect of Fifty Years (2 vols.; Baltimore: 1916), I, 22–3.

a comprehensive statement of Catholic belief, but he wanted it to be that, and not a compilation and refutation of errors. Repeating the approach which he had taken at the Second Plenary Council of Baltimore, he called for a simplified decree in conformity with the usage of past councils.[8] Finally, he warned against confusing theological argumentation with the actual doctrines being proposed, "lest reasons brought forward to prove the faith seem to pertain to faith itself." Kenrick closed his speech with the recommendation that the *schema* be reworked along the lines which he had indicated.[9]

The French-born Sulpician Augustin Vérot had spend thirteen years as a bishop in Florida and Georgia. A dedicated and zealous pastor, he quickly identified himself with his people. During the War between the States he was a staunch Southern patriot. His active concern for the conversion of his non-Catholic neighbors led him to preach a Catholicism which, while it was wholly orthodox, was closely geared to the practical demands of the apostolate in a predominantly Protestant area. Vérot had become thoroughly American and he was convinced that the Church could become American too, without being any the less Catholic. This American outlook was a theme that ran through all his speeches at the council. He was also possessed of a quick mind and a sharp wit, and was ever ready to spot the incongruous and the ridiculous and to use them to illustrate his argument. Unfortunately these humorous sallies frequently distracted his hearers from the point which he was making, and the memory of them has earned him the reputation of having been *l'enfant terrible* of the council.

The debate ended at the ninth general congregation on January 10, with no further American participation. However, Vérot had made a considerable impression, both on his hearers in the council and on those outside who heard somewhat garbled reports of what he had said. Perhaps the most eloquent comment

[8] Rothensteiner, p. 12.
[9] Kenrick's speech is in Mansi, L, 126.

was the one penned in his diary by Dupanloup. It read simply: "Vérot—en voilà un!"[10] Johann Friedrich recorded the fact that the American's homely examples had amused the fathers and caused laughter in the hall.[11] The Chicage *Tribune* paid the bishop the dubious compliment of stating that his speech had been "the most remarkable ever heard in the eternal city since the days of [Cola di] Rienzi," the fourteenth-century demagogue.[12] The Boston *Advertiser* had its own fanciful account of the speech and quoted Vérot as having said: "As a man of the age and of progress, I protest against the doctrines of the Jesuits, which are not those of the Church of Jesus Christ. The Church should not, cannot put science on the Index."[13] Catholics in the United States were not yet used to the idea that some of their bishops were going to speak out strongly at the council, and their information was as confused as that reaching the secular press. Sometime early in 1870, Father Joseph O'Reilly of Madison, Indiana, wrote to James A. McMaster that the *Catholic Telegraph* of Cincinnati had printed a dispatch said to be from the hand of Archbishop Purcell, which reported Vérot as having "denounced emphatically, calmly, firmly, the Roman Congregation of the Inquisition and its judges" for having condemned Galileo's theories. O'Reilly added that the same assertion now made by the archbishop had been made by John Quincy Adams in a public speech on Mount Adams in Cincinnati in 1844, and he recalled that at that time the former President of the United States had been censured for his statement by the *Telegraph*.[14] One final piece of reporting occasioned by the lack of any official facilities for the press at the council appeared in the Baltimore *Catholic Mirror*, which printed as an example of "that malevolent spirit which is sure to err against truth and charity whenever Catholicity is in question," the following item from the *Courier*

10 ASS, Dupanloup Journal, January 3, 1870.
11 Friedrich, *Tagebuch*, p. 61.
12 Chicago *Tribune*, February 6, 1870, in Beiser, p. 243.
13 Boston *Daily Advertiser*, January 27, 1870, quoted in Beiser, p. 265.
14 UND, McMaster Papers, O'Reilly to McMaster, Madison, . . . 1870.

des États-Unis: "The Bishop of Savannah delivered a discourse which was a curiosity in its way to us who are behind the times. He demands a revision on the judgment in the case of Galileo, on the ground that there is no such thing as revealed science; and that the plain duty of the Church is to refrain from imprudent meddling in things which do not concern her."[15]

Bishop Vérot's forthrightness and his knack for colorful illustration made his maiden speech memorable, but again these features tended to obscure somewhat the points which he had made. Granderath dismissed his effort with the remark: "He said of himself that he had been a professor of astronomy; and his speech is indeed the best proof that he had occupied himself more with experimental science than with theology and philosophy."[16] The German historian of the council also observed that Vérot reflected the national characteristics of the United States, but he neglected to point out that the bishop had demonstrated his pronounced pastoral interest as well. In Vérot's speech we can see clearly the different emphasis in this regard that marked off so many of the bishops from the theologians who had framed the *schema.*

Bishop Vérot asked for a positive, simple, clear-cut conciliar pronouncement on the nature of man and the human species. It may be that in this demand for a "market-place theology" he misunderstood the function of an ecumenical council. He certainly spoke in categories different from those of the scholastic theologians who had formulated the *schema.* His suggestions for a revision of the terminology with regard to original sin and the fate of unbaptized infants were likewise foredoomed to failure. The technical expressions to which he objected, and which explained the underlying reality accurately only when provided with a theological exegesis, had become too deeply embedded in tradition and past conciliar teaching to be eliminated. As matters turned out, neither of the issues he raised were acted

[15] *Catholic Mirror,* February 19, 1870.
[16] Granderath, II, 1, 127.

upon by the council, and, as will be seen later, the final constitution on Catholic faith differed considerably from the first *schema*. Both Kenrick and Vérot played a part in bringing the deputation on faith to effect the revision, but it cannot be said that their individual suggestions had any traceable effect, except insofar as they were part of the ensemble of objections made by many fathers. The final decree was simpler and shorter, as Kenrick had wished. It did not adopt any of the specific recommendations made by Vérot.

Before the conciliar debates were quite two weeks old, some of the bishops had begun to have their doubts that the sessions would ever come to an end. Relaying news received from his brother, the Archbishop of Cincinnati, the Reverend Edward Purcell wrote to a nun: "I fear you will be without a Bishop for years. The last accounts from Rome intimate that the council will most probably continue for years, or as they say—it will not be one of the shortest. Indeed it is most probable that many a mitred head will lie down to rest on Roman soil."[17] Bishop McQuaid was no more optimistic, as he told Father James Early:

Unless an escape is found from the present way of getting on, the council will not be over for *years,* I would not like to say how many. One book or pamphlet of matter has been under discussion for two weeks; the discussion is not yet over, and the probability is that the book will have to be rewritten. There are, we are told, some twenty such books. The first one now under discussion was supposed to have been so easy that it would be adopted almost without discussion. We have listened to some twenty speeches, in duration from 15 to 60 minutes. Saturday next will bring on five more.[18]

There was one break in the monotony of the initial debate. It took place on January 6, when the members of the council made

17 AAC, Purcell Papers, Purcell to M. Baptista Freamer, O.S.U., Cincinnati, January 14, 1870.
18 McQuaid to Early, Rome, n.d., in Browne, pp. 417–8. The Saturday session referred to must be that of January 8. The debate had begun on Tuesday, December 28, and the letter was, therefore, probably written toward the end of the week of January 2–8.

their solemn profession of faith in the presence of Pius IX. The ceremonies at this second public session resembled those which had been held on the opening day. Forty-five Americans were present, all of those who were actively participating in the council with the exception of Bishops Amat and Wood.[19]

After the ninth general congregation on January 10, the constitution on Catholic doctrine was referred to the deputation on faith. Two new *schemata* had been given out on January 8. They dealt with canonical matters concerning the episcopal office and with the government of vacant sees. Debate on these questions began at the tenth general congregation on January 14 and continued until the sixteenth congregation on January 25. It is surprising that none of the bishops from the United States had any comments to make on either constitution, since they covered areas in which the Americans had had some experience, such as the holding of synods and local councils, and also raised pastoral problems like the residence of a bishop in his diocese, diocesan visitation, the selection of candidates for the episcopacy. It is probable that they were discouraged by the wording of the decrees, which had been prepared by the commission on ecclesiastical discipline and reflected the absence of any American intervention in their formulation. That on vacant sees was written wholly in terms of a diocese which had a cathedral chapter and a vicar capitular, a form of government virtually unknown in the United States. The constitution on the office of bishop was phrased largely in terms of the duties of bishops and called, among other things, for close co-operation between the hierarchy and the civil power. This last point was one which came in for criticism during the debate. Several fathers also complained that the *schema* spoke only of the duties of bishops, while ignoring their rights and the dignity of their office. Perhaps the most lively clash followed the call of Cardinal Schwarzenberg, seconded by Bishop Strossmayer, for a reform of the College of Cardinals and of the Roman Curia. Cardinal Camillo di Pietro

[19] Mansi, L, 218–32.

made a spirited defense of the Roman cardinals at the sixteenth congregation in which, without naming him, he informed Strossmayer that the subject was not one for conciliar discussion, but that anyone was welcome to present a petition about it to the pope.[20] The debate ended inconclusively, and the *schemata* were sent to the deputation on discipline, from which the one on vacant sees emerged briefly during the following summer. Whatever the reason for their abstention, the American prelates gave in this instance some substance to the charge of the New York *Evening Post* that in the council they were "as silent as the grave."[21]

Two more minor constitutions were considered by the fathers during January and February. The first of these dealt with clerical deportment. It was brief—only three chapters long—but it gave rise to a comparatively lengthy discussion which lasted through eight congregations. This debate revealed more clearly than anything which had gone before the great divergence of opinion which existed in the Church on what constituted the proper role of the priest in the modern world. The Bishop of Paderborn ran into strong opposition when he asked that priests be forbidden to accept decorations from the civil government, but no one spoke for or against his further suggestion that the clergy of the western Church be allowed to wear beards. Many of the Spanish and Italian bishops delivered impassioned pleas for the wearing of the tonsure and soutane, and one of them alleged as a scriptural warrant for the latter practice the fact that Christ had worn a long robe at His ascension into heaven. Another pointed out that riding a horse was no excuse for adopting a shorter version of the clerical habit, since the Lord had not done so when He entered Jerusalem on the first Palm Sunday. The Latin prelates also wanted strict precautions taken

20 Granderath, II, 1, 199–208, outlines the *schemata,* and pp. 208–36, summarizes the debate.

21 The *Evening Post* (New York), February 8, 1870, quoted in Beiser, p. 75.

against concubinage, and they emphasized the need for priests to shun the contagion of the world by avoiding all places where lay people gathered.

Augustin Vérot was the only American prelate to speak in the debate on clerical life. He prefaced his remarks at the seventeenth general congregation with an explanation of an incident which had happened after his last appearance in the pulpit on January 3. The next speaker on that occasion had been Lorenzo Gastaldi, Bishop of Saluzzo, whose statements sounded suspiciously like the long-condemned doctrines of Michael Baius, the precursor of Jansenism. Specifically, the Piedmontese bishop seemed to have defended the thesis that immortality and integrity (or freedom from concupiscence) were natural to man and not gratuitous gifts of God that had been lost by Adam.[22] Vérot understood the regulations of *Multiplices inter* as permitting intervention from the floor, and he had risen to a point of order. But Cardinal de Angelis refused to recognize him, and the Bishop of Savannah waited until January 27 to explain the matter.

Vérot's speech on the life of the clergy concentrated on three issues, namely, the recreations permissible to priests, their obligation to make formal retreats at stated intervals, and the divine office which they were obliged to recite daily. Once more the Georgia prelate's somewhat humorous presentation distracted his audience from the solid arguments which he advanced, and he was interrupted twice and finally compelled to quit the pulpit by the president, Cardinal de Angelis.

The first contretemps occurred when Bishop Vérot recommended deletion of lessons such as the one in which St. Augustine discussed the cure of the paralytic who had been sick for thirty-eight years. Augustine, Vérot said, proved that thirty-eight was the "number of infirmity" by an algebraic process. Taking forty as the "perfect number," he subtracted two—representing the precepts of love of God and neighbor—and thus came up with

---

[22] Gastaldi's original statement is in Mansi, L, 175. He defended himself on February 8 (Mansi, L, 677–9).

thirty-eight. On this the Bishop of Savannah commented: "I must admit that I have never been able to read this without distractions." Cardinal de Angelis interrupted with the admonition, "Let the Most Reverend orator speak with greater reverence of the holy fathers." Vérot's answer was immediate: "I wish to speak with all reverence of the holy fathers, Eminence, but even good Homer nods sometimes. I shall say nothing more about that."

The bishop's next target was St. Gregory, but the cardinal presidents were in no mood to listen to further argument, and he did not get very far. He pointed out that, in one of his homilies, Gregory had predicted the proximate end of the world. This had been 1,200 years ago, and the end had not yet come. Vérot then started to discuss a fact which he found "certainly curious enough," that the Church had its priests read an office from which it was sufficiently clear that St. Gregory had incurred excommunication. He was about to prove this when Cardinal de Angelis sounded the bell. The following dialogue ensued:

De Angelis: We are dealing here with the *schema* on the life and deportment of clerics, and the most reverend bishop has already sufficiently expressed his desire for a reform of the breviary, and it is enough.

Vérot: I would also like to add something about corrections which have been made, and I shall say it in a word, although the matter is serious, and very serious.

De Angelis: If he does not speak of the deportment of clerics, let him make way for another speaker.

Vérot: I shall obey willingly, Eminent President, although it seems to me that I can say this, that it has a necessary and intimate relation with the divine office, namely that that office be recited with due reverence. Nevertheless, I acquiesce in your decision, Eminent President, and leave the pulpit.[23]

There is no need to evaluate the merits of Vérot's various proposals. They would seem to be obvious. He received support in some particulars, notably from Archbishop Melchers of

23 For Vérot's speech, see Mansi, L, 539–43.

Cologne and from Archbishop Haynald of Kalocsa, but in the end all the speeches came to nothing. The constitution was returned to the deputation on discipline on February 8 and was never brought to the floor again.

Along with the *schema* on the clergy, a second constitution had been distributed to the fathers on January 14. It proposed adoption of a universal elementary catechism based on the one composed by Robert Bellarmine which was then used in Rome. Once more there was a division along national lines. Those bishops who opposed the centralizing tendencies of the Roman Curia saw the universal catechism as another step toward unnecessary uniformity. Archbishop Guibert of Tours and Bishop Dupanloup of Orléans both spoke in this sense. Further opposition came from the Germans, who were loath to abandon the catechism of Peter Canisius, which had served their people well since the time of the Reformation. The debate lasted through six general congregations, and forty-one prelates spoke. Again Bishop Vérot was the only American participant.[24]

The Bishop of Savannah, for all his good humor, had been hurt by the treatment accorded him at his last appearance in the pulpit. When he rose to speak on the catechism at the twenty-fifth congregation on February 14, he began with an allusion to the former occasion and promised to deliver his message without explanations or recriminations. He was wholeheartedly in favor of a common catechism and said that the need for such a book was obvious in the United States where there were so many immigrants who had come to America with a wide variety of catechetical training. The bishop was so anxious for a standard catechism that he offered to accept it immediately in place of the work which he had issued just before coming to the council. To expedite matters, he suggested that the translation into various vernaculars be done right in Rome while the council

[24] Granderath, II, 1, 256–83, has a somewhat unbalanced account of the debate, which is hostile to those who opposed the *schema*. See also Butler, I, 228–30. Interruptions by the presidents and murmuring from the floor became more common during this debate.

was in session. "There are so many bishops," he said, "who are not burdened with many occupations, for whom the translation of a few pages will certainly not be an intolerable task."

These minor constitutions are less important for themselves than they are for the effect which the debates on them produced in the council. February 22, the last day of discussion on the *schema* about the common catechism, was really a turning point. For one thing it marked the beginning of a three-week recess, ostensibly to allow the council hall to be renovated and to permit the deputations to catch up with the mass of material which had been submitted to them for revision. Secondly, a new set of regulations for the conduct of the council was promulgated. Thirdly, the fathers were asked to submit written observations on the first ten chapters of a new constitution, the one on the Church, within a like number of days. Before considering the new regulations and the reaction to them, it will be well to retrace our steps and see the reaction of the American bishops to the whole procedure of the council.

Protests came from both the majority and the minority. Writing to his vicar-general, Henry Muehlsiepen, on March 6, Archbishop Kenrick summed up his feelings as follows:

Most of us are very tired of Rome and would willingly leave it. The Council has now been three months in session and nothing has been done. The body is too big for work, unless divided into sections; and those who had the management of matters were, and are, unwilling to attend to the suggestions made to them by those who had experience in similar assemblies.[25]

The archbishop recommended that Muehlsiepen read an article which had appeared several weeks previously in the French newspaper *Moniteur Universel* on the state of affairs at Rome, which contained, he said, a detailed and realistic account of the difficulties which had attended the sessions. The *Moniteur* article summarized the problems under seven headings, then recapitu-

[25] Kenrick to Muehlsiepen, Rome, March 6, 1870, in John Rothensteiner, *History of the Archdiocese of St. Louis* (2 vols.; St. Louis: 1928), II, 305–306.

lated them and offered its own solutions. In the process it presented most of the complaints of the fathers of the minority.

The first complaint antedated the council itself. It was about the composition of the preparatory commissions and the seeming semi-finality of their work. The French journal pointed out that the task of framing *schemata* had been entrusted to a body of theologians better known for speculative knowledge than for practical experience. Bishops had been refused advance knowledge of the agenda and in consequence had had no opportunity to prepare themselves for the discussions. It looked very much as if the intention of the organizers had been to bring the fathers to Rome simply to ratify a *fait accompli*. Everything was in the hands of the pope. Ardent papal partisans like Louis Veuillot did not help matters, the paper continued, by stating that this had been done deliberately so as "to take from bishops freedom to do evil." The *Moniteur* also rehearsed all the complaints which had been made at the time of the deputation elections and concluded that the power of the five commissions, backed up by the omnipotence of the pope who had reserved final judgment to himself, effectively excluded 700 bishops from any really decisive role in the council's business. On the matter of numbers there was another grievance. It was said that the Italians and the vicars apostolic taken together counterbalanced the votes of all the German, French, and United States bishops combined. Alone, the Italians outnumbered the Germans and the French by a ratio of about three to one. The article estimated that 140 of the 700 fathers represented more than ninety million Catholics, or over half the population of the Church. And, it added, these 140 prelates came from the most civilized nations. A final difficulty was inadequate information about what was going on in the debates. The council hall was said to be hopeless from an acoustical point of view. Voluminous *schemata* on complicated questions were handed out piecemeal only a few days before they were to be debated, the discussion was disorganized, printing of speeches was forbidden, and many fathers refused to speak since they could not be heard. The result of all this was a notable lack of common deliberation with the fathers being deprived of the opportunity to share their views with one another. The *Moniteur* considered this last as essential to a genuine council. It suggested that a partial solution to the many problems which were vexing the fathers would be to allow formation of smaller groups which could discuss issues and come to some common policy, which several of their members would then present to the deputations. This was, of course, a plan that had already been rejected by the pope. It will be seen, however, that many of the American bishops were among those who agreed substantially with the criticisms outlined by the French writer.[26]

As early as December 16, Bishop McQuaid had written home about the difficulties of the council hall. He remarked to Father Early that not even the best voice could fill an auditorium that measured 150 by 90 by 150.[27] A week later, Bishop Ullathorne reported that he had made an appointment to go with an American bishop to check on the suitability for debates of the great hall of the Quirinal Palace, but nothing came of the effort.[28] Several of the Americans recorded the ennui that had settled over the fathers. On January 8, James Roosevelt Bayley of Newark informed Father Michael Corrigan: "The Council is very tedious, will kill off a great many Bishops before it will be over." He added that some had fainted at the second public session on January 6.[29] Two weeks later the Bishop of Newark came up with a gloomy prediction: "The Council is going on very slowly—and if things be not accelerated some way or other, we will be here three years."[30] Bernard McQuaid of Rochester gave further details in a February letter to Corrigan: "How I

[26] The article from *Moniteur Universel,* "La situation des choses à Rome au 14 février 1870," is reprinted in Johann Friedrich, *Documenta ad illustrandum Concilium Vaticanum anni 1870* (Nördlingen: 1871), pp. 131–46.
[27] McQuaid to Early, Rome, December 16, 1870, in Browne, p. 414.
[28] Butler, I, 177.
[29] AANY, C-2, Bayley to Corrigan, Rome, January 8, 1870.
[30] AANY, C-2, Bayley to Corrigan, Rome, January 20, 1870.

long to go home!" he wrote, "At home there is work for me and here the whole life is so contrary to my notions and habits that I am fairly sick of it." He reported that they had spent two months without completing action on a single decree. There was no telling when the council would end—it might be in June, or it might not be for years. McQuaid found the sessions "very long and quite tiresome," and, while many of the speeches were "interesting, eloquent and practical," others were "long, tedious and not to the point." Sessions were held three or four times a week, and each one lasted for four hours, which he thought must be trying to the patience and endurance of the older bishops. His own health, he wrote, was good, but his spirits were flagging "under this enforced do-nothingness." He closed his letter with a reference to Corrigan's own ordinary: "Rome does not agree with Bishop Bayley; he is often 'out of sorts' although he has not had anything seriously the matter with him."[31] Two days after this letter from McQuaid, Bayley confirmed the diagnosis and summed up his own feelings when he wrote: "My eyes are very bad. The weather is very bad. There is much sickness." He told Corrigan that Bishop David W. Bacon of Portland had already left for home, and said that he was going to try for the same permission "by and by."[32]

The letters of Bayley and McQuaid reflect accurately the atmosphere of Rome in the winter of 1870. They also summarize some of the principal complaints against the management of the council. These were the inadequacy of the council hall, the lack of any concrete achievement, the time-consuming, boring, and pointless debates, and the fact that the talents of so many bishops were going to waste while work piled up in the deputations. This last point recalls Vérot's suggestion that some of the idle fathers could profitably be employed in translating the new universal catechism. Dissatisfaction with the proceedings was fairly general, but there was a large area of disagreement as to

[31] AANY, C-3, McQuaid to Corrigan, Rome, February 6, 1870.
[32] AANY, C-2, Bayley to Corrigan, Rome, February 8, 1870.

the proper remedy. Hovering always in the background was the big question of the council, papal infallibility. Although it had not yet been officially proposed, it was on everyone's mind. In his monumental study of the council's history, Granderath sees this as the crux of the matter and judges everything else by it. His explanation is disarmingly simple: There were two parties among the fathers. One of these (the majority) wanted to work within the rules of *Multiplices Inter*. If they had had their way, all would have proceeded smoothly. The second party (the minority) was composed of malcontents who were abusing the liberty allowed them to engage in a filibuster. Their aim was to delay as long as possible any discussion of infallibility.[33] Émile Ollivier had long since made a similar analysis of the minority's tactics. He wrote that the leaders of the opposition had adopted the policy of prolonging the discussions by lengthy speeches in the hope that the heat of the Roman summer would force an adjournment before infallibility could be brought to the floor. While they had no hope of converting their minority into a majority, the contemplated departure of the vicars apostolic for their far-flung mission stations would reduce the majority's advantage, and, with time, other factors might enter in to alter the situation.[34]

Abbot Butler's chapter, "Atmosphere of the Council," is a better-balanced account. He discusses the fears, reasonable and unreasonable, which had been aroused by the organization of the council and by the considerable extra-conciliar agitation, and he concludes with a summary of some of the legitimate apprehensions of the bishops of the minority.[35] There is no doubt at all that the idea of a "delaying action" entered into the calculations of the opposition. But to deny them the right to that parliamentary tactic raises a much more fundamental question which is beyond our present scope. It would involve an investiga-

[33] Granderath, II, 1, 284–6.
[34] Ollivier, II, 67.
[35] Butler, I, 254–68.

tion into the deliberative nature of an ecumenical council, and its relation to the monarchical papacy.

Whatever may be said of the French or the Germans or others, it is obvious that no Americans engaged in a filibuster during January and February. Apart from Kenrick's brief opening address, none of them had spoken except Vérot, and he spoke for himself and for the causes in which he believed, with no ulterior motive. American complaints referred principally to the inefficient conciliar machinery and represented a plea that the bishops be allowed to get on with the job for which they had come to Rome. It is true that most of the objectors belonged to the minority, and that American supporters of infallibility were more ready than some to acquiesce in whatever was put before them by the authorities of the council; but this was the result of conflicting views on the nature of the Church's hierarchical structure and on the function of bishops in council. It was entirely possible to call for a greater degree of episcopal responsibility without at the same time being completely, or at all, motivated by the narrower political aim of blocking consideration of a particular dogma. As time went on, the latter goal became inextricably linked with the fortunes of those who felt that bishops should have a greater role in church government. The dogma of infallibility went, in fact, to the heart of the papal-episcopal question. Nevertheless, in the early stages of the council the American bishops gave little sign that they had fully grasped this deeper implication. As will be seen, they did engage in petitions for and against presentation of the infallibility question. But all their objections to the running of the council were not subsumed under this one all-embracing objective. They were still very much interested in the more comprehensive goal of working out of all the *schemata* which had been prepared.

Among the flood of petitions which went to the pope and to the presidents of the council on the subject of a more efficient operation of the council was one signed by Archbishops Kenrick and Purcell and by the Bishop of Wheeling Richard V. Whelan.

The other signers were predominantly French, but Hungary, Canada, and Ireland were also represented. The petitioners had two requests to make. They asked that another assembly room be found, in which speeches could be heard. Pointing out that the bad acoustics in St. Peter's provided a pretext for those who claimed that freedom of speech had been denied the fathers, they said that a remedy was imperative now that the time was approaching when the council would be called upon to make solemn definitions and pronounce anathemas. The second request was an old one. It called for the division of the bishops into smaller groups which would meet before general congregations to discuss the *schemata* and then appoint representatives to speak for them in the plenary sessions. The secretary Bishop Fessler noted that an effort would be made to accede to the first demand, and that the second was under consideration.[36] The answer actually came with the new rules of February 22. The reasonable tone of the petition, which was the only one on this subject signed by any Americans of the minority, seems to confirm the judgment which has already been made on their frame of mind in January and February.

Not all the Americans were unduly disturbed by the state of affairs. Bishop James Gibbons of North Carolina, a moderate infallibilist, sent home a whimsical description of the sessions in mid-January. His letter was addressed to his brother John, a grain dealer in New Orleans. Gibbons wrote as follows:

There is the most ample liberty of discussion in the Council. No matter how much a speaker in the chamber may tire his audience, he is patiently heard to the end of the chapter. Those that desire to speak have only to notify the president the day before. It is true you will not hear fifty bishops shouting at the top of their voices, "Mr. President, Mr. President," nor will you hear Mr. President "bringing down" his hammer and making confusion more confounded. You will not see bishops proving the liberty of the Council by taking the liberty of throwing ink-bottles at their brothers on the opposite side. You will observe no bishop trying to assert his independence by reading a

36 Mansi, LI, 1–2.

New York *Herald* in a horizontal position. Such exhibitions, fortunately for the reputation of the Vatican Council, are hardly essential to true freedom of debate.[37]

Another bishop from the United States was even more pleased with the way the sessions were going. John Baptist Miége, the Jesuit Vicar Apostolic from Kansas, wrote the following lines to an old friend in France, Canon Joseph-François Alliaudi of Moûtiers:

> These long sessions, where we have to listen to endless repetitions, are fatiguing enough, but it's always agreeable to attend them. It is a whole world, but a world of men from 55 to 80 years old, almost all aged workers in the vineyard of the Lord, who love the Church and the venerated Pontiff who governs it. You have there all the manners, all the costumes, all the colors of beards, all the diversity of languages. But the good Latin language is understood by all, save for some orientals who use interpreters. You have there all the oriental majesty, French and Italian style and gravity, American candor, German dullness, Spanish fire. In a word, it is beautiful, my dear canon, but I would have to have the ability to describe it and have the time to do so. Both are lacking to me.[38]

Two American bishops who belonged to the majority expressed their opinions during February. Bishop Augustus Mary Martin of Natchitoches, an ardent proponent of infallibility, wrote on February 7 to Father Napoleon Perché of New Orleans that nothing was happening at the council. He reported that obstacles were being thrown up to delay as long as possible the discussion of the question that was on everyone's mind.[39] Bishop Michael Heiss of La Crosse was the only prelate from the United States to sign a majority petition about the debates. It was a moderate document, and Heiss's co-signers were the

[37] Gibbons to Gibbons, Rome, January 19, 1870, in *Morning Star and Catholic Messenger,* February 20, 1870.

[38] Miége to Alliaudi, Rome, January 30, 1870, in J. Garin, *Notices Bibliographiques sur Mgr. J.-B Miège, Premier Vicaire Apostolique du Kansas et sur les Prêtres de las Paroisse de Chevron (Savoie)* (Moûtiers: 1886), 148. Miége altered the accent on his name after coming to the United States. Garin uses the traditional form.

[39] UND, New Orleans Papers, Martin to Perché, Rome, February 7, 1870.

78

Archbishop of Udine, the Bishops of Treviso and L'Aquila, Bishop Senestréy, and Bishop Mermillod. They protested the lengthy and repetitive speeches which had been tolerated and which took no account of the temper of the fathers. The petition also noted that some speakers had been lacking in reverence for the Roman congregations and for the usages of the Roman Church. Among the suggestions they made was that a time limit be set on each speech, and that the speeches themselves be concise and to the point. They also brought up the idea of cloture and proposed that, when a sufficient number of speakers had been heard, the council should vote whether to continue the debate. As alternatives, they suggested that this vote could recommend adoption of the *schema* as it stood, minor modifications to it, or its consignment to the appropriate deputation.[40]

Account was taken of the various proposals and protests, and on February 22, a new set of conciliar regulations was distributed to the fathers. There were fourteen points. Five of these outlined a new feature, the submission of written observations prior to debate in general congregation. These comments were to be handed in to the secretary of the council, who would pass them along to the proper deputation, where they would be duly considered. In the congregations, speeches were to be given either on the whole *schema* or on some part of it. Representatives of the deputations would be recognized out of their normal turn if they wished to speak on some objection that was raised. A provision for cloture was introduced. Any ten fathers could petition the chair to bring the matter to a vote, and a simple majority would be sufficient to end the debate. The new rules further provided that voting should take place in three stages. First came the ballot on individual parts of a constitution and on the emendations proposed for each section. A member of the deputation would report on these written emendations before the vote and recommend their adoption or rejection. The fathers would signify their "yea" or "nay" by rising in their place at the appropriate time. The second stage of the balloting was the

40 Mansi, LI, 57–9.

vote on the *schema* as a whole. Here it would still be possible to vote *placet, non placet,* or *placet juxta modum.* However, this last conditional approval had to be accompanied by a written explanation of the voter's reservations on the constitution. The third vote was left as before, and it would take place in solemn session. With these regulations the cardinal presidents hoped that the work of the council would be speeded up and the legislative deadlock broken.[41] The reaction to the new arrangement was, predictably, varied, and American bishops found themselves adopting contradictory positions.

The first indication of American displeasure came in a letter from Acton to Döllinger, written on February 25. He reported that many bishops were upset by the fact that unanimous consent was no longer to be demanded for doctrinal decrees. Among those who had spoken to him on the matter were Archbishop Kenrick, Bishops Dupanloup, Clifford, and Maret, and Arch-bishops Landriot and Haynald.[42] Protests along these lines were formalized in a series of petitions signed by representatives of a variety of countries. One such document, drawn up by the German-Austro-Hungarian group, attacked virtually every pro-vision of the new rules and added that if moral unanimity of the fathers were not demanded for the promulgation of dogmas, the signers feared that the council's acts would be called into question. Ignatius Mrak, Bishop of Sault-Sainte-Marie and Marquette, added his name to those of twenty-one prelates from the three central European nations on this petition[43] Mrak was the only bishop from the United States to lodge a formal protest. Döllinger later reported that the Americans had held a meeting to discuss their stand, but that they could come to no decision.[44] His informant, Acton, complained to him that the bishops from North America did not fully appreciate the significance of

[41] Mansi, L, 854–6.
[42] Conzemius Transcripts, Acton to Döllinger, Rome, February 25, 1870.
[43] Mansi, LI, 23–8.
[44] Quirinus, pp. 324–5.

the new decree and he reported that Kenrick felt that it was so impractical that its net result would be to delay the council proceedings still further.[45]

Whatever might have been his views as to the practical effect of the decree, the Archbishop of St. Louis was not at all pleased with its terms, and he told Father Muehlsiepen that he found the new regulations "highly objectionable and scarcely reconcilable with the liberty a Council should have."[46]

The story of the practical operation of the new regulations belongs to the later history of the council. Their promulgation on February 22 brought to an end the first phase of the debates. From a technical standpoint, the results achieved in two months' work were so minimal as to be almost unnoticeable. Five *schemata* had been proposed, and none of them had passed. All were in the hands of the deputations. The Roman authorities had not foreseen the extent of the opposition, and they were unprepared to cope with it. The most sensible thing to do seemed to be to prorogue the council for some weeks and then to attempt a fresh start. This was done with the adjournment of February 22 to March 18. As will be seen, a great deal of activity went on during those three weeks which was to have a dramatic impact on the future work of the council. But even if no decrees were adopted, the first two months had hardly been wasted. It must be remembered that the council numbered some 700 fathers, most of them previously unknown to one another, from every quarter of the globe. Moreover, the last general council had finished its sessions 300 years before that of the Vatican opened. The world of 1869 was a great deal different from the world of 1563, and the Church had undergone drastic, although not essential, changes in its internal structure and in its relations with the nations and people among whom it worked. A period of adjustment was inevitable.

[45] Conzemius Transcripts, Acton to Döllinger, Rome, February 25, 1870.
[46] Kenrick to Muehlsiepen, Rome, March, 6, 1870, in Rothensteiner, *History,* II, 305.

III

Preliminaries to the Debate on Infallibility

THE somewhat bewildered state of mind of the American hierarchy at the state of affairs which confronted them upon their arrival in Rome was expressed by Bernard McQuaid in a letter written on December 1 to Father James Early:

Since coming to Europe, I have heard much of the question of the infallibility of the Pope, which with us in America was scarcely talked of. The feeling is very strong, *pro* and *con*. It seems that the Jesuits have been at the bottom of it, and have been preparing the public mind for it for the past two years. They have not made friends for themselves by the course they have followed, and if in any way the harmony of the Council is disturbed it will be by the introduction of this most unnecessary question. The probability now is that in consideration of the opposition already manifested that it will not come before us. Still there is no telling what the Jesuits will do, and from the manner in which they are sounding out the Bishops, I am inclined to think that they will succeed in having the question forced upon us. In my humble opinion, and almost every American Bishop whose opinion I have heard agrees with me, it will be a great calamity for the Church. My great hope is on the prayers of the whole Church that the Holy Ghost may guide us aright.[1]

McQuaid's forebodings proved correct, and the question of infallibility did come before the council. Very nearly every other issue which arose among the fathers bore some relation to it, although it was not placed on the agenda until March and was

[1] McQuaid to Early, Rome, December 1, 1869, in Browne, pp. 412–3.

not debated until mid-May. During the intervening months the particular merits of various proposals engaged the attention of the bishops, but infallibility was always in the background and very often in the foreground, even when the discussion ostensibly centered on the nature of the human species or the composition of a universal elementary catechism.

Acton's initial letters to Döllinger traced the evolution of the American impact on the Roman scene. On November 22 he reported that the bishops from North America were not as submissive as had been reported.[2] Two weeks later he reported that Isaac Hecker, Johann Friedrich, and Bishop Dupanloup had arrived in the city and at this point gave his first summary of probable opponents of the dogma of infallibility. According to the Englishman's calculations, the opposition could count on the following votes: the majority of the French; half the Bavarians; all the Prussians, except Conrad Martin of Paderborn and Mieczislaw von Ledóchowski of Gniezno; the majority of the Austrians; most of the oriental-rite bishops, and some of the Americans and Irish. Acton also reported that the opposition was not yet organized, since three of its leaders had not put in an

2 Conzemius Transcripts, Acton to Döllinger, Rome, November 22, 1869. Reports of on-the-scene observers testify to the fact that Acton was in a good position to know the sentiments of the English-speaking bishops. Albert du Boÿs, the lay confidant of Bishop Félix Dupanloup, termed the Englishman's residence "the center of an anti-infallibilist opposition which included all the countries of the English and German languages." Among the fifteen or twenty American prelates who frequented Acton's salon, du Boÿs noticed particularly Archbishop Connolly of Halifax and Archbishop Kenrick of St. Louis. (ASMP, du Boÿs Papers, "Memoirs of the Council.") The American author and educator, Charles Eliot Norton, called Acton "the lay Head of the opposition to the Ultra-Clerical Party." (Sara Norton and M. A. DeWolfe Howe [eds.], Letters of Charles Eliot Norton [Boston: 1913], I, 379.) The British diplomatic agent in Rome, Odo Russell, later said of Acton in a letter to Lord Clarendon, the Foreign Secretary: "To Lord Acton's marvellous talents, science, energy and zeal the enlightened opposition in the Council owes its present existence and strength. Without him the Germans, French, Americans and English could not have agreed and acted together, so different are their national theological standpoints." (Noel Blakiston [ed.], The Roman Question; Extracts from the Despatches of Odo Russell from Rome, 1858–1870 [London: 1962], p. 419.)

appearance.[3] By mid-December the predicted American opposition had risen to "at least half" of the prelates from the United States and Canada, and the whole of the Portuguese hierarchy had been added.[4] On December 22, Acton sent Döllinger a quotation which perhaps explained why so many Americans were flocking to the anti-definition party. It was taken from the *Controversial Catechism,* which had been recommended by Archbishop John Hughes of New York and four other bishops, and had sold 24,000 copies in North America and England in the past quarter of a century. The citation read as follows:

Q. Must not Catholics believe the Pope in himself to be infallible?
A. This is a protestant invention; it is no article of the Catholic faith: no decision of his can oblige under pain of heresy unless it be received and enforced by the teaching body; that is, by the bishops of the Church.[5]

In the summations which Döllinger made from the reports reaching him from Rome and published as the Quirinus letters, he was at first hesitant about the attitude of the American bishops, but toward the end of December he had grown more confident and in the fifth letter he devoted a long paragraph to an analysis of their position:

The opposition of German and French Bishops to the new dogma was more or less anticipated here; what was not expected was that the

[3] Conzemius Transcripts, Acton to Döllinger, Rome, November 28/ December 5, 1869. Russell's breakdown of the parties was more general than that of Acton. On December 8 he reported to Clarendon: "The Roman Papal, Jesuit or ultramontane party is said to be composed of the Italian, Spanish, South American, English, Irish, Belgian and half of the French Bishops, whilst the other half led by Dupanloup commands the votes of the Austrian, German, North American, Bohemian, Hungarian and Portigese Bishops. The orientals are still wavering. . . ." (Russell to Clarendon, Rome, December 8, 1869, in Blakiston, p. 370.)

[4] Conzemius Transcripts, Acton to Döllinger, Rome, December 18/19, 1869.

[5] Conzemius Transcripts, Acton to Döllinger, Rome, December 22, 1869. The citation appeared in Stephen Keenan, *Controversial Catechism: or Protestantism Refuted and Catholicism Established* (2nd ed.; Edinburgh: 1849), p. 102. The second edition carried the recommendation of two Scots vicars apostolic and a notice to the effect that a first edition had been approved by Hughes.

Orientals, numbering about sixty, and the North American Bishops, would pronounce against it . . . . The Americans ask how they are to live under the free constitution of their Republic, and maintain their position of equality with their (Protestant) fellow-citizens after committing themselves to the principles attested by Papal Infallibility, such as religious persecution and the coercive power of the Church, the claim of Catholics to exclusive mastery in the state, the Pope's right to dispense from oaths, the subjection of the civil power to his supreme dominion, etc. The inevitable result would be that Catholics would be looked upon and treated as pariahs in the United States, that all religious parties would be banded together against them as common enemies, and would endeavour, as far as possible, to exclude them from public offices. One of the American Bishops lately said, 'Nobody should be elected Pope who has not lived three years in the United States, and thus learnt to comprehend what is possible in this day in a freely governed commonwealth.'[6]

While Döllinger was prone to indulge in overdramatization, there is no doubt that infallibility was beginning to loom large in the minds of the bishops from the United States. The Sulpician Superior-General Henri Icard had recorded a visit which he paid on December 1 to the American College. There he met Archbishops Spalding and Purcell and Bishops Vérot and Williams. Spalding was most interested in finding out the views of the French hierarchy about infallibility, and he told Icard that, although he did not doubt the doctrine itself, he was not at all sure that a definition was opportune. The Archbishop of Cincinnati did not speak directly about infallibility, but he was very upset that Pius IX had recently complained to the bishops about the supposedly lax state of discipline at the college. Purcell reported that he and others had protested that the house was quite regular and edifying, and he commented to Icard that the complaint had been inspired by the Jesuits, who wanted to take over direction of the seminary. Williams apparently maintained his customary taciturnity, but Bishop Vérot took the occasion to raise the question of Dupanloup. He told Father Icard that the

---

[6] Quirinus, pp. 107–108. Döllinger does not identify the American bishop whom he quotes.

Bishop of Orléans' position was amply justified by the provocative attacks which had been made upon him, and he singled out for special condemnation the intemperate polemic of Louis Veuillot and his newspaper, *L'Univers*.[7]

Archbishop Purcell was one who had for some time been interested in the evidence of tradition for the primacy of the Roman See and the infallibility of its occupant. In February, 1868, he had written to ask Martin J. Spalding's opinion on certain documents connected with the third-century controversy over the validity of baptism conferred by heretics. In that dispute St. Cyprian of Carthage had challenged the decision of Pope St. Stephen I that such baptism was valid. A letter, purported to have been written by Firmilian of Cappadocia, supported Cyprian's position. This letter was at the same time a violent attack on the pope's orthodoxy and, by a reverse twist, an indirect testimony to the pre-eminent position in the Church of the Bishop of Rome. Archbishop Vincenzo Tizzani, a professor at the Roman University of the Sapienza, had recently questioned the authenticity of the Firmilian letter, and Purcell remarked to Spalding that he was inclined to agree with him.[8] Nearly two years later, the Archbishop of Cincinnati was still wondering about Firmilian, as we learn from a letter written to him by Dr. Francis J. Pabisch of the seminary of Mount Saint Mary of the West. Pabisch cited a long list of authorities who had expressed doubts about the provenance of the letter attributed to the Cappadocian. He then went on, apparently in answer to another question posed by Purcell, to catalogue a wide range of evidence for the fact that Pope Honorius I had been condemned by the Sixth General Council, that of Constantinople, in the year 680.[9] Purcell had also come under the influence of Dupanloup, and he was reported to have written home as follows: "The powerful argument of Mgr. Dupanloup on Papal Infallibility

[7] ASS, Icard Journal, December 1, 1869.
[8] AAB, 35–s–31, Purcell to Spalding, Cincinnati, February 29, 1868.
[9] UND, Purcell Papers, Pabisch to Purcell, Cincinnati, December 19, 1869.

86

is the universal topic of conversation; even those who do not agree with him, admit that the pastoral [probably the "Observations" of November 11, 1869, addressed to the clergy of Orléans] was written in the spirit of truest devotion to the highest interests of the Church, and is remarkable, like the many productions of his pen, for its force and learning."[10]

Two other American bishops testified to the increased activity in late December. Bernard McQuaid informed Father Early on December 16: "It seems that disciplinary questions affecting the position of the Church in quasi-Catholic countries are most likely to stir up diversity of views and strong feelings. Fortunately it is not a matter that concerns the American Church to any great degree." But the same could not be said about infallibility, and the letter continued: "The other disturbing element is that of the definition of the infallibility, about which the Jesuits have been so busy to their own detriment. Nothing is said about the dogma, but a great deal about the expediency or advisability of any definition."[11] Archbishop Blanchet of Oregon City noted in his diary that the fathers were kept amply supplied with reading matter. On December 11 he received two pamphlets on the Gallican Church, on the 19th, several unspecified tracts were delivered, and on the 21st, four volumes on infallibility. On the last of these days Bishop Dupanloup left his calling card, and Blanchet also reported hearing from Paris that his companion at the Palazzo Malatesta, Bishop Demers of Vancouver, was ill in the French capital and unable for the moment to return to Rome. The letter that brought this news also conveyed the latest Parisian *bon mot,* a play on the name "Dupanloup." The wags were saying of the Bishop of Orléans, "de pavone lupus"—"the peacock has become a wolf."[12]

The role of the unofficial majority and minority committees in the deputation elections has already been described, and we

---

10 *Catholic Telegraph,* December 23, 1869.
11 McQuaid to Early, Rome, December 16, 1869, in Browne, p. 414.
12 AAS, F. N. Blanchet Journal, December 11, 19, and 21, 1869.

have seen that a series of petitions on procedural points also issued from the minority group. The main objective of both parties was to promote their own particular views on infallibility. There was a third group as well, which initially centered around Archbishop Spalding of Baltimore. The competing efforts of these organizations brought the infallibility question for the first time directly into the open.

The diary of Bishop Ignaz von Senestréy of Regensburg has provided us with a detailed account of the operations of the majority committee. Meetings of the majority leaders seem to have begun about the middle of December. Of the five prelates beside himself whom the Bishop of Regensburg mentioned as having been present at the first session, three were from the Tyrol and represented the only segment of the Austrian hierarchy which did not follow the lead of the cardinals of Vienna and Prague. They were Vincenz Gasser of Brixen, Benedikt von Riccabona of Trent, and Johann Zwerger of Seckau. Three of those in attendance were members of the deputation on faith, namely, Senestréy, Gasser, and Bishop Conrad Martin of Paderborn. Martin belonged to the congregation for receiving proposals. Two members of the deputation for disciplinary matters were also on hand. They were Zwerger and the Bishop of La Crosse Michael Heiss who seems to have been the only American associated with the majority committee at this point. Senestréy's diary added that others were present at the first meeting, but gave no more names. The committee's first project was to frame a petition for the admission of infallibility to the agenda of the council. Several different formulas for this petition were discussed at the initial session. The committee met again on December 23 at the Villa Caserta. The three Tyrolese bishops absented themselves, but the representation from the committees of the council was even more impressive than it had been at the first meeting. There were now three members of the all-important congregation on proposals: Archbishops Dechamps and Manning and Bishop Martin. The deputation on faith was represented by the same three and Senestréy and Bishop Pierre de Preux of Sion, Switzerland: the deputation for discipline by Heiss and Bishops Georg von Stahl of Würzburg, Stephan Marilley of Lausanne and Geneva, and Leo Meurin, S.J., Vicar Apostolic of Bombay. Other delegates were Baron Franz von Leonrod, Bishop of Eichstätt, a member of the deputation on religious orders, and the Vicar Apostolic of Luxembourg Nickolaus Adames.

The third meeting of the majority committee took place on December 28. The wording of the petition was decided upon and it was also agreed that no member of the congregation on proposals would sign, since it was to that committee that the petition had to be presented. The names of those fathers who were thought to favor the petition were printed on it. This document—petition and signatures—was then to be circulated among the bishops for further signatures. Bishop Gasser favored sending a copy to all the members of the council, but he was overruled and circulation was limited to known partisans of infallibility. Senestréy remarked that even many of these refused to lend their support. An added note asked recipients not to publicize the petition, but the committee later decided that this caution was neither necessary nor useful.

Most of the original signers came from Germany, Austria, and France, but Spain was represented by José Caixal y Estrade of Urgel and the oriental bishops by Patriarch Hassun of Cilicia. The sole American was Bishop Heiss. Two of those whose names had been printed on the petition, the Bishops of Seckau and of Ermland, asked that their signatures be dropped.[13] This first petition was circulated among the fathers under the date of December 30.[14] Four days later a second draft, with an enlarged list of names, was distributed. Attached to this second petition was a statement of the committee's proposition, that the authority of the Roman pontiff should be defined as "su-

[13] *Collectio Lacensis*, VII, 1695–6.
[14] Mansi, LI, 644.

preme, therefore free from error, when in matters of faith and morals he has set down and commanded what must be believed and held by all Christians and what must be rejected and condemned."[15] A list of reasons for the doctrine was appended, and then a summary of statements by recent local councils, including a long citation from the Second Plenary Council of Baltimore with pertinent phrases italicized. The passage read as follows:

Living and infallible authority exists only in that Church which was founded by Christ the Lord upon Peter, the head, prince and pastor of the whole Church, whose faith He promised would never fail, and which always has its legitimate pontiffs, who take their origin from Peter himself, who sit upon his chair and are heirs and vindicators of his doctrine, dignity, honor and power. And since the Church is where Peter is, and since Peter speaks through the Roman pontiff and through his successors continues to live and exercise judgment and offer the truth of faith to those who seek it, *therefore divine revelation must be accepted in that sense alone in which it is and has been held by the Roman chair of Blessed Peter,* which is the mother and teacher of all churches and has ever kept the faith given by Christ the Lord whole and inviolate, *and has taught it to the faithful, showing to all the path of salvation and the doctrine of incorrupt truth.*[16] . .

By the end of January, Bishop Senestréy counted some 410 fathers as having signed petitions favoring the definition of papal infallibility. There were several other petitions besides the one put out by the Villa Caserta, but, apart from the formula prepared by Archbishop Spalding, none of them bore any American signatures. Ten prelates from the United States lent their support to the main majority effort. The documents preserved in the Vatican Archives list the signers in groups, each of which put their names down on a separate page. The pages were then collected and attached to the petition. It is therefore possible to determine from the groupings something of the way in which individual fathers were approached. It has already been seen

[15] Mansi, LI, 645–6.
[16] Mansi, LI, 646–50.

that Bishop Heiss was a member of the committee which drew up the petition. His name appears alone, as do those of two Vincentian bishops, John Mary Odin of New Orleans and Claude Dubuis of Galveston. Apart from the notice of his death on May 25, this is the only mention of Odin in the acts of the council. Eugene O'Connell of Grass Valley signed together with the Prior-General of the Augustinians. Bishop Ignaz von Senestréy must have canvassed the Benedictine abbots since his name headed a list of them which included Boniface Wimmer of St. Vincent's. Louis Lootens, the Vicar Apostolic of Idaho, and Augustus Martin of Natchitoches added their signatures to those of the Archbishop of Toulouse and the Coadjutor Bishop of Three Rivers. The latter, Louis La Flèche, had been one of the three Canadian candidates proposed unsuccessfully by the minority for the deputation on faith. Archbishop Blanchet and Bishop Louis de Goesbriand of Burlington, Vermont, signed a page which contained the names of a number of bishops from Canada. Finally, John Baptist Miége's name is found among those of other Jesuit vicars apostolic in a list which also includes that of the general of his order, Petrus Beckx.[17] The fate of the majority petitions which made the rounds of the fathers during January will be seen presently. It is time to turn to the activities of the minority and then to those of Archbishop Spalding.

Like the Villa Caserta committee, the international committee of the minority had begun operations at the time of the deputation elections. Its complete failure at that juncture has already been noted. The next step was an effort to counter the infallibility petitions being prepared by the majority group. On December 26, Bishop Dupanloup held a strategy session with Archbishop Kenrick and the Archbishops of Halifax and Rheims.[18] Three days later he received a letter from Archbishop Darboy of Paris. Darboy reported that he had spoken with

[17] Mansi, LI, 650–60.
[18] ASS, Dupanloup Journal, December 26, 1869.

91

Cardinal Rauscher of Vienna about a meeting place for the minority bishops and that the cardinal did not think his own residence, the Palazzo Nardi, suitable. The Archbishop of Paris suggested instead that the minority meet on the following evening at the Palazzo Salviati. He asked Dupanloup to make the necessary arrangements with Duke Salviati for the use of his home. If this suggestion was not acceptable, Darboy offered his own apartment, or, as an alternative said that he would speak to Rauscher again about the Palazzo Nardi.[19] Bishop David Moriarty of Kerry supplied the rest of the story in a letter to John Henry Newman:

> We have made a little reunion at the Palazzo Salviati. Cardinal Rauscher of Vienna, Archbishop of Paris, Bishop [Jacques Ginoulhiac] of Grenoble, Bishop of Orléans, Archbishop Kenrick of St. Louis, Archbishop Connolly of Halifax, Strossmayer of Bosnia, Ketteler of Mayence, the Bishops of Ivrea [Luigi Moreno] and [illegible] representing north and south Italy, and I.
>
> It is well appointed with the sharp intellect of Mgr. Darboy, the ardent zeal of Dupanloup, the massive intellect of Ketteler, the strategic ability of Ginoulhiac of Grenoble, the Irish slap-dash of Halifax, and the brilliant eloquence of Strossmayer, all presided over by the aristocratic gentleness of Cardinal Rauscher. We are all thoroughly of one mind. Manning works hard and cleverly on the other side.[20]

On January, 4, Lord Acton informed Döllinger of the activities of the international committee, and he had the following comments to make on the North American representatives:

> The Americans Connolly (Halifax, therefore English subject) and Kenrick (St. Louis, brother of the late theologian) have expressed themselves already. Hecker is active in the same sense. Hopes are high. Yet I do not much believe in the depth of their conviction and

19 ASS, Dupanloup Papers, Darboy to Dupanloup, Rome, December 29, 1869.

20 Moriarty to Newman, Rome, January, n.d., 1870, in Butler II, 28. In late January, Odo Russell informed Lord Clarendon that the international committee was composed of twelve members, and he gave eleven of their names: Schwarzenberg, Rauscher, Darboy, Dupanloup, Ginhouliac, Strossmayer, Ketteler, Haynald, Connolly, Kenrick, and Clifford. (Russell to Clarendon, Rome, January 23, 1870, in Blakiston, pp. 383–384.)

count on only a few. The battle will be fought by the French and the Germans. Still Hecker speaks well of his own people.[21]

Bishop McQuaid was discouraged at the controversy which he saw shaping up and wrote to the rector of his cathedral: "The Jesuits and some others are bent on bringing out the definition of infallibility. If the question were left where it belongs, in the Council, no one could complain, but their schemes and tricks outside of the Council are many and mean. Pray God to direct all things for the best."[22] By the time the minority's petition was sent to the deputation, it had been divided into five separate addresses. The work of smoothing out differences and collecting signatures occupied almost the entire month of January.

As early at the first week of the new year, Döllinger's informants had advised him that there might be difficulty in coordinating the minority's forces. This apprehension was reflected in the eighth Quirinus letter which bore the date of January 8. Döllinger wrote: "The question now is, whether the minority of some 200 Prelates have spirit and harmony enough for a counteraddress."[23] On January 11 Dupanloup attended a meeting "at the cardinal's," probably at Rauscher's residence in the Palazzo Nardi. The American and English opposition bishops were present and put their names to a three-point petition drawn up by the former.[24] Three days later, the picture had clouded over, and Dupanloup was not so sure. The notations in his diary for January 14 read: "Sad reflections . . . the Americans hesitate . . . have not signed the three demands."[25] Acton had more optimistic news, and he informed Döllinger on the following day that there were already twenty-five signatures on the American address.[26] The main petition was that of the German-

[21] Conzemius Transcript, Acton to Döllinger, January 4, 1870.

[22] McQuaid to Early, Rome, n.d. [week of January 2–8], 1870, in Browne, p. 418.

[23] Quirinus, p. 132.

[24] ASS, Dupanloup Journal, January 11, 1870.

[25] *Ibid.*, January 14, 1870.

[26] Conzemius Transcripts, Acton to Döllinger, Rome, January 14/15, 1870.

Austrian bloc, and it seemed to be moving along well. By January 15, Quirinus was able to report that thirty-five prelates had agreed in writing to sign it. He added that one reason for the delay in getting out the petition was that papal censorship prevented its being printed, although this had been allowed in the case of the majority address, and that the minority had scruples about having the printing job done beyond the borders of the Papal State.[27]

Meanwhile, the Austrian and German bishops agreed on a formula prepared by Cardinal Rauscher at a meeting in the Palazzo Nardi on January 9.[28] Seven days later it was reported that all the Hungarian hierarchy except the primate Archbishop Simor of Esztergom and the Roumanian-rite Bishop Jozsef Papp-Szilágyi had accepted the German text. An Italian version which corresponded substantially to the German was being prepared. The French opposition fathers met on January 15 at the residence of Cardinal Jacques Mathieu of Besançon. Thirty-three of them adopted a wording which eliminated some of the clauses found in the German and Italian petitions, but retained the same essential ideas. The North American text followed that of the French.[29] Lord Acton was one observer who regretted the alterations made by the French and the Americans. He told Döllinger that he felt the German and Italian petitions made a splendid defense of the honor of the bishops, of the council, and of the Church, but that the French and American formulas, while they surrendered nothing essential, weakened the force of a united front by insisting on their own changes.[30] Archbishop Paulus Melchers of Cologne disagreed with Acton's view of the matter, as did the Archbishop of Salzburg, Maximilian von Tarnoczy, and at a meeting of the German bloc on January 20 it was only the strong protest of Archbishop Hay-

27 Quirinus, p. 153.
28 Friedrich, *Geschichte,* III, 384–5.
29 Quirinus, pp. 187–8.
30 Conzemius Transcripts, Acton to Döllinger, Rome, January 16/19, 1870.

nald of Kalocsa which prevented substitution of the American version for that proposed by Cardinal Rauscher. Melchers and Tarnoczy feared that some of Rauscher's passages might be construed in such a way as to promote disrespect for the Holy See.[31]

The collection of signatures continued during the third week of January. Johann Friedrich claimed that many American bishops were saying that they would not dare return to their dioceses if infallibility were proclaimed. He added that Archbishop Manning had declared that he could not return to England if the dogma were not proclaimed.[32] Considering the lack of any overwhelming American public interest in the question, Friedrich's report was obviously exaggerated. What was probably a more typical attitude among the United States bishops was that expressed by Archbishop McCloskey of New York. According to Acton, the archbishop refused to sign the petition of the Villa Caserta committee with the remark that he had enough to do in defending religion against its enemies, without having to defend it against Catholics also.[33] Maurice de St.-Palais, the Bishop of Vincennes, was one American prelate who refused to sign petitions for either side, but he told Father Icard something which helped to explain the tendency of his fellow countrymen to opposition. They were still smarting, he said, at the almost universal rejection of the candidates whom they had proposed for the deputations.[34] Another report which circulated in the city during this period was not calculated to win for the majority the good will of the American bishops, who depended on the Congregation de Propaganda Fide for the conduct of their Roman business. According to Friedrich, Archbishop Connolly of Halifax had let it be known that Cardinal Barnabò, the Prefect of Propaganda, had threatened him with

[31] Friedrich, *Tagebuch,* p. 126.
[32] *Ibid.,* p. 108.
[33] Conzemius Transcripts, Acton to Döllinger, January 16/19, 1870.
[34] ASS, Icard Journal, January 16, 1870.

the weight of the congregation's displeasure if he did not cease his collaboration with the international committee.[35] Friedrich later claimed that Connolly subsequently severed formal relations with the committee and alleged that his reason for so doing was the pressure to which he had been subjected by Propaganda.[36]

Two bishops from the United States viewed the mounting support for the opposition with some dismay. John Baptist Miége regretted that his "dear Americans" had allowed themselves to be "taken a bit in tow by the Gallicans and the Germans," but he was confident that at the decisive moment the great majority of them would be found on the side of the definition. He felt that the French were less dangerous adversaries than the Germans and Hungarians, but he expressed his hope that the Holy Spirit would influence even the latter. There were some hopeful signs, Miége thought, and he reported that three Portuguese bishops who had been dissuaded from signing the majority petition by Dupanloup had changed their minds after reading the attacks made on the doctrine by the French priest Auguste-Alphonse Gratry. His own convictions were clear, and, after communicating this last bit of information, he added:

It is thus that the good work is done and will continue to be done. If the Holy Father lives, and if the Council can continue its work, despite the underhanded scheming and intrigues of certain spirits, the personal infallibility of the Pope will—*positis ponendis*—be defined, declared and proclaimed for the happiness of the children of the Church and for the good even of its enemies.

In another passage of the same letter Miége continued in the same vein: "What day more beautiful than that when, by an almost unanimous vote, the Pope will be declared infallible! Let us pray that this may be one of the alleluias of Easter."[37]

Bishop Augustus Martin of Natchitoches was much less

35 Friedrich, *Geschichte,* III, 409.
36 *Ibid.,* III, 811.
37 Miége to Alliaudi, Rome, January 30, 1870, in Garin, pp. 147–8.

happy about the situation than was Miége. He penned a forceful denunciation of the minority in a letter to Father Napoleon Perché of New Orleans on January 18:

What shall I say to you about the council? It moves, but slowly and in the midst of a thousand difficulties. In truth, human nature is a sad thing, and the frailty of the human element of the Church is the most evident demonstration of the presence and the power of Him who alone is its light and its way. Two-thirds and more of the council have but one heart and one soul: but we have to wrestle with a turbulent and agitated opposition which considers all means good. Freedom of discussion is unlimited, but unlimited also is the abuse that is made of it. Some are real revolutionaries, others servile creatures of power, others more or less avowed enemies of the Holy See, others those who from their youth have sucked the poison of heresy. They form together a phalanx which grows tighter each day. They wish, and they admit it, to impede the progress of the council, and to drag it out, so as to force the Holy Father to adjourn it, or at least to force the withdrawal of at least 300 missionary bishops who are a hindrance to them and who do not have, as they do, the means to choose at Rome a very expensive residence. I am ashamed of the French episcopate, ashamed also of our own, of which 25 or more let themselves be taken in tow by 2 factious Archbishops and the celebrated ex-Redemptorist, Father H. *Tu quoque* . . . . The Holy Father is saddened. His cardinals are discouraged. Nevertheless let us hope. The good God remains the master.[38]

Martin's letter had its effect in Louisiana, and the Lenten pastoral for 1870 which Perché issued as Administrator of the Archdiocese of New Orleans exhorted the faithful to pray for the success of the Roman assembly, which was, the administrator said, threatened by "diabolical machinations of Gallicanism, Caesarism and liberalism seeking to disturb and impede the operations of the Council and make it fruitless." All religious communities in the archdiocese were requested to offer a weekly general Communion of reparation for the same intention.[39] The letters of Miége and Martin, and Perché's reaction to the

---

[38] UND, Perché Papers, Martin to Perché, Rome, January 18, 1870.
[39] Roger Baudier, *The Catholic Church in Louisiana* (New Orleans: 1939), p. 434.

latter, revealed again the deep division that existed in the ranks of the American hierarchy, a division that was further aggravated by the feverish activity over the petitions.

As January moved into its fourth week, the tempo increased. On Saturday, January 22, Cardinal Rauscher wrote to Cardinal Schwarzenberg that he had learned from the Archbishop of Cologne that the majority address was already in the hands of the congregation on proposals. Archbishop Melchers had received this information from Bishop Conrad Martin of Paderborn. Rauscher added that the French fathers of the opposition had best not delay longer over their own petition.[40] On the next day, the cardinal reported that he had the French address in hand, and that it bore forty-one signatures, including those of some Portuguese bishops. He had also been assured that the petitions of the Italians, the Greeks, and the Americans would be delivered to him by the evening of January 24th. He found the delay disagreeable, but he felt that the sacrifice was worth the possibility of presenting all five petitions simultaneously. He hoped, he said, that this could be done on the 24th.[41] The difficulties of the minority were a well-kept secret. On Sunday, January 23, when Rauscher was in possession of only two of the five petitions, the British diplomatic agent in Rome, Odo Russell, paid a visit to the Austrian embassy in the Palazzo Venezia and came away with the following misinformation, which he communicated to Archbishop Manning:

I have tried in vain to get the opposition petition, which is not printed, but I heard to-night at the Austrian embassy that Cardinal Rauscher had sent it up to the Pope to-day under cover to Monsignor Pacca. It was to have been presented to his Holiness by four archbishops, but each of them declared that three would be sufficient!

The petition is composed of five documents signed by different nationalities, the German one has forty-seven signatures, of the other ones I know nothing positive.[42]

[40] Rauscher to Schwarzenberg, Rome, January 22, 1870, in Granderath, II, 1, p. 185.

[41] Rauscher to Schwarzenberg, Rome, January 23, 1870, in Granderath, II, 1, 185–6.

[42] Russell to Manning, Rome, January 23, 1870, in Purcell, II, 438.

98

A meeting of either the international committee or of the German-Austrian group was scheduled for Wednesday, January 26, but the minority's problems had not yet been ironed out, and Cardinal Rauscher told Cardinal Schwarzenberg:

> I still have no news from the Archbishop of Paris; doubtless he does not know what to say; I believe that Your Eminence should not wait any longer for the Orientals, but send your package to the *Maestro di camera* before today's meeting. If the bishops learn to-day that nothing has yet been done, it could produce upon them an impression very prejudicial to the affair, and discourage them.[43]

It is not clear whether Schwarzenberg, who had been commissioned to submit the petitions, attempted to get them to the pope or not. This had been the original intention of the international committee, and each of the documents was addressed to Pius IX. In any case, the pope refused to entertain any petition, whether from the majority or from the minority, and referred them all to the congregation on proposals.[44] Schwarzenberg's covering letter to the congregation is dated January 29. The German and French memorials bore the date of January 12, that of the English-speaking bishops January 15, and those from the orientals and the Italians January 18.[45]

Forty-five Austrian, German, and Hungarian prelates signed the main petition. The sole outsider to join them was Bishop Ignatius Mrak of Sault-Sainte-Marie and Marquette, Michigan, a native of the Austrian Empire. The signers freely conceded the primary place of the See of Rome in the Church, and they acknowledged that obedience was owed to its decrees. They mentioned that pious and learned men taught that papal decrees *ex cathedra* were to be considered irreformable. Their present objections they phrased under four headings. First, they expressed astonishment that members of the council had been asked to commit themselves to a definition of papal infallibility

[43] Rauscher to Schwarzenberg, Rome, January 26, 1870, in Granderath, II, 1, 186.
[44] Ullathorne to Newman, Rome, February 4, 1870, in Butler, I, 215.
[45] Mansi, LI, 677–84.

before any discussion on the subject had taken place. Next, they declared that the struggle of the Church in the nineteenth century was not with internal enemies, but with those outside who were hostile to its interests. Since no Catholic called the prerogatives of the Holy See into question, the petitioners saw no reason for adding to the obligations in this regard which had already been laid down by the Councils of Trent and Florence. The final point in the petition was a reminder that the definition would provide a weapon for the Church's enemies and afford European governments a pretext for interference in ecclesiastical affairs. The French and Italian texts—neither of which was signed by bishops from the United States—covered these same arguments. What they omitted was another section of the German memorial which declared that it was impossible to propose the doctrine of papal infallibility as divinely revealed dogma until the many historical problems which attended it had been solved. Like the French and Italian versions, the address presented by the Eastern-rite bishops did not incorporate the German reference to historical difficulties. Instead, the oriental prelates simply suggested that the conciliar declaration of Florence on the subject be accepted.[46]

The fifth petition was entered over the signatures of twenty-seven English-speaking bishops. The burden of its argument was that a definition would be inopportune. There were only three paragraphs. In the first of these the signatories declared that discussion of the question would serve to reveal a lack of unity and especially of unanimity among the fathers. Secondly, they claimed that in the peculiar circumstances of their own countries, which were predominantly non-Catholic, the result of a definition would be to alienate those whom they were trying to gain for the Church. The third point looked to the future and foresaw interminable quarrels which would impede the work of the Church and prevent any beneficent effect that

[46] Schwarzenberg's covering letter and the German petition are in Mansi, LI, 677–80; the other petitions follow these.

the work of the council might have among those outside its ranks. The names of five archbishops headed the list of signatures. They were Purcell, Kenrick, Mc Closkey, Connolly, and George Errington—the former Coadjutor Archbishop of Westminster. England was also represented by Bishop William Clifford of Clifton, and Canada by two bishops from New Brunswick, James Rogers of Chatham and John Sweeny of St. John. The only Irish prelates to affix their signatures were David Moriarty of Kerry and the Dominican Bishop of Dromore John Leahy. The remaining seventeen were from the United States and, together with the archbishops, brought the total American count to twenty. The following bishops were listed: Thaddeus Amat, C.M., of Monterey-Los Angeles; David W. Bacon of Portland; James Roosevelt Bayley of Newark; Michael Domenec, C.M. of Pittsburg; Patrick Feehan of Nashville; Edward Fitzgerald of Little Rock, John Hennessy of Dubuque; John Martin Henni of Milwaukee; John Joseph Hogan of St. Joseph; Patrick N. Lynch of Charleston; Francis McFarland of Hartford; Bernard J. McQuaid of Rochester; Joseph Melcher of Green Bay; Tobias Mullen of Erie; James M. O'Gorman, O.C.S.O., of Nebraska; Augustin Vérot, S.S., of Savannah; and Richard V. Whelan of Wheeling.[47]

Caution must be used in attempting to determine the exact intention of any individual bishop who signed the minority petition. The most that can be said without further evidence is that as of January 15, 1870, each of the signatories believed that it would be unwise to raise the question of papal infallibility in the council. This was the gist of the statement to which they lent their names. Bishop McQuaid later filled in something of the background of the petition in a letter to Father James Early. He emphasized that the Americans had asked only one thing, namely, that the question not be brought before the council. Their arguments were external to the doctrine itself, and did not enter into its merits, as did the German text. McQuaid dis-

[47] Mansi, LI, 681–2.

tinguished four categories among the bishops who were approached for their support. One group refused to sign any petition at all. Others agreed that a definition was inexpedient, but did not want to appear hostile to the doctrine. Of the twenty who actually signed the petition, the bishop wrote: "All who signed it were opposed to the doctrine, as understood by the leaders of the other side, except two or three."[48]

The qualifying phrase in the sentence just quoted from McQuaid's letter is of supreme importance, not only for an understanding of the mind of many of the bishops from the United States, but also for a balanced understanding of all the subsequent discussion of the question in the council. As of January 15, no official formula for a definition of papal infallibility had been laid before the fathers. The majority had expressed their own understanding of the prerogative in words that were susceptible of a very broad interpretation. Before the doctrine had been discussed and refined in the council, there existed a wide divergence of views as to the meaning, object, and extent of infallibility. There was certainly room for legitimate apprehension, even on the part of those who might be willing to accept a clear-cut and theologically precise formulation of the dogma. Overzealous partisans fed this apprehension by statements which were at best theologically unsound and at worst approached the blasphemous. We have already seen examples of the mentality of James A. McMaster. In England, William George Ward summarily dismissed the role of theologians as interpreters of papal pronouncements and found infallible declarations even where they were not so intended by the pope. Louis Veuillot perpetrated some of the worst outrages. Two of the more celebrated instances occurred in the pages of L'Univers during October and November, 1869. In one case, he printed as a hymn to the "pontiff-king, Pius IX" words taken from the Veni, Sancte Spiritus, which the liturgy of the Church applied to the Holy Spirit on Pentecost Sunday. On another

[48] McQuaid to Early, Rome, May 24, 1870, in Browne, p. 433.

occasion he published a parody of the breviary hymn for the canonical hour of None, beginning with the words, "*Rerum, Pius, tenax vigor.*" In the original, the hymn is addressed to God. Excesses were not confined to lay dabblers in theology. Auxiliary Bishop Gaspard Mermillod of Geneva, one of the leaders of the majority committee and a future cardinal, had preached openly before the council on "the three incarnations of the Son of God," that is, in the womb of Our Lady, in the Eucharist, and in the pope. This sort of theologizing was certainly sufficient to give pause to any member of the council who took seriously his role as judge of the faith.[49]

In addition to theological difficulties the fathers were also influenced by political and by what we should call today ecumenical considerations. Ultimately each one of the opponents must be considered as an individual, and his individual reasons for opposition must be weighed on their own merits. There was no necessary correlation between a signature on the petition of January 15 and a vote against the definition in July. In many cases, the correlation existed. A more profound study of the issues caused some bishops to pass over to the majority, while others moved in the opposite direction. Still others who were inopportunists in January had conceived theoretical and historical difficulties before the debates were finished. These developments will be revealed in subsequent chapters.

In the case of three of the American signers of the minority petition, there is explicit evidence that they were not opposed to the doctrine of infallibility. Even before the petition had been handed in, Acton told Döllinger that Bishop Lynch of Charleston was one of "several friends of the dogma" who had nevertheless agreed to go along with the protest.[50] Two months later, Bishop Hogan wrote from Paris to Archbishop Spalding

---

[49] An excellent survey of the thought of Ward and Veuillot is found in Ward, pp. 234–74. See also Roger Aubert, *Le Pontificat de Pie IX (1846–1878)* (Paris: 1952), pp. 301–303. The examples are taken from these sources.

[50] Conzemius Transcripts, Acton to Döllinger, Rome, January 22, 1870.

and asked him, in his capacity as a member of the deputation on faith, to have his name erased from the document. He had been influenced, he said, by the fears of some prelates that a definition would mean the end of state subsidy to the Church in France and the withdrawal of French troops from Rome. But now that he had spent two weeks and three days in France, the Bishop of St. Joseph was convinced that such apprehensions were groundless, and therefore the reason for his opposition had vanished.[51] James M. O'Gorman was another who later formally retracted his signature. It is probable that he had originally consented to the petition at the behest of Archbishop Kenrick, his metropolitan, upon whom he had long been dependent for advice in matters affecting the Church at large. His retraction did not explain the reasons for his change of heart on infallibility, but it did make it quite clear that he had never been more than an inopportunist. After his return to the United States in the spring of 1870, he wrote to the Secretary-General of the Trappists: "I wish to repair any offense that I may unintentionally have given by signing my name to the letter of the inopportunists." If it were at all possible, O'Gorman wanted his vote cast by proxy in favor of the definition and he asked the secretary to commission either the Abbot of La Grande Trappe or Bishop James Gibbons to do this favor for him.[52]

The name of Martin J. Spalding was conspicuously absent from both the majority and minority petitions. In his letters to Cardinal Barnabò and Dr. Corcoran during 1869, he had been inclined to take an inopportunist line. Although he later claimed that he had come to realize the extent of Gallican influence in the Church from the reading which he did while enroute to Rome—and stated that this had determined him to a more positive course in respect to the definition—he was, as we have seen, still wavering on the question when he spoke to

[51] AAB, 34-G-8, Hogan to Spalding, Paris, March 8, 1870.
[52] O'Gorman to Father Stanislaus, Omaha, June 9, 1870, in Mansi, LI, 682.

Father Icard on December 1. Archbishop Purcell claimed that Spalding had encouraged the American minority petition of January 15, and had refrained from signing it himself only because he was a member of the deputation on faith, to which it would presumably be referred. This incident was said to have occurred during a meeting of twenty bishops at the American College.[53] There is no other evidence to connect Spalding with the January 15 petition, although its tenor coincided with his own previously expressed views. Certainly, Döllinger's informants saw in the Archbishop of Baltimore an enemy of their own projects. On January 7, for example, Acton wrote: "Despite Hecker's assurances, Spalding's example will draw over many of the Americans."[54]

Further confirmation of this estimate of Archbishop Spalding as hostile to the minority was contained in an erroneous notation which Johann Friedrich made in his diary. Although the German theologian's information was incorrect, in that he associated Spalding with the leaders of the majority, he did make it clear that the Baltimore prelate was considered no friend of his party. The diary passage read: "The infallibilists, with their priority-petition, which has gone out from Archbishops Manning, Spalding and Dechamps, have finally brought the opposition to a determined stand."[55] Döllinger summed up reports reaching him from Rome in the ninth Quirinus letter, which was dated January 9. He claimed that pressure from Napoléon III's government was about to force Piux IX to make Archbishop Georges Darboy of Paris a cardinal, and he added: "Some consolation for it is found on the now openly proclaimed apostasy from the anti-definition side of Archbishop Spalding of Baltimore, who had hitherto been wavering, for it is hoped that other

[53] Purcell made this statement in a speech delivered on August 21, 1870, at Mozart Hall in Cincinnati. (Catholic Telegraph, August 25, 1870.)

[54] Conzemius Transcripts, Acton to Döllinger, Rome, January 6/7, 1870.

[55] Friedrich, Tagebuch, p. 87. Odo Russell reported to Lord Clarendon on January 10 that the leaders of the infallibilist group were Spalding, Mermillod, and Manning. (Russell to Clarendon, Rome, January 10, 1870, in Blakiston, p. 379.)

American Bishops will follow his example."[56] In these statements, the Quirinus group drew a picture of Spalding that was too simple. Whatever may have been his relations with the minority, one thing is certain, and it is that in early January he was not associated with the activities of the Villa Caserta committee, of which Manning and Dechamps were among the chief representatives. Instead, he was attempting to find a middle ground which would be acceptable to all factions.

Canon Roger Aubert has pointed out that it is an oversimplification to speak as if there were only two parties at the council, one of them for the definition of infallibility and the other against.[57] There were clearly defined extremes, but within the extremes there existed a considerable body of opinion which may be called moderate. Even within this moderate camp, a distinction must be made. One group wanted the council to make some affirmation of infallibility, another thought it inexpedient, but was open to possible compromise. Among the bishops of the United States, many of the Franco-American prelates belonged to the strongly infallibilist party, but Augustin Vérot opposed the definition, while Amadeus Rappe of Cleveland and Maurice de St.-Palais of Vincennes were moderate proponents. Bishops Elder and Heiss were also strongly in favor of the definition. Archbishop Kenrick was the most prominent American anti-infallibilist. The support which he was able to muster for his position will be seen presently. Spalding was the leader of the American moderates. Aubert claims that his position was shared by most of the prelates close to Pius IX, including the Secretary of State Giacomo Antonelli. He summed up their stand in a delightful phrase: "Italians have a ready appreciation for adjustments, and the Roman prelates in particular have little taste for violent solutions." Other moderates, all of whom accepted infallibility as a doctrine, were Archbishop Dechamps of Malines, Bishops Ullathorne and Martin of Pader-

[56] Quirinus, p. 146.
[57] Roger Aubert, "Documents concernant le tiers parti au concile du Vatican," *Abhandlungun über Theologie und Kirche; Festschrift für Karl Adam* (Ed. Marcel Reding et al.; Düsseldorf: 1952), p. 241.

born, and the General of the Jesuits, Petrus Beckx.[58] However all the moderates were not of one mind, as Spalding was to discover. For example, three of those just mentioned, namely, Dechamps, Martin, and Beckx, were signers of the majority petition.

The move to find a middle-of-the-road solution was encouraged and even promoted by official circles in Rome. On January 18, Bishop Karl Joseph von Hefele told Johann Friedrich that he had been asked by the secretary of the council Bishop Fessler to accept the leadership of a moderate group.[59] Hefele rejected the suggestion, but Fessler continued his activities, and Count Trauttmansdorf, the Austrian Ambassador, reported them to Vienna on January 22.[60] Four days later the French Ambassador, the Marquis de Banneville, informed his government that a compromise document was already being circulated among the fathers. This was apparently a formula drawn up by Archbishop Spalding.[61]

According to his nephew and biographer, Spalding had prepared his text for an indirect and implicit definition of papal infallibility before being named to the congregation on proposals.[62] It is probable that James A. Corcoran had a hand in its composition, if he was not completely responsible for its wording.[63] There were two separate texts. The first and shorter version found its way into the acts of the council over Spalding's own signature. It contained three condemnations. The first of these was directed at anyone who appealed to a future council as if it were superior to the pope. The second condemnation referred to those who held that only external assent was owed to papal pronouncements, and the third recalled the tortuous evasions of the Jansenists by proscribing the opinion of those who held that the pope, in condemning certain propositions, had

[58] *Ibid.*, pp. 241–2.

[59] Friedrich, *Tagebuch,* pp. 111–2.

[60] Aubert, "Documents," p. 243.

[61] *Ibid.*, p. 244.

[62] John Lancaster Spalding. *The Life of the Most Rev. M. J. Spalding, D.D.* (New York: 1873), p. 395.

[63] Corcoran's authorship is affirmed by James F. Loughlin, "James Andrew Corcoran," *The Catholic Encyclopedia* IV, 356.

107

not fully understood their meaning.[64] The second Spalding *schema* included the same three points and added a fourth condemnation, namely, of those who attempted to divide the pope and the bishops by entering into disputes as to the relative importance of the pontiff and the episcopate, "as if an assembly of brothers, whom Peter is commanded, even in his successors, to confirm, could ever be severed from him whose faith, by the promise of Christ, shall never fail; or as if they who are to be taught and confirmed by Peter could ever lawfully teach and confirm in opposition to him."[65]

There is no date on either text, so that it is impossible to determine when they were presented. One or both were accompanied by a pair of covering letters. The first, written in Italian, commended the proposals to Cardinal de Angelis, the first president of the council. It was signed by Bishop James F. Wood of Philadelphia. The second letter, in Latin, was addressed to Cardinal Constantino Patrizi, the senior member of the congregation on proposals. Wood's name headed the list of signatures. He was joined by Bishops John Quinlan of Mobile, John Conroy of Albany, John Williams of Boston, and William Henry Elder of Natchez.[66] Appended to the second formula were two long quotations confirmatory of the doctrine just enunciated, and a list of six reasons why the *schema* was thought to be expedient. The first quotation repeated the address of loyalty made to Pius IX by over 500 bishops on the occasion of the eighteenth centenary of the martyrdom of Saints Peter and Paul in 1867.[67] The second passage was the citation from the Second Plenary Council of Baltimore which had been incorporated in the majority address. It consisted in a concatenation

[64] Mansi, LI, 663–4.

[65] Mansi, LI, 664. Also, in English and Latin, in Spalding, pp. 386–7. Martin Spalding's manuscript copy is in AAB, 39-N-4, and 39-L-2 and 3.

[66] Mansi, LI, 664.

[67] Dupanloup had had a hand in preparing the 1867 address and had seen to it that the word "infallible" was left out, despite the protests of Manning. See Aubert, *Pontificat de Pie IX*, p. 310.

of statements from the Councils of Chalcedon, Ephesus and Trent, from Saints Ambrose and Peter Chrysologus, and from an encyclical letter of Pope Pius IX.

Archbishop Spalding's first reason for preferring his formula was the hope that it would win nearly unanimous approval from the bishops. In one of his early drafts he wrote that it contained "principles already settled & accepted by all except Gallicans, who are a mere hand full [sic]," but this comment was omitted in the copy submitted to the cardinals.[68] He felt that unanimity in such a serious matter was not only good, but seemed to be demanded, and he felt that whatever definition was made should, if possible, be made with no one dissenting. This second point is one to which we shall have to return, since it later involved the archbishop in an acrimonious controversy with Bishop Dupanloup. Thirdly, Spalding warned that the Church had enough external enemies without having to stir up discord within its own household. His fourth reason was that the formula which he proposed was clearer and simpler and more comprehensive than a formal and explicit definition, and less open to theological quibbling. The fifth point was that the *schema* made the pope's infallibility the logical corollary of his primacy, and its limits the same as the infallibility of the Church. Finally, Spalding felt that he had avoided one of the great difficulties that seemed to be looming ahead, since his definition was prospective and not retrospective. He hoped that it would escape the historical arguments that were certain to be used against a formal definition.[69]

Circulation of Spalding's proposal gave rise to considerable speculation in Rome. Albert du Boÿs wrote in his memoirs that the scheme had been elaborated without consultation of either

---

[68] AAB, 33-M-8.

[69] All the official documents connected with the Spalding proposal are in Mansi, LI, 663–6. They are found, in both English and Latin, in J. L. Spalding, pp. 387–94. Manuscript copies of the *schema* are in AAB, 39-L-2 and 3, and 39-N-4. Manuscript copies of Spalding's reasons for preferring his *schema* to a formal definition are in AAB, 33-M-8 and 39-N-1.

majority or minority fathers, and that the text has been distributed without its author's name being mentioned.[70] Odo Russell sent two reports on the affair to Archbishop Manning. In one of these, he said that he had been shown a document which was supposed to have emanated from Bishop Conrad Martin of Paderborn, Spalding, and Manning himself, and he declared that the minority found it "quite inadmissable."[71] In a second note to the Archbishop of Westminster, Russell relayed the information that the Prussian and Bavarian diplomatic representatives to the Holy See had told him that the compromise plan was the work of Manning, Spalding, and Dechamps. He had, he went on, expressed his surprise and doubt at the truth of the rumor since he could not see that any compromise was necessary in the matter.[72]

One further piece of contemporary evidence strikes an oddly jarring note. On the evening of February 6, Henri Icard paid one of his periodic visits to the American College. He found the Archbishop of Cincinnati highly exercised over portions of the text of the recently distributed *schema de ecclesia.* Purcell also confirmed what Icard said he had himself thought all along, that the formula which had come to be known as that of the "third party" was the work of "the Bishop of St. Louis and the Archbishop of Baltimore."[73] This is the only suggestion that has been found of collaboration between the two archbishops— Kenrick and Spalding—in the matter of the petitions. On the face of it, such collaboration would appear to have been unlikely, although in January their aims did coincide to the extent that both wanted to avoid an outright confrontation of the council with the question of infallibility. It must be remembered that Kenrick was the prime mover in the American minority petition of January 15, and that that petition relied solely on the argument of inexpediency. Even the gingerly German approach

[70] ASMP, Du Boÿs Papers, Memoirs of the Council, pp. 14–5.
[71] Russell to Manning, Rome, n.d., in Purcell, II, 441.
[72] Russell to Manning, Rome, "Sunday," *Ibid.,* II, 440.
[73] ASS, Icard Journal, February 6, 1870.

to historical difficulties connected with the dogma had been deliberately omitted in the American version. It is also possible that Acton was referring to the Spalding petition when he remarked to Döllinger on January 28: "Archbishop Kenrick of St. Louis, one of the calmest men in Rome, does not at all believe in the count of 400 [claimed by Manning for the majority petition]. Consequently, this will be withdrawn, and the opportune assistance of the milder address will become necessary through want of success."[74]

Archbishop Purcell is the sole certain witness for the supposed Kenrick-Spalding collaboration—if Icard understood him correctly. His is also the only testimony we have about Spalding's encouragement of the petition of January 15. Interpretation of the Acton letter just quoted as confirmatory of the collaboration is rendered doubtful by the general tone of the Englishman's other comments on Spalding's plan. He was quite hostile to it, and at the same time he was extremely close to Kenrick. We would expect him to have informed Döllinger if the Archbishop of St. Louis were connected with a proposal that conflicted with the views held by the Quirinus group. Kenrick and Spalding had previously disagreed sharply over the management of the Second Plenary Council of Baltimore. Their disagreement on the question of infallibility erupted into a public and rather bitter debate during April, 1870.

On January 20 Lord Acton reported that the Archbishop of Baltimore had put his program before the French minority group. The French prelates rejected the scheme, he said, and told Spalding that they were not interested in any compromises.[75] The next piece of evidence we have comes from Ullathorne's letter of February 4 to Newman. According to the Bishop of Birmingham, Cardinal Bilio, president of the deputation on faith, had told an American archbishop—presumably

[74] Conzemius Transcripts, Acton to Döllinger, Rome, January 28, 1870.
[75] Conzemius Transcripts, Acton to Döllinger, Rome, January 19/20, 1870.

Spalding—that there had originally been no intention of presenting the council with a *schema* on infallibility, but that attacks made by the two Frenchmen, Bishops Dupanloup and Henri Maret, had forced the issue. However, the cardinal promised that the proposal would be moderate in tone. Ullathorne commented, in an obvious reference to the Spalding plan which he had already mentioned in his letter, "My general knowledge enables me to say that this, amongst other things, implies the omission of the word 'infallible,' and I apprehend also the limitation to some such terms as the obedience due to Pontifical decisions and their irreversibility." Parenthetically, it should be added that the majority bore at least equal responsibility for forcing the issue. Ullathorne wrote: "I, of course, do not forget that one of these prelates [Dupanloup] was roused up by excesses on the other side, nor do I forget who roused him."[76] The reference is to the epistolary controversy between the Bishop of Orléans and Manning, which had begun in November, 1869.[77] Moreover, the first to bring the infallibility question to the formal notice of the council had been Bishop Anton Pluym of Nicopoli, who presented a petition for the definition on December 18.[78]

The Belgian Minister to the Holy See informed his government of the activities of the "third party" in a letter dated February 5. He reported that the leading figures in the effort to organize those who were not "fettered by prejudice or preoccupation with self-love" were Archbishop Spalding and Cardinal Henri de Bonnechose of Rouen. The diplomat was not, however, optimistic about the success of the project.[79] Isaac Hecker reflected the *malaise* which had settled over the fathers when he wrote to Orestes Brownson: "The council is in the via purgativa or discussiva, and from appearances it will be some time before it will enter upon the via illuminitiva." He expressed his

---

[76] Ullathorne to Newman, Rome, February 4, 1870, in Butler, I, 214–7.
[77] *Ibid.*, pp. 149–50.
[78] Mansi, LI, 639–40.
[79] Aubert, "Documents," p. 243.

confidence, however, that God's will would in the end prevail, and he concluded: "Light will come and action follow in due season."[80]

Spalding's fruitless efforts continued throughout February. On February 13, Cardinal Mathieu of Besançon asked Father Icard's opinion of a communication which he had received from the Archbishop of Baltimore. In his letter Spalding identified himself as the author of the four-point *schema* and asked Mathieu to use his influence for its adoption by the French minority bishops. If the four points were unacceptable, Spalding had said, then he would like to know what modifications might make it acceptable, or what alternative program could be substituted for it to secure agreement. Icard told the cardinal that he considered the first and fourth points superfluous. Number one was already in the *schema* on the Church which had been distributed to the fathers, and number four belonged to the section on the infallibility of the Church, rather than to that on the infallibility of the pope. He thought that paragraphs two and three might be allowed to stand if they were modified. In particular he objected to the term "perverse quibbling" as applied to those who held that only external assent need be given to papal pronouncements and he also felt that the third paragraph should be revised so as to skirt controversies which might be aroused by its wording.[81] Cardinal Mathieu brought the Spalding *schema* to the attention of the French minority at their meeting on February 15, but Dupanloup indicated in his diary that there was no great enthusiasm for its provisions. Archbishop Darboy of Paris, he said, opposed it, while the Archbishop of Rheims, Jean-Baptiste Landriot, dismissed it as "more than a definition."[82]

Archbishop Spalding made one final attempt to persuade the French bishops. On the morning of February 17 he went to Cardinal Mathieu and asked if he might not be permitted to

80 UND, Brownson Papers, Hecker to Brownson, Rome, February 4, 1870.
81 ASS, Icard Journal, February 13, 1870.
82 ASS, Dupanloup Journal, February 15, 1870.

address the minority prelates in person and explain his *schema* to them. The cardinal answered that he could make no promises, and that same evening the bishops voted to reject all compromise and to stand by their own original counterpetition.[83] Spalding was no more successful with the German-Austrian group. On February 16, Cardinal Rauscher wrote to Cardinal Schwarzenberg: "I heard yesterday from reliable sources that attempts will be made to enlist the support of the Austrian and German bishops for the Spalding proposition, which has been put out from the American College. I hope without result."[84] The obituary notice to these efforts to gather minority support was written by the Norbertine canon Franz Mayer, a confidant and theological advisor of the Cardinal Archbishop of Prague: "The compromise proposed by Spalding is evidently no compromise at all, and embraces in its indistinct generality much more than an explicit definition of *ex cathedra* statements."[85]

After the failure of Archbishop Spalding's proposal, Cardinal Henri de Bonnechose of Rouen and a group of French bishops continued to work for a compromise solution, but their endeavors had no more success than the American attempt. The Bonnechose party differed from Spalding in that they were all inopportunists, while he was considered a moderate infallibilist. At first there were hopes that a settlement acceptable to all factions might be achieved, but the new regulations of February 22 and the pressures for a strong definition exerted by the majority disappointed those of the minority who were tempted to compromise, and in the end nothing was accomplished.[86]

Reaction to Spalding's plan from anti-infallibilist sources outside the council was unfavorable. This, added to the lack of

---

[83] Friedrich, *Tagebuch*, pp. 189–190. Friedrich had his information from Archbishop Haynald, who had just visited Mathieu. This and the two following citations are also found in Aubert, "Documents," p. 257.

[84] Rauscher to Schwarzenberg, Rome, February 16, 1870, in Wolfsgruber, III, 245.

[85] The quotation is from Mayer's diary, cited *ibid.*

[86] Aubert, "Documents," pp. 244–55, tells the story of the Bonnechose group.

any perceptible ground swell in support of it from the infal-libilist side, spelled its doom. Döllinger was an outspoken critic. On February 8 he instructed Acton to see to it that an answer was made to the archbishop's use of the episcopal address of July 1, 1867 as an argument in support of his proposals. The German professor suggested that Dupanloup might undertake this task.[87] Three days earlier he had summarized the *schema* as demanding "that everybody must assent to every doctrinal de-cision of the Pope on pain of everlasting damnation," and this, he commented, beyond even the desires of Manning and De-champs, who would at least restrict infallibility to decrees addressed to the whole Church. He concluded confidently:

Every theologian must declare this invention of the Archbishop of Baltimore's to be the most monstrous demand ever made on the con-science and understanding of the Catholic world. It is as if a courtier at Teheran were to say, 'I will not indeed affirm that our Shah is al-mighty, but I do assert confidently that he can create out of nothing what he will and that his will is always accomplished.' The reverend fathers who torment themselves with inventing such devices would perhaps do best if they were to make a collection among themselves, and offer a prize of 100 ducats for that form of circumlocution or involution most securely adapted for entrapping the innocent souls of Bishops. Then the most ingenious heads from all Europe would com-pete in sending in their suggestions, and the right bait might be dis-covered among them.[88]

Three weeks later, Döllinger was still disturbed at the Spalding petition, and he returned to the attack in the twenty-sixth letter of the Quirinus series:

Archbishop Spalding of Baltimore has not receded from his ludicrous notion that his infallibilist formula is milder and more tolerable than that of the 400 . . . . Its essence consists, as was mentioned before, in asserting that everybody must receive with unconditional inward assent every Papal decision on every question of faith or morals or Church life. On all theological principles such faith can only be accorded in cases where all possibility of error is excluded, or, in other words,

87 Conzemius Transcripts, Döllinger to Acton, Munich, February 8, 1870.
88 Quirinus, pp. 213–4.

where a revealed truth is concerned; and therefore to accept this formula would be to set aside the limitation of Papal Infallibility, hitherto recognized even in Rome, to decisions pronounced *ex cathedra*. And thus, in the crush and confusion of the innumerable and often contradictory decisions of Popes, theology would degenerate into a lamentable caricature of a system—"science" it could not longer be termed—involved in hopeless contradictions. If the good Spalding had the slightest acquaintance with Church history, he would know that he was bound, in virtue of his inward assent paid to all Papal decrees, first of all to reject his own orders as invalid.[89]

The German theologian's attack, for all its polemical sarcasm, did single out the major defect in Spalding's proposal. The archbishop had deliberately made his *schema* more comprehensive than an explicit definition. This was not the way to conciliate the opposing parties and it betrayed a lack of understanding of the minority's mentality. Their objection was not primarily to the word "infallibility," as Spalding seemed to imply. They were not mere nominalists. The principal labor of the council was destined to be a gradual refinement of the definition formula until it expressed accurately and precisely the limits, conditions, and objects of infallible papal pronouncements. This was the process which Spalding attempted to avoid with his vague general statements. It was an approach which pleased neither side.

Back home in the United States, the press was still bedeviled by lack of exact information on the proceedings in Rome. On January 29, the New York *Tribune* tried to line up the contending forces. Its correspondent listed three parties: those who believed with Archbishop Manning that the pope was infallible in both spiritual and temporal matters, those at the opposite extreme who held with Archbishop Darboy and Bishop Maret that infallibility rested with the hierarchy, and, finally, a middle

[89] Quirinus, pp. 313–4. The reference to invalid orders had been explained in Döllinger's earlier work, published under the pseudonym of "Janus." He claimed that there was so much confusion on the point in Italy during the eight and ninth centuries that many ordinations conferred by popes were annulled by subsequent popes and synods. See Janus, *The Pope and the Council* (Boston: 1870), pp. 42–4.

group of inopportunists headed by Dupanloup and Schwarzen-berg. These last were said to hold the infallibility of the pope only when he spoke *ex cathedra*. The *Tribune* stated that an "important" part of the French and Belgian bishops and the majority of the Americans belonged to the inopportunist party.[90] The inaccuracies in the report are obvious, but they demonstrate the fallacy of a policy that had refused the world press adequate opportunity to cover the council. In mid-February, a full month after the minority addresses had been signed by twenty-one American prelates, the *World* carried an item to the effect that some bishops from the United States had refused to sign the majority petitions[91] The *Herald* was better informed when it reported on February 28 that a "third party" had grown up among the fathers, and it gave a reasonably accurate summary of the Spalding proposals.[92]

Some Catholic sources had access to more direct information. On January 23, Paulist Father Augustine F. Hewit, the acting editor of the *Catholic World* in the absence of Isaac Hecker, wrote to Orestes Brownson:

> I hear the bishops are all deeply studying the question of papal infallibility and it is supposed about one fourth are against the op-portuneness of the definition. If they are obliged first to vote on the question is it definable as a dogma, the opposition will be in straits, & I feel sure we shall have a definition. The memorial against the Papal Bull regulating the council got only fourteen signatures, & on Xmas Day the Pope gave them a beautiful sermon on despising human respect & listening with humility to his teaching as the Vicar of Christ.[93]

Two weeks later, Hewit wrote again to Brownson: "I am very glad to see you writing on papal infallibility and I hope you will keep up the fire, as I am somewhat restricted in these things."[94]

90 New York *Tribune*, January 29, 1870, in Beiser, pp. 82–3.
91 The *World* (New York), February 14, 1870, *ibid.*, p. 86.
92 New York *Herald*, February 28, 1870, *ibid.*, pp. 90–91.
93 UND, Brownson Papers, Hewit to Brownson, New York, January 23, 1870.
94 *Ibid.*, Hewit to Brownson, New York, February 9, 1870.

James A. McMaster of the *Freeman's Journal* was kept supplied with news by two correspondents. One of them, William Faulkner Browne, M.D., reported on February 3 that he had arranged a subscription to *Civiltà Cattolica* for McMaster. He added that the other Italian papers—*Giornale, Osservatore Romano,* and *Unità Cattolica*—were all very good "to light your cigar with—or for some other purpose—but as newspapers Oh!" Browne warned McMaster to beware of using too much imagination in his comments on the situation in Rome, and said that there was actually very little news available. He had tried without success to get hold of a copy of the petition against the definition, but had learned that many of the United States bishops were among the signers. He concluded: "I think that the opposition to the definition of dogma is good because it will insure its definition."[95] McMaster's second informant was Father Eugene M. O'Callaghan of the Diocese of Cleveland. O'Callaghan was in Rome on behalf of another of the crusades sponsored by the *Freeman's Journal,* a campaign for the establishment of canonical parishes in the United States. He wrote on February 26:

The question of the infallibility of the Pope is convulsing the assembled prelates considerably. It has strong opposition and will give rise to a great deal of bad will. It will almost without doubt be introduced. The question De Ecclesia is now up for deliberation and afterwards comes the Question De Summo Pontifice, when it will be introduced. There are many grave reasons offered *contra,* and many objections, but I understand each party gives the opposite party credit for conscientious and sincere motives. Notwithstanding this, there is a great deal of excitement. There have been also objections—and it would seem from the statement of the Bishop who informed me—not unreasonable ones to the manner in which some of the "Committees" have been formed. But I trust and pray that the issue may be peaceful and the end productive of harmony.[96]

[95] UND, McMaster Papers, Browne to McMaster, Rome, February 3, 1870.

[96] UND, McMaster Papers, O'Callaghan to McMaster, Rome, February 26, 1870.

The editor of the *Freeman's Journal* was not disposed to the same degree of magnanimity as the correspondent. On February 5, he reported that a petition had been submitted for the definition and went on to say that there were rumors that a second and contrary memorial was being prepared. His only comment was to add in brackets: "Feebly signed by a very few. Ed. F. J."[97] A month later the news had been confirmed, and McMaster had heard that "a very respectable minority" had signed the inopportunists' petition. He remarked of this minority, "a small one either as to number or character."[98] By March 19, the facts were clear and the New York editor could not contain his hurt astonishment. He refused to believe that Archbishops Purcell and Kenrick were involved in the affair and that they had the support of a considerable number of the American bishops. It must be "idle Roman gossip," he thought, although it was obvious to McMaster that there was a "spirit of heresy and schism rampant."[99]

Other Catholic newspapers were not so outspoken. The *Catholic Telegraph* of Cincinnati had been a strong supporter of the definition until March. On the third of that month, it printed a letter which had been received from its Roman correspondent, "Viator." The letter was dated February 5, and said in part: "The question of infallibility has assumed a new character; many prelates are in favor of a compromise, if there can be any such thing . . . . I have known since I came to Rome (Nov. 10, 1869) that the majority of the *working* Bishops were opposed to it."[100] Two more Viator letters appeared in the *Telegraph's* March 10 edition. On February 12 he had written that "few of the American, Canadian, English or Irish Bishops are in favor of the dogma," and that many were annoyed over the "petition business," which had originated with Archbishop Manning. In a letter sent on February 14, Viator declared that Archbishops

[97] *Freeman's Journal,* February 5, 1870.
[98] *Ibid.,* March 5, 1870.
[99] *Ibid.,* March 19, 1870.
[100] *Catholic Telegraph,* March 3, 1870.

McCloskey, Purcell, and Kenrick had lost their chances for a cardinal's hat because of opposition to the "new dogma."[101] The *Telegraph* later apologized for this "unbecoming and untrue reference . . . concerning the relations of the Holy See and some of the American episcopacy," and its subsequent treatment of the whole question of infallibility was marked by a more detached approach than had been used in the earlier months of the council; it was no longer a strong advocate of the definition.[102]

The Pittsburgh *Catholic* also modified its stand as a result of dispatches from Rome. On February 19, its columns contained a defense of the temporal power of the pope and also some remarks on the fallacious reasoning of the inopportunists. On the temporal power, the editor remarked that its opponents reminded him of the parishioner who "saves a few dollars by practicing his creed of spiritualizing the clergy." Only "weak-kneed persons," he went on, feared the definition of papal infallibility. "It is not by toning down the truth, by covering up its stern outlines, that the Church is to be spread, as some romantic lackadaisical Christians seem to think."[103] It was not until May 7 that the *Catholic* obtained a copy of the minority petition, which was then printed without comment, although it included the name of the Bishop of Pittsburgh among the signers.[104] Two weeks later, the editor remarked that the petition proved that there was freedom of discussion in the council, and he placed the best possible interpretation on the intentions of those who had presented it.[105] Neither the *Catholic* nor the *Telegraph* turned into anti-infallibilist journals, although the latter did lean towards inopportunism. The American Catholic press in general continued to favor the definition, although none was quite so violent in their partisanship as the *Freeman's Journal*. All through the council they labored under the double handicap

[101] *Ibid.*, March 10, 1870.
[102] The apology is in the March 19 issue of the *Telegraph*.
[103] The *Catholic*, February 19, 1870.
[104] *Ibid.*, May 7, 1870.
[105] *Ibid.*, May 21, 1870.

of inadequate and delayed information. By the time the issues before the council were discussed in the United States, the fathers had already moved on to a new phase of their work. The result was that comments in American journals were most often nothing more than out-of-date reprints, culled principally from the pro-infallibility newspapers of Europe.

The three-week adjournment which began on February 22 marked, as we have seen, a turning point in the council. There is only one more incident which must be mentioned before summing up the situation of the American bishops at that time. This was the visit of Pope Pius IX to the American College on January 29. The occasion was the promulgation of a formal decree declaring that the apostle of sixteenth-century Corsica, Giovanni Giovenale Ancina, was to be considered venerable. The pope, attended by Cardinals Patrizi, Capalti, and Barnabò, presided at a Mass in the college church at which all the American bishops assisted. Afterwards he delivered a short sermon in Italian on the virtues proper to the episcopate. When the ceremonies were over, a reception was held in the great hall of the college and Archbishop Spalding spoke on behalf of the Americans. He traced briefly the history of the Church in the United States and ended his discourse, as Bishop Gibbons remembered, with "a few touches of true American wit." The pope entered into the spirit of Spalding's talk and seemed to enjoy these lighter touches, although his attendants were taken aback by the unexpected informality.[106]

James Gibbons interpreted the pope's visit as "a very signal and very agreeable mark of his good will" towards the American bishops. Others were inclined to a more cynical interpretation. The sixteenth Quirinus letter reported:

The North American Bishops too are being gradually educated to ecclesiastical maturity in the school of Rome and the Council, and have already grown out of that naïve belief in the disinterested generosity and superhuman wisdom of the *Curia* which most of them brought here. To-day the Pope paid them a visit at the American

[106] Gibbons, I, 57–63.

College, conversed in a friendly way with the Bishops individually, said obliging things, and, in a word, displayed those well-known powers of fascination he has such a command of. "A month ago this would have taken effect," said an American priest who was present, "but now it comes too late."[107]

The source of Döllinger's information was Lord Acton, who had written on February 2: "[The pope] made a visit three days ago to the American College and spoke very cleverly with each of the bishops. Hecker was there and said to [Archbishop Xavier de] Mérode: 'It is too late. A month ago he would have been able to accomplish something.'"[108] Johann Friedrich's account was even more at variance with that of Gibbons and he also succeeded in transforming the festival of the sixteenth-century Italian bishop into an American national holiday. His diary entry for February 4 read:

In the last few days, the pope gave a talk at the American College on the occasion of a national holiday, in which he complained quite openly and frankly about the opposition of a segment of the American bishops, so that a bishop said to my informant, Count . . . , "This is too much. Now the pope goes from house to house and exerts pressure on the bishops."[109]

It is not difficult to see the wishful thinking that crept into the reports of both Acton and Friedrich. While it is true that a personal visit from the pope was calculated to impress the American bishops, there is no evidence, apart from the accounts of two scarcely impartial observers, neither of whom was present, that any overt attempt was made to win votes for the definition.

[107] Quirinus, p. 208.
[108] Conzemius Transcripts, Acton to Döllinger, Rome, February 1/2, 1870. Mérode, a member of a noble Belgian family, had been Pius IX's Minister of War and was the chief architect of the many civic improvements made in Rome during his reign. But he remained until the final balloting an opponent of the definition.
[109] Friedrich, *Tagebuch,* p. 155. The informant was probably Count Louis Arco-Valley of the Bavarian Legation, Acton's brother-in-law, who provided Friedrich with information on other occasions. See Johann Friedrich, "Römische Briefe über das Konzil (1869–1870)," *Revue Internationale de Théologie* XI (1903), 621–8.

Whatever subtle purposes the celebration might have had in the minds of some, the bishops of the United States preferred to see in it a gracious gesture to themselves and to their country on the part of the pope.[110]

Bishops McFarland and McQuaid were quick to take advantage of the recess which was announced on February 22, and they left Rome for a holiday in Naples.[111] Among the fathers who remained in the city, the battle over the competing petitions temporarily gave way to equally heated controversy over the new regulations for the council. The adjournment also permitted the various parties to take stock of their situation and to evaluate their relative strengths and weaknesses. The prospects of the majority were encouraging. Approximately 500 bishops and abbots had signed the several petitions for the definition. The minority could count only 136 signatures, or some twenty per cent of the fathers, but it represented an imposing segment of the non-Latin countries.[112]

The American bishops had been practically unknown when the council opened in December. By the end of February they had become an important factor in the calculations of both majority and minority. In two letters to Father John Henry Newman, Bishop Moriarty of Kerry reported that all, or nearly all, of them would support the opposition.[113] Gaspard Mermillod, the Auxiliary Bishop of Geneva, partially confirmed this when he wrote to his vicar-general, Monsignor Dunoyer: "The Gallican group, joined to the bishops of Hungary and to some American bishops, creates many difficulties for us."[114] The

---

110 Gibbons, I, 57–63.
111 AANY, C-2, Bayley to Corrigan, Rome, February 25, 1870.
112 Aubert, *Pontificat de Pie IX*, p. 332.
113 Moriarty to Newman, Rome February 3 and February 20, 1870, in Butler, II, 28–9, 30.
114 Mermillod to Dunoyer, Rome, January 21, 1870, in Charles Comte, *Le Cardinal Mermillod d'après sa Correspondance* (Geneva: 1924), p. 103. Although technically an auxiliary bishop of the Diocese of Lausanne and Geneva, Mermillod ruled the Geneva section of the diocese as if he had been its ordinary. The anomalous situation was caused by the Swiss constitutional prohibition against the erection of new dioceses. (*Ibid.,* pp. 84–8.)

opinions of both Moriarty and Mermillod were based on general impressions or on the activity of individuals like Archbishop Kenrick. The records show that less than half of the United States bishops present in Rome had taken a stand against the definition, and we now know that at least three of those who did sign the petition of the inopportunists were not firmly committed to opposition.

Ten American prelates, including two archbishops and one abbot, had signed the petition put out by the Villa Caserta majority committee. Another six, headed by Archbishop Spalding, asked for an indirect and implicit definition of papal infallibility without mentioning the term. Twenty archbishops and bishops signed the English-speakers' minority petition of January 15, and one other put his name to the German-Austrian version. These signatures accounted for thirty-seven of the forty-eight American fathers who were at the council in the winter of 1869-70. Another affirmative vote had been sent in by Celestin de la Hailandière, the retired Bishop of Vincennes, Indiana, who asked Archbishop Godefroid Saint-Marc of Rennes to have his name added to the majority petition.[115] Eleven bishops refused to sign any petition.

As a tentative conclusion, it can be said that as of February 22 there was a barely discernible tendency toward following the lead of the respective metropolitans. This was particularly true in the case of Archbishop Kenrick and, to a lesser degree, of Archbishop McCloskey. The least united province was that of Baltimore. The small size of the representation from Cincinnati, Oregon City, and San Francisco renders any attempt to categorize them fatuous. New Orleans was the strongest center of pro-infallibility sentiment, with only Bishop Fitzgerald in open opposition.

February also saw the first rash of American departures from Rome. Apparently Archbishop Odin of New Orleans was one of the first to leave. At the suggestion of the pope he retired to France, where he died at Ambierle (Loire) on May 25.[116] Bishop

---

[115] Saint-Marc to Fessler, February 27, 1870, in Mansi, LI, 677.
[116] Baudier, pp. 434-5.

David Bacon obtained leave of absence on January 31, and Bayley reported his departure in a letter to Michael Corrigan dated February 8.[117] Five more bishops were excused on February 14, but the exact time when they left Rome is not known. These were Patrick Feehan, John J. Hogan, John Baptist Lamy, Joseph Melcher, and James O'Gorman[118] To the observer who judged solely on the basis of the petitions, the minority seemed to have suffered the greater losses. Five of the departing bishops had been signatories of the opposition memorial of January 15, one had not committed himself, and another had signed the majority request. We have, however, already seen that Bishops Hogan and O'Gorman later retracted their signatures. Nevertheless, the minority could ill afford to lose any votes, and so the early departures represented a net gain for the majority.

A writer in *Conservatore* of Naples summed up the various nationalities at the council in an article which eventually found its way, via the *Vatican* of London, into the pages of the Pittsburgh *Catholic*. The bishops subject to Propaganda, he said, were "one body with the Holy See." This was a reference to the numerous vicars apostolic who generally supported the definition. The Spaniards were noteworthy for their strict and edifying lives, and, said the commentator, "they are all, to a man, red hot supporters of Papal Infallibility." He found the Italians fully the equal of the Spaniards in erudition, but more knowledgeable about "the duties of the ecclesiastical state." The French he reported as having attempted to take Rome by storm with an active social life, while the "cold, speculative" Germans and English kept to themselves. The "honors of notoriety" fell to the Hungarians, who were used to riding about with hussars as a military escort. They were excellent Latinists who wanted the whole Christian world to look through Magyar spectacles. As for the North and South Americans, the Italian writer said: "They are a little more uncouth, and if I may speak in so delicate a

---

[117] Mansi, L, 571; AANY, C-2, Bayley to Corrigan, Rome, February 8, 1870.
[118] Mansi, L, 725.

matter, more careless of external forms. They pay less regard to ecclesiastical costume, they talk more loudly and gesticulate more freely and do everything in a more offhand way than their European prototypes."[119] These views are interesting as indicative of the impression created by the foreign bishops, and they are also illustrative of the proprietary mentality toward the Church on the part of some Italians which was responsible at times for the insufficient attention paid to the needs of Catholics whose situation differed from that existing in Italy.

Comments by three bishops from the United States will sum up the state of affairs which obtained as the council went into recess. James Roosevelt Bayley wrote to Michael Corrigan on February 25 that progress had been slow and the weather miserable. He cautioned Corrigan that many of the stories circulating about the deliberations were false, although some were true. Unfortunately, he did not go into further detail.[120] Bishop McQuaid had been more explicit when he wrote to Corrigan on February 6:

The great question of the infallibility has not come before us as yet, although it is the great question outside the Council. Should it come before us then the war begins in earnest. The present skirmishing is only child's play to what will be. The ablest Bishops by far that have spoken in the Council are Bishops whose views are known to be adverse to any definition. Another difficulty will be to define what is meant by "ex cathedra" etc. Should this question come up the discussion will be endless. I am afraid that there is a determination to pass abstract questions as decrees, that may be true enough in themselves, but will be highly injurious to us in America from the handle they will give to our enemies. If I had not confidence in God's protecting hand, I would run from the Council in despair, so strangely ignorant are many men of what is going on in the world. We need the earnest prayers of all good Catholics.[121]

Bishop Augustus Martin of Natchitoches agreed with Bayley and McQuaid in only one particular. He informed the newly

[119] The *Catholic,* April 23, 1870.
[120] AANY, C-2, Bayley to Corrigan, Rome, February 25, 1870.
[121] AANY, C-3, McQuaid to Corrigan, Rome, February 6, 1870.

126

appointed Coadjutor Bishop of New Orleans Napoleon J. Perché that the cold and humidity of Rome had kept him from writing many letters, since the climate was very bad for his rheumatism. But his description of the council had nothing in common with that supplied by the prelates from the north. It was instead a strong manifesto of infallibilist faith and as such will bear extensive quotation. Martin wrote as follows:

The council is a real arena, in which 650 bishops devoted to the [illegible] faith, which is the life of the Church, and to the supreme pontifical authority which is its strength, have been battling for three months against the old Gallicanism, modern rationalism and a wicked spirit of independence. The chiefs of this triple school have rallied a hundred men of different types, without fixed principles, such as are found even in the ranks of the episcopate. The evident purpose of the council was to remedy the actually existing evils of society by exposing and striking at the numerous errors which have overrun it since the council of Trent, to tighten again the bonds of discipline and to strengthen the unity of the Church by affirming more distinctly and more solemnly than ever the supreme authority of its head. The last purpose was particularly hateful to the opposition, which is in reality nothing more than the revolutionary element introduced into the Church. According to the order of matters to be discussed, the question of pontifical authority was not to have been presented until towards the end of the council. The password, today perfectly well known, has been to drag out the discussion, opposing everything, multiplying speeches without end, wearying the patience of the majority, which had counted on a council of only three or four months, putting half of the fathers to the necessity of returning to their dioceses, coercing the Holy Father, whose exhausted treasury cannot for long pay all the expenses of the more than 300 bishops who are his responsibility, to prorogue the council—a prorogation which would be the equivalent of a miscarriage. This plan has been followed, and after three months, not a question has been settled, not a Decree formulated.

That is not all. The very pronounced stream of aspirations of the immense majority of the clergy and *faithful* has been calling for a Definition of the Dogma of infallibility. To lead opinion astray, the academician Gratry, Oratorian of the drawing-rooms, has let loose to counteract this stream, and has already published and distributed gratis by the hundred thousand, 4 pamphlets in which the historical lies, the most brazen falsifications, the blasphemies, the insults to the Roman Curia are prodigious. The impious writings of this madman, worthy of Luther, have been judicially condemned and censured by 13 Archbishops and Bishops of France, but they are rightly honored by the applause of the liberal and atheist press, by the encouragement of the [two words illegible] purveyors of insults, Montalembert and de Falloux, and by the unfortunate letters of congratulations of the Croat Strossmayer and the Bishop of St.-Brieuc, which the press has printed in full, &tc., the reading of which has drawn tears from the Holy Father. Yielding to our repeated requests, the Most Holy Father, who had declared that he did not wish to take the initiative in the matter of a Decree for the definition of infallibility, has had it drawn up and distributed to the residence of each of the fathers, subject to study and written observations within ten days, which expire on the 18th, the vigil of St. Joseph. However, the calendar of business adopted would demand that ten other [schemata] take precedence over it. We are now pressing to have it declared urgent and that it have precedence, so that it may be voted before Easter. We await the result. There is a great deal of talk that the French government would intervene to prevent a definition of the doctrinal infallibility of the Holy See. The fact is, that pressure of this type has been asked for by some Gallican prelates. For myself, I don't believe it. Whether the pope is or is not subject to error in matters of doctrine concerning faith and morals is indeed the last concern of the present ministry. It is much more concerned about decrees which would affirm the imprescriptable rights of the Church over the education of its children and their matrimonial unions. It is likewise probable that in a few days the doors of the council will open to a representative of the cabinet of the Tuileries. They speak of M. De Broglie, whose liberal opinions are known to you. Look at where we stand. You see that we move slowly. Many complain at this slowness, but I bless God for it. It cannot have for its effect but to bring into focus the wounds from which the Church suffers, and to throw a great light on serious questions. Rome does not move quickly, because He of the all-powerful word to whom it owes its past of eighteen centuries has also given it the future.

After a recess of two weeks at Easter, the council will resume its work, to finish by the feast of St. Peter. We can say that the most difficult part is done, each one of us having worked on the decrees and formulas, of which the last on the list have as their object modern dances, loss of souls and the shameless theatres which make [illegible] the corruptions of paganism.

Martin concluded his letter by telling Perché that he would unfortunately have to leave Rome within the week, since he had to think of the needs of his diocese. However, he concluded, "to the edifice which is rising, I have brought my humble stone."[122]

Bishop Martin was obviously strongly partisan, and his letter is a good example of the attitude of the extreme infallibilists, but it also summarizes the facts of the situation. The long debates had been barren of tangible results, however much they had contributed to a deeper understanding of the manifold problems of the Church and of the opinions of others within the Church. The broad gap between opposing sides which Spalding had sought to bridge had grown wider, and any sort of compromise seemed out of reach. Discussion of infallibility was inevitable. The only question that remained was whether the definition could be made without causing a schism in the Church. It was with thoughts such as these that the fathers began their three-week vacation on February 22.

[122] UND, Perché Papers, Martin to Perché, Rome, March 12, 1870. On Gratry, see Granderath, II, 2, 191–217; Ollivier, II, 49–64; Aubert, *Pontificat de Pie IX*, pp. 344–5. Auguste-Alphonse Gratry had left the Congregation of the Oratory ten years previous to the council. Dupanloup, Strossmayer and Bishop Augustin David of St.-Brieuc encouraged him in his polemical exchange with Archbishop Dechamps and Abbot Prosper Guéranger of Solesmes. Of the others mentioned by Martin, Count Charles de Montalembert and Count Frédéric de Falloux had both encouraged the ex-Oratorian, while Duke Jacques-Albert-Victor de Broglie was an associate of Montalembert. For the French government's attitude, see Ollivier, II, 87–242.

IV

The Constitution *Dei Filius*

THE *schema* on the Church, in the elaboration of which James A. Corcoran had expended so much energy before the council opened, was distributed to the fathers on January 21. The document contained fifteen chapters and twenty-one canons.[1] Although the *schema* was supposedly secret, its full text was published in Germany during February, and the publication raised for the first time the specter of possible interference with the council on the part of several European governments. Chapter X, which treated the power of the Church, caused the most difficulty. The *schema* claimed for the Church a legislative, judicial, and coercive authority which was completely independent of the State. It further asserted that ecclesiastical authority was not restricted to the internal forum of conscience, but extended to the right of imposing external punishments on offenders against church discipline, even without their consent. The canons attached to the chapter were written in the assumption that a union of Church and State was the most ideal form of government. There was no mention of papal infallibility in the entire constitution.[2]

On February 22, a month after the *schema* had been distributed, the fathers were advised that observations on the first ten

[1] Mansi, LI, 539–53.
[2] On the agitation among the governments, see *Collectio Lacensis*, VII, 1546–1607; Ollivier, II, 102–242; Granderath, II, 2, pp. 362–425; Butler, II, 3–25.

chapters should be handed in within ten days for referral to the deputation on faith. Consideration of the relations of Church and State, of the primacy of the Roman Pontiff, and of the temporal power of the papacy was thereby postponed, since these topics occurred in the last five chapters of the constitution.

Eight American bishops responded to the call for written observations, but even before that, several of them had expressed views on problems raised by the *schema*. William Ewart Gladstone, the Prime Minister of Great Britain, indicated that he hoped that these views would coincide with his own when he wrote to Lord Acton:

> Of all the prelates at Rome, none have a finer opportunity, to none is a more crucial test applied, than to those of the United States. For if there, where there is nothing of covenant, of restraint, or of equivalent between the church and the state, the propositions of the Syllabus are still to have the countenance of the episcopate, it becomes really a little difficult to maintain in argument the civil rights of such persons to toleration, however conclusive be the argument of policy in favour of granting it.[3]

Bishop McQuaid's initial reaction, as we have seen, was that he thought the Americans could avoid involvement in what seemed to be peculiarly European preoccupations, and he wrote in that vein to Father Early on December 16.[4]

Before the new regulations of February 22 made provision for the submission of written comments to the deputation on faith, the bishops of the German-Austrian minority bloc had presented a suggestion of their own. They asked for ample time to consider the *schema* and recommended that a vote on it should be preceded by exhaustive discussion of each section. Bishop Mrak of Sault-Sainte-Marie and Marquette was the only non-Central European to sign the petition, which was handed in on February 9.[5] Mrak was not, however, the only American bishop

[3] John Morley, *The Life of William Ewart Gladstone* (3 vols.; New York: 1903), II, 511. The letter is undated, but from the context seems to have been written in December, 1869, or January, 1870.

[4] McQuaid to Early, Rome, December 16, 1869, in Browne, p. 414.

[5] Mansi, LI, 636–8.

to give serious consideration to the original, fifteen-chapter constitution. On February 6, Archbishop John Baptist Purcell of Cincinnati told Father Icard that some of its provisions disturbed him greatly and he promised that, when the time came, he would deliver a speech on it in a general congregation.[6] As matters turned out, Purcell never had the opportunity to deliver his planned discourse on the relation of the Church to civil government, although he incorporated some of its ideas in a later speech on papal infallibility. After his return to Cincinnati, he gave an outline of his ideas to an audience gathered to hear him in Mozart Hall. He told his listeners that a copy of the speech would be found among the acts of the council, and he then went on:

In it I took occasion to show that ours is, I believe, the best form of human government. That the source of government is placed by God in the people. That kings rule for their benefit, and that they were not created for kings. That the Church of God has no need of kingly patronage or protection; that for the first three hundred years of her history she managed to exist without the aid of kings, and in despite of them; that she was persecuted for these three hundred years, but that she throve and prospered. As Tertullian says, "the blood of martyrs is the seed of the Church," and when kings pretend to take her under their favor and patronage she was suffocated. Happy would it have been if kings had never pretended to be her nursing fathers! I said that our civil constitution grants perfect liberty to every denomination of Christians; that it grants perfect liberty to them all; and that I verily believe this was infinitely better for the Catholic religion, than were it the special object of the State's patronage and protection; that all we want is a free field and no favor. Truth is mighty and will prevail; and as we are here side by side with every sect and denomination of Christians, it is for the people to judge which of us is right, which of us teaches that which is most conformable to the Holy Scriptures. If they approve our religion, they will embrace it; if not they will stay away from it. I believe this is the best theory.

I illustrated all I was saying by contrasting all the nations of Europe with American Catholics; that in Spain the Catholic religion is perse-

[6] ASS, Icard Journal, February 6, 1870.

cuted; that in Portugal the Catholic religion is persecuted, the very Sisters of Charity driven out of the country; that in Italy monks, priests and people are driven away from their homes. I had seen the desolation that Victor Emmanuel has made, and all this contrasts, I said, with the best form of government which, I thanked God we had adopted.[7]

We can only speculate what might have been the effect of this speech, which dealt with the relations of Church and State, not in terms of theses and hypotheses, but in terms of history and of contemporary facts. Purcell enunciated his ideas bluntly, but they were ideas shared by the majority of his fellow bishops from the United States, and they recalled the representations which Dr. Corcoran had made during the meetings of the preparatory commission on dogma. It is probable that a good deal of the private discussion among the Americans centered on the Church-State problem. The special correspondent of the Boston *Pilot*, "P.L.C.," wrote on February 19 that they had achieved a reputation for fairness and clearness in the matter, and that they were especially opposed to groups like the Italians, who wanted to universalize their own sad experience of government and make it the basis for general laws.[8] The order of February 22, which limited comments to the first ten chapters of the *schema*, and the subsequent abandonment of all but the section on the primacy and an added chapter on papal infallibility, prevented what might have been a most enlightening confrontation between the representatives of the Old and the New World. Some of the American ideas found expression, especially in the comments made on Chapter X of the constitution, but the occasion never arose for a full-scale debate on Church and State.

The eight American bishops who submitted observations by March 4 commented on nine of the ten chapters, on the *schema* in general, on the title and introduction, and on the canons appended to the constitution. Some of the changes which they requested were stylistic, others looked to greater clarity of ex-

[7] *Catholic Telegraph,* August 25, 1870.
[8] Boston *Pilot,* March 19, 1870.

pression, and still others attempted to tone down the harshness of certain formulations. None of the Americans proposed wholly new constitutions, as did, for example, Bishop Wilhelm von Ketteler of Mainz and the Dominican Archbishop of Bologna, Cardinal Filippo Guidi. Butler has estimated that some 300 bishops participated in the preparation of a total of 600 separate amendments.[9] It must have seemed to the managers of the council that the story of the constitution on faith was going to be repeated, but on a larger scale, and this realization must, in turn, have been a factor in determining them to abandon the general treatment of the Church without any debate and to pass on instead to the question of infallibility.

The first American observation listed in the conciliar acts was that of Bishop Patrick N. Lynch of Charleston, whose remarks were among sixty-five amendments which were directed at the constitution as a whole. Lynch commented: "Very often the *schema* does not speak accurately, nor clearly, and its ideas are not expressed in an orderly way." He added specific examples; presumably these were his objections to individual parts of the constitution.[10] William Henry Elder, Bishop of Natchez, was the only prelate from the United States to make a suggestion about the introduction to the document. He felt that arguments from Sacred Scripture should be added, so as to enhance the decree's appeal to non-Catholics.[11] An interesting emendation to Chapter I was proposed by Archbishop Joseph Sadoc Alemany of San Francisco. The chapter asserted that the Church was the mystical body of Christ. Alemany asked that a statement be added to the effect that the Church was one society of the faithful professing one faith under one pastor, the Vicar of Christ.[12] The archbishop was a moderate proponent of the doctrine of papal infallibility, and it may be that he hoped to avoid a division in the council on the latter point by having a mitigated affirmation of the

[9] Butler, II, 15.
[10] Mansi, LI, 740.
[11] Mansi, LI, 747.
[12] Mansi, LI, 756.

pope's supremacy in matters of faith inserted at the very beginning of the constitution on the Church.

The fourth chapter asserted that the Church was a visible society. Alemany suggested that this would be better placed after Chapter V, which explained its visible unity.[13] Bishop Richard V. Whelan of Wheeling wanted the scriptural basis for the claim explicitated.[14] Like Lynch, he thought in terms of the apologetic value of the decree. Chapter III brought comments from three American prelates, Whelan, Lynch, and Bishop Thaddeus Amat of Monterey–Los Angeles. The last-named merely mentioned that there was no need to underline the unity of faith and cohesion of the members of the Church in this chapter on its nature as a perfect society. He felt that the notion had been overstressed, since it appeared in three separate sections of the constitution.[15] Both Lynch and Whelan asked that emphasis be placed on the fact that the Church was a society of the supernatural order. As the Bishop of Wheeling expressed it, the Church's function was to procure the eternal salvation of men through faith and charity.[16] Behind these comments lay, of course, the fear that the council would seem to be setting up a conflict between two societies—ecclesiastical and civil—which operated in the same sphere of men's lives and disputed their allegiance.

There were no observations from the American fathers on Chapter IV, which stated that the Church was a visible society, but three bishops proposed emendations to the next section on its visible unity, which excluded all other religious bodies from participation. Alemany wanted this chapter and Chapter II transposed, and he asked that the note of apostolic origin be added.[17] Once again, Bishop Whelan called for enunciation of the scriptural foundation for the assertions made, while Bishop

[13] Mansi, LI, 765.
[14] Mansi, LI, 764.
[15] Mansi, LI, 777.
[16] Mansi, LI, 771–3.
[17] Mansi, LI, 787.

Tobias Mullen of Erie felt that the introductory sentences could be simplified.[18]

The sixth chapter said that the Church was not a "free" society, but that it was altogether necessary for salvation. Four American prelates braved the technicalities of theological language and called for a simpler and clearer declaration. Whelan and Lynch questioned the use of the term "free." The former felt that the sense was ambiguous, and asked that the adjective be dropped, while retaining the affirmation that the Church was a society "into which it is altogether necessary that all men enter." The Bishop of Charleston delivered a learned disquisition on the several meanings of the word "free," none of which he thought fitted the present context. Whelan further questioned a statement in the chapter which said that membership in the Church was necessary for participation in truth. He noted that heresy often retained a great deal of truth along with error.[19] Bishop Amat's amendment expressed his wish for an explicit statement that we are saved in the name of Christ.[20] Both Lynch and Bishop Augustin Vérot of Savannah asked that the assertion of the absolute necessity of the church membership be modified, so as to leave room for the doctrine of invincible ignorance which was mentioned in the following chapter. They were afraid that the text was susceptible of too rigid an interpretation which would not state the mind of the council with complete accuracy.[21]

Chapter VII enunciated the ancient doctrine that "outside of the Church no one can be saved." It then continued with an explanation that God would not condemn to eternal punishment, on that ground alone, those who because of invincible ignorance did not know that the Catholic Church was the true Church. Bishop Mullen noted only that he approved very strongly of the doctrine as formulated.[22] Vérot was not so pleased, and he asked

18 Mansi, LI, 787.
19 Mansi, LI, 788, 790.
20 Mansi, LI, 794.
21 Mansi, LI, 790, 796.
22 Mansi, LI, 798.

that a clear acknowledgment of the possible good faith of non-Catholics be given a prominent place in the opening sentences of the paragraph.[23] Amat asked that two examples which had been used to illustrate the doctrine be deleted. One of these had compared the faithful to those who went into the ark with Noah.[24] Bishop Whelan was annoyed at the description of religious indifference as "either impious or repugnant to reason." He declared that when Christ spoke of the obligation of believing in Him, He also promised certainty about the teachings of faith, whereas in modern times there was so much prejudice against the Church as a result of schisms and heresies that great care had to be taken in judging the motivation of those who could not bring themselves to accept Catholicism, or for that matter, any religion.[25]

The eighth chapter asserted that the Church remained immutable in the constitution which it had received from its founder, although it admitted that with changing times, different expression was found for the same fundamental truths. Whelan was the sole American commentator, and he asked that this last idea be expanded and stated more accurately, so as to read: "The Church explains itself variously in matters of discipline and more clearly (or more fully) in matters of doctrine."[26] Three fathers proposed amendments to the chapter on the infallibility of the Church.

Chapter X of the *schema,* which asserted the external, public, and absolutely independent power of the Church and its authority to impose salutary punishments, provoked the most outspoken criticism from the United States bishops. Thaddeus Amat pointed out an error of fact. The text stated that "pastors have this [external and absolute] power from Christ, and exercise it freely and independently of any secular domination." The Spanish-born Vincentian suggested that this be rephrased to read that pastors

[23] Mansi, LI, 798.
[24] Mansi, LI, 798.
[25] Mansi, LI, 799.
[26] Mansi, LI, 808.

"should exercise" the power freely and independently, since the simple declarative statement of the original did not describe a situation which corresponded to reality.[27] Amat was the only one of the six Americans who addressed themselves to this chapter to accept without qualification the doctrine proposed in it. Bishops Vérot and Domenec asked that the adjective "ecclesiastical," or else "spiritual" replace "salutary" in describing the punishments which the Church claimed the right to impose. Vérot wanted a further qualification on the assertion that the Church possessed "coercive power" by the phrase "by means of ecclesiastical penalties."[28] Tobias Mullen of Erie was another prelate who was clearly haunted by memories of the Inquisition. He expressed his dismay at the prospect of the hatred and persecutions that were liable to be stirred up by the chapter. Like Vérot and Domenec, he proposed that the reference to "salutary punishments" be dropped. The penalties, he thought, should be termed "ecclesiastical" or "canonical." In any case, he demanded that the Church explicitly abdicate any claim to use of the death penalty or corporal punishment.[29]

Bishop William Henry Elder of Natchez was less perturbed about the possible consequences of Chapter X than were some of his colleagues. Nevertheless, he was dissatisfied with its wording, and he rewrote the section completely. He recommended that the Church's claim to possess judicial power and to inflict salutary punishments be modified with the condition, "insofar as it sees that these will really be for the good of souls and the glory of God and will not do greater harm."[30] The Bishop of Wheeling was much more positive in his views. His first suggestion read: "The entire chapter should be omitted, as calculated to arouse hatred." If this could not be done, Whelan demanded that the document at least be made more moderate in tone, so that it would not give offense. He thought that a good starting point

27 Mansi, LI, 830.
28 Mansi, LI, 834.
29 Mansi, LI, 833.
30 Mansi, LI, 833–4.

would be the words of Christ, "Render to Caesar the things that are Caesar's, and to God the things that are God's." His amendment continued: "In particular, I do not agree that we should, as the heretics do, reason about the Church in the same way that we do about civil society. Nor should rights of the Church be asserted which it has never exercised, nor, it seems, ever will exercise. We should claim only those rights which are of divine origin, or which are absolutely necessary for the Church's conservation and extension and for the fulfillment of the mission given to the apostles." Whelan summed up this part of his argument with a reminder that "the more authority the Church tries to claim for itself, the less it is permitted to have in practice." He also proposed three concrete amendments. The *schema* described the external triple power of the Church (legislative, judicial, and coercive) as absolute and entire. This sweeping assertion, the bishop remarked, was false and should be dropped. If the phrase "coercive power" had to be retained, he asked that it be defined as referring only to spiritual penalties. Finally, he felt that the entire section on the autonomy of the Church's external power ought to be deleted, since it was "harmful rather than useful."[31]

In large part, American criticism of the twenty-one canons which accompanied the ten chapters corresponded to the amendments already suggested for the body of the text. The chief emphasis was on points which touched upon the relations of Church and State. Stylistic revisions for the first two canons were submitted by Bishops Lynch, Vérot, and Elder. In each case, greater simplicity and precision was the object.[32] Bishop Amat brought up a topic which was to be discussed at very great length during the debates on the revised *schema* on faith. In the thirteenth canon, the Church was described as "holy, catholic, apostolic and Roman." The Bishop of Monterey wanted the last two adjectives combined as "apostolico-Roman," to indicate that

31 Mansi, LI, 835.
32 Mansi, LI, 862, 860, 850.

139

the Roman Church was founded by Peter and was therefore apostolic.[33] Archbishop Alemany and Bishop Vérot were both concerned about Canon Nine, which declared that the Church was infallible, not only in teaching doctrines contained in divine revelation, but also with regard to all truths necessary for preserving the deposit of faith. Alemany recommended that the word "contained" be replaced by "expressed," but Vérot thought that the whole canon should be suppressed.[34]

All the remaining American amendments dealt, in one way or another, with the Church-State question. Five bishops denounced the use of the word "intolerance" to define the Church's attitude toward non-Catholic religious groups. In this way they echoed Archbishop Spalding's letter to Cardinal Barnabò in August, 1869, and also the protest which had been made by an anonymous consultor—perhaps Corcoran—at the session of the preparatory commission on April 1, 1869.[35] Those who repeated the complaint in March, 1870, were Amat, Elder, Vérot, Domenec, and Lynch. Amat added that there should be no talk of "proscribing and condemning" non-Catholics, while Domenec noted that in the United States "intolerance" meant only civil and external intolerance. Spalding had already pointed out to Barnabò that there was a difference between this usage of the term and the technical theological meaning intended by Franzelin, who had framed the *schema*.[36]

Two other canons which aroused opposition were the tenth and the twelfth. Canon Ten asserted that the Church was a perfect society, and, as such, not subject to state control. Canon Twelve reiterated the claim to possession of coercive power. Bishop Whelan asked for their emendation on the grounds that "in their present form, they are fit only to arouse hatred, turn

[33] Mansi, LI, 849.

[34] Mansi, LI, 860, 861.

[35] AAB, 39-M-6, Memoranda pro Concilio Oecumenico; Mansi, XLIX, 682–685.

[36] Mansi, LI, 849 (Amat); 850 (Elder); 860 (Vérot); 860 (Domenec); 862 (Lynch).

men from the Church and leave everything confused in men's minds."[37] Thaddeus Amat requested clarification of the meaning of Canon Ten, and he declared that it ought to be made clear that penal legislation applied only to Catholics.[38] Patrick Lynch argued along the same lines, and reinforced his argument by adverting to the Protestant fear that if Catholics ever achieved political power they would be obliged by their religion to become persecutors of heretics. He had noticed, he said, that this apprehension was beginning to die away, but he was sure that the proposed canon would revive it.[39] Others who presented analogous amendments were the Bishops of Natchez and of Savannah.[40]

The council never considered the *schema* on the Church, and so the work of the American bishops—and of nearly 300 others—came to nothing. However, the opportunity had been provided for a reaffirmation of what was clearly a majority consensus in the Church of the United States on the proper relation of Church and State. No one could charge that the numerous amendments on this and other points represented an attempt on the part of the minority to delay the work of the council. Bishop Elder, for example, was one of the foremost American proponents of papal infallibility, and Archbishop Alemany also belonged to the majority. If there was any common bond among the prelates from the United States who contributed observations to the constitution, it was their acute sense of the contemporary religious situation and of the need to avoid giving needless offense to non-Catholics. European theorists might dismiss their effort as sheer pragmatism. It seems instead to have been prompted by a keen pastoral awareness and the desire to seek out the best way of carrying on their apostolic mission in the modern world. As such, it merited at least as much consideration as shopworn formulas which in many cases were them-

[37] Mansi, LI, 845.
[38] Mansi, LI, 849.
[39] Mansi, LI, 862.
[40] Mansi, LI, 850, 860.

selves only the relics of practical adaptations which had been achieved in past centuries and in other political and cultural climates.

Two weeks elapsed between the submission of observations on the *schema* about the Church and the resumption of general congregations on March 18. The usually pessimistic James Roosevelt Bayley reported on March 2 that Bishops McFarland and McQuaid were still vacationing in Naples, and he added an uncharacteristic note of optimism: The sun had finally come out in Rome. He commented that the Roman winter had been as bad as one might expect to find in England.[41] The Bishop of Rochester was back in the city by March 14, and on that day wrote to Father James Early from his new quarters in the Hotel Minerva: "We have now been over three weeks without a meeting of the Council. They seem to count time for nothing in this *'Eternal City.'* There are *rumors* of a meeting the end of this week, but only rumors, which in Rome are as thick and lively as their fleas."

The rumor which McQuaid had heard about the reopening of the debate proved to be correct. He had written to Early on a Monday, and the council resumed its sessions with the thirtieth general congregation on the following Friday, March 18. The revised draft of the constitution on the Catholic Faith had been laid before the deputation on March 1. It was the work of Joseph Kleutgen, S.J., and was sponsored by Bishop Conrad Martin of Paderborn. After some days of debate and emendation in the committee, a definitive text was adopted on March 11, and three days later it was distributed to the fathers. The division of the new *schema* was similar to that of its predecessor, but it contained only nine chapters, half as many as there had been in the constitution rejected by the council during the debates of December and January. Four of these chapters were proposed for immediate consideration. They corresponded roughly to the

[41] AANY, C-2, Bayley to Corrigan, Rome, March 2, 1870.

THE CONSTITUTION *Dei Filius*

first eleven sections of the original draft, and dealt with creation, revelation, faith, and the relation of faith and reason.[42]

Archbishop Janos Simor of Esztergom, the sole minority member of the deputation on faith, opened the discussion on March 18 with an explanation of the new text. The three orators who followed him to the rostrum were generally favorable to the proposals, although Bishop Luigi Moreno of Ivrea, the last to speak on the first day of the debate, offered several amendments before he was interrupted by the presidents with the comment that the initial speeches should be confined to general commentary on the *schema* as a whole. The session was then adjourned, because of the fact that the pope was coming down into the basilica to make the weekly visit which was customary on all Fridays of Lent.[43]

The fourth speaker at the thirty-first general congregation on March 22 was Peter Richard Kenrick. His comments recalled the speech which he had delivered at the fourth congregation on December 28. The Archbishop of St. Louis was not a man to waste words. He began by saying that he had many objections to the *schema*, but that he would confine his remarks to two themes. The first of these was a call for greater simplicity. Kenrick analyzed the role of bishops in council. "We must remember," he said, "that we have been summoned to the council not to compose a course in theology, and still less to pass judgment on philosophical systems, but to protect the faith by explaining it and condemning errors opposed to it." While it was true that the fathers were judges, he went on, their function was that of witnesses rather than that of men who put forth their own opinions. Their mandate was to guard the deposit of faith. The archbishop defined this in the words of Vincent of Lérins: "The deposit, not what had been found; what you have received, not what you have discovered; what you have learned, not what you have excogitated." Almost in passing, he added what was

42 The text of the new constitution is in Mansi, LI, 31–40.
43 Mansi, LI, 42–61.

in fact a capital point with the minority, that decisions in matters of faith should be by unanimous consent. Becoming more specific, he spoke out against incorporation of philosophical systems into the constitutions. He reminded the fathers that their task was to condemn errors which were plainly in opposition to to the faith. They were, he said, scarcely capable of forming adequate judgments on philosophical theories. His second point also recalled the earlier debates at the council. Although he admitted that the term "anathema" was borrowed from the apostles Paul and John and that it had been consecrated by long conciliar usage, he was disturbed by the excessive employment of it in the *schema.* He pointed out that in modern times men were attracted to the Church by its inherent goodness and not by repeated threats of punishment. If the term could not be omitted completely, Kenrick recommended that it at least be reserved for very serious errors and open impiety.[44]

The debate on the *schema* as a whole ended with the speech of Bishop Jean-Pierre Bravard of Coutances, who followed Archbishop Kenrick. According to the new rules, a spokesman for the deputation which had presented the constitution under discussion had the right to take the floor and explain any difficulties which had been raised. Archbishop Simor availed himself of this privilege before the debate on the introduction to the constitution began. He mentioned none of Kenrick's points except that on the proliferation of anathemas. The merit of this he left to the council to decide. For the rest, he contended that the new draft reflected accurately the demands made by the fathers during December and January.[45]

Granderath has dismissed Kenrick's effort as a mélange of truth and error, and he claimed that the archbishop's thought was somewhat obscure in the passage about introducing philosophical systems into a dogmatic decree.[46] Lord Acton was, of

[44] Mansi, LI, 62–3.
[45] Mansi, LI, 65–7.
[46] Granderath, II, 2, pp. 39–40.

144

course, more favorably disposed to the speech, and he grasped its import more clearly than did the German historian, who never made any great attempt to conceal his bias against the minority. Acton told Döllinger on March 27 that Kenrick, whom he styled one of the most impressive figures in the council, had in effect explored the reasons for the minority opposition to the management of affairs in his treatment of the function of bishops as witnesses and judges of the faith.[47] What Kenrick's speech revealed, and what Granderath professed not to understand, was that there was a fundamental disagreement among the fathers on the nature of an ecumenical council and on the role of bishops in it.

From the outset, the policy of the Roman authorities had been to have decrees framed by a body of professional theologians using precise and technical theological language and employing concepts and patterns of thought drawn from scholastic theology and philosophy. It had not been anticipated that the bishops would do much more than suggest minor revisions, and no one had foreseen the massive resistance which the first constitution encountered. The motivation of the opposition bishops has been obscured by the fact that it is nearly always explained in terms of their determination to prevent a definition of papal infallibility. This explanation recognizes in their tactics only political moves, and it fails to realize that in the minds of many fathers— among them Peter Kenrick—papal infallibility was part of a larger picture. Kenrick had already opposed the move to send a Roman theologian to assist at the Second Plenary Council of Baltimore. He had protested to Cardinal Barnabò that the decrees adopted at that council did not represent the real wishes of the bishops who took part in the assembly. He had objected to the form in which the decrees were framed. His whole approach was to place greater emphasis on the episcopal role in determining essential truths. Their further elaboration he was content to

---

[47] Conzemius Transcripts, Acton to Döllinger, Rome, March 27, 1870; Quirinus, pp. 385–6.

leave to the theologians, but he did not want to see this elaboration form part of dogmatic constitutions.

Emphasis on the role of the episcopate brought Kenrick and others into conflict with the process of centralization which was already far advanced in the Church by the time of the Vatican Council. It led logically to a reluctance to accept the definition of papal infallibility, particularly if that definition was to be proposed, as some of the majority wished, without sufficient time for long and serious consideration. The same emphasis on the role of the episcopate led, in the present instance, to a reluctance to define theological and philosophical formulations as belonging to the deposit of faith. The minority bishops thought that a council should restrict itself to enunciation of clearly and universally held doctrines. Kenrick and his colleagues were consistent in their opposition. They may have been wrong, but this does not excuse the historian from trying to understand and appreciate their point of view.

After Archbishop Simor had finished his defense of the *schema* against the general remarks directed at it, the debate on the introduction to the four chapters began. Four speakers were heard on this subject at the thirty-first general congregation. The last of them was Bishop Strossmayer whose speech provoked a vehement outburst. The Bishop of Diakovár made some preliminary comments on the unsuitability of the hall for any real discussion and on the papal prohibition against having the speeches printed. This *exordium* was scarcely calculated to render either the presidents or the majority of his hearers benevolent. He announced that he would raise three points. The first of these was the omission of the word *definientibus* in the introductory paragraph's description of the bishops. Strossmayer, like Kenrick, was sensitive to anything that seemed to detract from the bishops' role in the framing of dogmatic definitions. The proposed constitution was written in the form of a decree emanating from the pope in collaboration with the fathers, but the function of the latter was absolved in the one word *judicantibus.* Strossmayer wanted it made clear that they not only "judged," but also "defined."

The Croatian prelate's second point—and, as it turned out, his last—was to object to the attribution of the whole spectrum of modern errors to Protestantism. He began by indicating that not all Protestants were in bad faith, and he stated that a great many of them loved Christ. At this point murmuring broke out in the hall, and Cardinal de Angelis asked the speaker to refrain from words that were causing scandal to some of the fathers. There then ensued a long dialogue between the bishop and the presidents which came to an end amidst a general uproar in the council. Strossmayer finally left the pulpit with bishops shouting at him: "He is Lucifer, anathema, anathema," and so on.[48] The congregation was adjourned hastily, and one of the bishops from the United States said to Acton as he left the hall: "There is certainly one assembly in the world rougher than the American Congress."[49]

On the day following this incident, Bishop Richard Vincent Whelan of Wheeling was the sole American representative in the discussion of the preamble to the *schema.* He and two other speakers advocated some of the points which had been made by Strossmayer, but their enunciation of them was received in respectful silence.[50] The Bishop of Wheeling had three substantial amendments to propose, but he first addressed himself to what he felt was a series of inaccuracies in the text. The first of these was caused by a collocation of words which seemed to imply that the cornerstone of the Church was Holy Scripture and not Christ. The bishop noted that this was a Protestant way of looking at things. Bishop Whelan also wanted a more accurate analysis of the origins of naturalism. The draft constitution named materialism, rationalism, and indifferentism as the errors

[48] Mansi, LI, 75–7; Butler, I, 270–73; Granderath, II, 2, pp. 45–61; Quirinus, pp. 386–9.
[49] Conzemius Transcripts, Acton to Döllinger, Rome, March 27, 1870.
[50] *Ibid.*

which led to naturalism. He suggested that it be made clear that this was only a partial enumeration, and he objected to the sweeping assertion that religious indifferentism turned men into materialists, pantheists, or atheists. This statement, he thought, should be modified to read that indifferentism had these re-results in the case of "many" men. Another phrase that caught his attention was the declaration that naturalism was "a plague that was raging unchecked (*impune*)." He felt that this smacked of a desire to persecute and asked that the word *impune* be replaced by *liberrime* or "freely." As he reminded the bishops, those who take the sword die by the sword, "and this is the reason why the Church has already suffered so much."

Whelan's three principal amendments played upon themes which were recurrent in the thought of the minority. The final paragraph of the preamble began with a eulogy of the pope's role as defender of Catholic truth. The same had been said in a more general sense of the Church in the preceding paragraph, and the preamble concluded with another similar reference to the pope. The Bishop of Wheeling thought this repetition excessive and proposed its elimination. Secondly, he repeated Archbishop Kenrick's request that the word *definientibus* be added to the phrase *sedentibus nobiscum et judicantibus* which was applied to the bishops. Again the point was to emphasize that in the council the pope *and* the bishops defined doctrine. Recalling Bishop Strossmayer's comments of the previous day, he insisted that the bishops had an obligation to defend the divinely conferred rights which belonged to them as a body. These were rights, said Whelan, which could not be renounced, since they belonged to the essential constitution of the Church as created by Christ. We all know of the primacy and rights of the Holy Father, he went on, but "let there not be silence about the rights of bishops, and more especially when questions of grave moment are proposed to us." Finally, he repeated another of Kenrick's suggestions by asking that the preamble end, not with a threat of proscription and damnation, but with a warning that all who hoped to be saved must recognize and avoid the errors to be mentioned in the constitution.[51]

In accordance with the new rules, all amendments had to be proposed in writing. These written amendments were given to the deputation on faith for consideration.[52] Nine bishops submitted emendations on the preamble. The only ones which the deputation thought worthy of refutation were those proposed by Bishop Whelan.[53] Archbishop Simor took them up at the thirty-fourth general congregation on March 26. He made an impassioned plea for the rejection of the amendment which suggested deletion of the eulogy of the pope, argued that the episcopal function in the council was adequately expressed by the word *judicantibus,* and refused the suggestion that the final words of the preamble be changed.[54] Preparations were then made to vote on the amendments, but Whelan went to the President's desk and asked that they be withdrawn. The vote was not taken, and the preamble was sent back to the deputation for a last revision.[55] While Whelan's three major proposals were unsuccessful, the text as revised by the deputation did incorporate some of the other modifications which he had requested. The confusion as to whether Christ or Holy Scripture was the cornerstone of the Church was avoided by treating the Church's relation to Our Lord and to the Bible in separate paragraphs. Rationalism was equated with naturalism, instead of being styled its parent. The broad sweep of the general condemnation of the religiously indifferent was modified, so that "many" of them were said to fall into the errors enumerated. And, lastly, the word *impune* was replaced by *circumquaque*

[51] Mansi, LI, 85–7.

[52] For the contributions of Archbishops Alemany and Spalding at deputation meetings between March 4 and April 20, see Mansi, LIII, 186–230. Alemany was consistently present; Spalding was regularly absent after April 3. Both took an active part in the discussions of the deputation and proposed emendations in the text of *Dei Filius.*

[53] Mansi, LI, 126.

[54] Mansi, LI, 129–30.

[55] Mansi, LI, 130–1.

or "everywhere."[56] Simor also announced that the fathers would be permitted to sign the decrees with the traditional phrase, *definiens subscripsi,* so that, as Acton wrote to Döllinger, the principle for which Strossmayer and Whelan had fought was recognized, even if they had not been able to have it written into the constitution.[57]

Whatever may have been Bishop Whelan's motives for withdrawing his amendments, the action raised a minor procedural point. Friedrich later reported that Dupanloup had entered a protest on the grounds that the rules made no provision for such a retraction and he felt that it was prejudicial "because other fathers would perhaps have proposed the same modification and abstained from doing so since someone had done it before them."[58] In any event, the president ruled that it could be done. The issue did not come up again at the council.

Debate on the four chapters and on the canons of the *schema* began at the thirty-third general congregation on March 24. No American spoke on the first chapter, which treated of the existence of God and of creation, but Bishop Thaddeus Amat, C.M., of Monterey-Los Angeles more than made up for this lack at the following session, where the topic was divine revelation. He proposed a long series of technical theological emendations, which were also submitted in writing. Vincenz Gasser, Bishop of Brixen, discussed these amendments at the fortieth congregation, and they were then voted upon.[59]

The Bishop of Monterey's first two changes were rejected. His third emendation took on no less an adversary than St. Thomas Aquinas. The supernatural end of man had been described as a participation in the divine goodness which surpassed the comprehension of human reason. Amat rightly pointed out that

---

[56] Mansi, LI, 429–30.

[57] Conzemius Transcripts, Acton to Döllinger, Rome, March 29, 1870.

[58] Friedrich, *Geschichte,* III, 788.

[59] Amat's speech is in Mansi, LI, 146–7. His written observations occur *ibid.,* 263–70. Gasser's answers are found *passim* in columns 277–94. The record of voting is also found in the last-named place.

under no circumstances could reason ever "comprehend" the supernatural, although it could come to "know" the divine goodness and supernatural truths by revelation. He asked that the word "understanding" be substituted for "comprehension."[60] Gasser recommended the change as clearer and more definite than the original text, which had been borrowed directly from St. Thomas, and the vote was affirmative.[61]

The subject of the third chapter was the supernatural virtue of faith. Once more, Bishop Amat was the only American prelate to speak. At the thirty-eighth general congregation on March 31 he presented a total of nine amendments. Five of these which dealt mainly with stylistic changes were rejected, two more were replaced by other emendations, one was accepted in its entirety, and one was combined with several other proposals to form a new text for Canon Three.[62]

Amat's third amendment was the one adopted. He had asked that the whole scriptural definition of faith from Hebrews 11:1 be included at the close of the first paragraph, and this was done.[63] He also wanted it made clear that internal experience could play a part in moving men to faith. Canon Three defended the proposition that revelation could be made credible by external signs. Amat did not deny this, but he felt that the proposed wording of the canon seemed to exclude the possibility of any influence from the individual's subjective experience.[64] The canon was rephrased to accommodate this and similar objections.[65] The only other significant modification, in which the Bishop of Monterey-Los Angeles' recommendations played a

[60] Mansi, LI, 265.

[61] Mansi, LI, 281.

[62] Amat's speech is in Mansi, LI, 231–2. His written observations are found *ibid.*, 300–302, *passim*. Bishop Conrad Martin of Paderborn acted as spokesman for the deputation in discussing the amendments. His comments are found *ibid.*, 315–35, *passim*.

[63] Mansi, LI, 301; 317–8. The proposal was also made by Bishop José Caixal y Estrada of Urgel.

[64] Mansi, LI, 300.

[65] Mansi, LI, 332.

part, was the introduction of a clearer division between what had to be believed on the authority of divine revelation and what had to be believed on the authority of the Church. His proposal was not accepted, but its substance was contained in another amendment which was written into the constitution.[66]

Debate on Chapter X ended on March 31. On the following day, twelve speakers mounted the rostrum to discuss the interrelation of faith and science. None of them came from the United States, but the Archbishop of San Francisco contributed to the general discussion by handing in an amendment concerning revision of the second canon of the chapter. It touched upon a problem which had been raised in the council by Bishop Jacques Ginoulhiac of Grenoble. The canon was framed in broad terms and condemned those who held that scientific disciplines could be pursued without any reference to divine revelation. Ginoulhiac objected that there were some disciplines which by their very nature could not conflict with revelation. Speaking for the deputation, Bishop Louis Pie of Poitiers agreed with this proposition, but pointed out the difficulty of enumerating the sciences which did or did not impinge upon areas in which the Church, as the custodian of divine revelation, had a legitimate interest. Archbishop Alemany thought that the problem would be solved if the canon were changed to read: "If anyone say that *all* human disciplines are to be treated without regard for supernatural revelations; or that the conclusions of these disciplines, even if they are repugnant to Catholic doctrine, cannot be proscribed by the Church, let him be anathema." Alemany's addition was the word "all," which he hoped would reconcile the views of Pie and Ginoulhiac.[67] His wording was not accepted by the deputation, but the definitive text of the canon managed to skirt the dilemma which Ginoulhiac's objection had raised.[68]

Although they took no further part in the debates, a number

[66] Mansi, LI, 322–33.
[67] Mansi, LI, 343.
[68] Mansi, LI, 372.

of the bishops from the United States became involved in two disputes connected with the constitution on faith. The first of these had to do with the opening words of Chapter I, and had been brought to the floor of the council on March 24 in a speech by the Benedictine Bishop of Birmingham, William Ullathorne. The chapter began with the words, "The holy Roman Catholic Church . . . ." Ullathrone objected that this qualification of "Catholic" by "Roman" gave countenance to the branch theory espoused by Anglicans and could be interpreted as an admission that there were really three Catholic churches, namely the Roman, the English, and the Eastern. He suggested that the text be reworded to read "Catholic and Roman," or that a comma be placed between the two words.[69]

The subsequent history of Ullathorne's proposal is murky. On March 29, Bishop Gasser stated that the deputation had no objection to the placing of a comma between "Roman" and "Catholic."[70] A standing vote was then taken on the formula "Catholic and Roman," which was clearly rejected by the fathers, as was the substitute offered by Bishop William Clifford of Clifton, who wanted to say simply, "the Catholic Church." The next amendment to be voted upon was the insertion of the comma. The presidents declared that they could not determine the result of this vote, and a count was ordered. While this count was in progress, the voting was suddenly adjourned until the following day. When the council reassembled on March 30, Gasser again went to the pulpit. He announced that he had consulted many of the fathers, and many, although not all, of the members of the deputation on faith, and had come to the conclusion that the comma could not be allowed. He went on to explain his reasons:

What is the meaning of the words "Roman Catholic Church?" It means the same as the Roman Church, that is, the mother and teacher of all churches, joined with the Catholic Church, that is, with that

69 Butler, I, 277–82; Mansi, LI, 105.
70 Mansi, LI, 187.

church which is in the whole world, and indeed so joined that the Roman Church is the Catholic Church and the Catholic Church Roman.

It was a proper name, he continued, and he asked if any of the fathers had ever thought of separating their Christian and family names by a comma. Finally, the bishop concluded, the comma could not be tolerated, because "that church which is the mother and teacher of all the churches cannot have or hold second place in the proper name of the Church."[71] After this exhortation, the council voted to reject the amendment.

Despite this defeat, the last had not been heard of the Ulla-thorne proposal. On the day following Gasser's sudden reversal and the consequent vote in the council, nine bishops from English-speaking countries addressed a strong protest to the cardinal presidents over the way in which the affair had been managed. Bishop Michael Domenec, C.M., of Pittsburgh represented the United States in this protest. The signers recalled that the amendment for the introduction of the comma had been approved by the deputation, and they declared that it had apparently been adopted by standing vote. But, the memorial continued, while the vote-counters were checking the results, a conference was held at the rostrum. A bishop who was a member of the deputation had then come to the English-speaking delegates and asked them if they would be satisfied with the change —"holy, Catholic, apostolic and Roman Church"—instead of the comma. He was told that this was satisfactory, and in turn assured the Anglo-American group that the deputation would recommend the new formula. On this note, the session had been adjourned. On the next day Gasser had rejected all compromise, and admitted in so doing that he had not even consulted all the members of the deputation. The nine bishops who signed the protest of March 31 felt that they had been deceived.[72]

The question lay dormant until the preliminary vote on the entire constitution, which took place on April 12. At that time,

71 Mansi, LI, 200.
72 Mansi, LI, 200–201.

154

thirty-six amendments were handed in which supported Ulla-thorne's demand. Nearly all of these came from bishops of the British Empire and the United States. The seventeen American protests cut across all previously established party lines. Those who voted *placet juxta modum* and gave as at least one of their reasons for so doing the name which had been adopted for the Church were: Archbishop Martin J. Spalding, Archbishop John B. Purcell, and Bishops John J. Conroy, Michael Domenec, William H. Elder, Edward Fitzgerald, James Gibbons, John Lough-lin, William McCloskey, Bernard J. McQuaid, Tobias Mullen, William O'Hara, Maurice de St.-Palais, Jeremiah Shanahan, Augustin Vérot, Richard V. Whelan, and John J. Williams.[73]

Only a handful of prelates who did not belong to the Anglo-American group protested against the word *Romana* at the congregation on April 12. However, forty-four bishops of the opposition made the cause their own in a written protest submitted to the presidents on April 18. They informed the cardinals that they were anxious that the vote for the constitution at the third public session should be unanimous, but they demanded two changes before they would consent to add their *placets*. The first change asked that a clearer distinction be introduced between the faithful in general and the episcopate. The peroration of the constitution seemed, they thought, to minimize unduly the episcopal role. The second demanded that the Church be entitled "holy, Catholic, apostolic and Roman." Among the signers were Archbishop Kenrick and Bishops Domenec, Fitzgerald, and Mrak.[74]

These repeated representations finally had some effect, and on April 19 Gasser recommended to the council that it adopt the style "holy Catholic apostolic Roman Church." This had been another formula suggested by Clifford. Ullathorne wrote exultantly to a friend, Canon Edgar Estcourt, on the very same day:

[73] Mansi, LI, 381–92.
[74] Mansi, LI, 411–2.

To-day in General Congregation my amendment was carried unanimously, two only rising against it: after it had been first proposed and voted, the votes left uncounted; the substance of the question retracted and shelved; and then voted again in another form by the 'placet', except about forty who stood by me; and then protested against on the score of informality; then reopened by private correspondence; then taken up anew and unanimously approved by the special deputation; then to-day finally voted . . . . But many Americans voted with me, and I owed the reopening and working of the question in Council to the Archbishop of Baltimore. I shall I hope be able to show some day what a mess it has saved us from, in England especially. Our Archbishop [Manning] behaved very well in the last act of the special deputation.[75]

The final form of the amendment adopted, as well as the initial impulse, had come from England, but the bishops of the United States had provided indispensable help in accomplishing something that was very rare in the Vatican Council, namely, the reversal of a decision already taken by both the deputation on faith and a general congregation.

The second problem which threatened unanimous approval of the constitution has already been hinted at. It involved the two concluding paragraphs. They were written in the first person, and therefore in the name of the pope. This was in itself a sore point with the minority, which would have preferred that decrees be issued in the name of the council. The first paragraph exhorted the faithful, and particularly those charged with the pastoral or teaching office, to protect the Church against the errors which had just been condemned, and to strive to teach the faith which had been enunciated. The second paragraph said:

But since it is not sufficient to avoid heretical perversity, unless those errors are also avoided which more or less approximate it, we admonish all of their duty to observe also the constitutions and decrees by which this Holy See has proscribed and condemned similar evil opinions which are not here enumerated in detail.[76]

[75] Ullathorne to Estcourt, Rome, April 19, 1870, in Butler, I, 297.
[76] Mansi, LI, 38.

156

Both of these paragraphs had originally belonged at the end of the entire constitution on Catholic faith, of which only the first part had been discussed. The deputation had wavered on the proper placing of them, but finally decided that they should be put at the end of the truncated decree. Messengers had been sent to the home of each of the fathers on April 9 to tell them that they would be asked to vote on the concluding paragraphs before the vote on Chapter IV of the *schema*. This inversion of the order of voting brought a letter of protest from nine minority bishops on April 10. Among them were Archbishops Kenrick and Purcell.[77] The protest was disallowed, and the council approved the two sections on April 12.[78] Kenrick later explained the reasons behind the minority objection. They feared—and their fears were subsequently confirmed in a speech of Archbishop Manning—that they were being asked to put their names to an implicit acknowledgment of the infallibility of the pope. Kenrick claimed that a spokesman for the deputation had expressly denied that this was the intention of the paragraphs.[79]

As in the case of the word *Romana,* last minute protests were entered against the paragraphs. At the general congregation of April 12, when the ballot on the entire constitution was taken, Archbishop Kenrick and Bishops McQuaid and Mullen joined thirty-seven other prelates in submitting requests that the section be dropped.[80] The letter of April 18, which was signed by forty-four bishops, including five Americans, made the same point. As an alternative, they declared themselves ready to accept the amendment of Bishop Matthias Eberhard of Trier, who proposed that prelates and teachers be distinguished from the faithful, and that all be asked to work for the elimination of error according to their position in the Church.[81]

[77] Mansi, LI, 378.
[78] Mansi, LI, 378–80.
[79] Peter Richard Kenrick, *Concio in Concilio Vaticano habenda at non habita* (Naples: 1870), pp. 66–7.
[80] Mansi, LI, 409.
[81] Mansi, LI, 411–2.

The third public session of the council, at which the formal vote on the constitution on Catholic faith was to take place in the presence of the pope, was set for Low Sunday, April 24. Three meetings of the international committee of the minority were held during Easter Week in an effort to decide whether they should make a public show of opposition by voting *non placet*. Bishop Clifford opposed the move, while Bishop Strossmayer favored it. A compromise was ultimately agreed upon and those who could not bring themselves to vote *placet* were asked to abstain altogether, so that the decree would be adopted unanimously.[82]

Several of the more outspoken leaders of the minority were not content with this halfway measure. On the eve of the public session, eight bishops, headed by Peter Richard Kenrick, transmitted a formal explanation of their stand to the cardinal presidents. They regretted, they said, that they would be unable to explain their vote at the session, as had been customary in the Council of Trent. Despite that fact, they intended to vote for the constitution, since they admitted the essential doctrines contained in it. They wanted to go on record, nevertheless, with three objections. The first of these was to the generous use of anathemas. Secondly they complained that the conclusion of Chapter IV—by which, presumably, they meant the two paragraphs discussed above—was "too general and indeterminate." The third objection brought into the open one of the principal reasons why the minority had contested the constitution so vigorously. The eight signatories declared that in giving their *placet* they did not retract or minimize any of the expostulations which had been made about the management of the council. They insisted, the letter went on, that these demands be met, for the sake of the liberty of the council and for the preservation of conciliar tradition and the rights and prerogatives of bishops. In addition to Kenrick, the protest was signed by Strossmayer, Archbishop Jean-Paul Lyonnet of Albi, Bishop Augustin David of St.-Brieuc, Bishop Henri Maret, titular of Sura, Bishop Félix

[82] Friedrich, *Geschichte,* III, 835–6.

de Las Cases of Constantine, Bishop Charles-Philippe Place of Marseilles, and Bishop Luigi Moreno of Ivrea. Seven of the eight voted *placet* on April 24; only Strossmayer abstained. Bishop Fessler, the secretary, placed the letter in the files with the notation that it had not been delivered until April 25.[83]

Consideration of the struggles over the word *Romana* and over the terminal paragraphs has carried us beyond the forty-fifth general congregation on April 12, when the test vote on the whole constitution was held. When the roll call had been completed, it revealed that the representation from the United States was down to forty prelates. Nine had already left Rome, while Bishop William McCloskey of Louisville had arrived. Sixteen Americans gave an unconditional *placet*, eighteen voted *placet juxta modum*, and six others who were still in the city absented themselves.[84] No one had voted *non placet*, and the over-all tally stood at: *placet*, 510; *placet juxta modum*, 85.[85]

As required by the rules of February 22, each of the fathers who had given only conditional approval to the constitution handed in his objection or objections in writing. For many of the Americans, this amounted to a briefly stated demurrer on the word *Romana*. Some, like Bishop Shanahan of Harrisburg, specifically associated themselves with the speech given during

[83] Mansi, LI, 425–6.
[84] Mansi, LI, 381–2. Affirmative votes were cast by Archbishops Blanchet and Alemany, by Bishops Amat, Dubuis, de Goesbriand, Heiss, Henni, Lootens, Martin, Miége, Mrak, O'Connell, Persico, Rappe, and Ryan, and by Abbot Wimmer. Conditional ballots came from Archbishops Spalding, Kenrick, and Purcell, and from the following bishops: Conroy, Domenec, Elder, Fitzgerald, Gibbons, Loughlin, William McCloskey, McQuaid, Mullen, O'Hara, St.-Palais, Shanahan, Vérot, Whelan, and Williams. The six temporary absentees were Archbishop John McCloskey and Bishops Bayley, Hennessy, Lynch, McFarland, and McGill. The nine who took no further part in the council were Archbishop Odin and Bishops Bacon, Feehan, Hogan, Lamy, Melcher, O'Gorman, Quinlan, and Wood.
   In this balloting, Bishop Ignatius Persico, O.F.M. Cap., participated for the first time as a full-fledged member of the American hierarchy. In March, 1870, he became Bishop of Savannah and Bishop Vérot was transferred to the new See of St. Augustine.
[85] *Collectio Lacensis*, VII, 739.

the debates by Ullathorne.[86] Elder of Natchez was not content with any such general statements. He presented seven amendments, and in some of them backed up his argument with a half-dozen reasons.

Bishops Whelan and Vérot were two others who explained their opposition to the word *Romana* at some length. The Bishop of Wheeling recalled that it was a comparative late-comer to the official name of the Church, and said that it was completely unknown to the ancient councils. He lamented the fact that an accessory and accidental title, which belonged properly to a local church, was to be emphasized at the expense of two of the four notes of the universal Church, namely the qualifications "one" and "holy." If it had to be included in the constitution, he said, it ought to be placed last, only after all the notes of the Church had been enumerated, and separated from them by a conjunction.[87] Bishop Vérot, appearing for the first time in the minutes of the council under his new appellation as Bishop of St. Augustine, proved to be as sprightly and humorous as ever. His preference was for the description "holy Catholic Church," as an answer to those Protestants who claimed that the Roman Catholic Church was not the Catholic Church of the creeds. The matter was more than a question of apologetics and theology to Florida's new bishop, as he proceeded to explain. Some years previously, he declared, a farm had been left to his diocese. The will specifically stated that the property was to go to the "Catholic Church." However, the Episcopalians had taken the case to court and had won the farm with the contention that Vérot's church was not Catholic, but Roman Catholic.[88]

Another amendment on the same subject was submitted anonymously, but the editors of Mansi have identified the handwriting as that of Archbishop Spalding. His arguments paralleled those of the preceding bishops, but he added one more by referring to the profession of faith of Pius IV, which was in

[86] Mansi, LI, 396–8.
[87] Mansi, LI, 395.
[88] Mansi, LI, 395–6.

standard use. There the term "Roman" was used to designate a specific church, the mother and teacher of all churches. Spalding feared that indiscriminate use of the term with reference to the whole Church would result in ambiguity. Like Whelan, he asked that all four notes of the Church be included if the added title also was employed.[89] No American emendations were suggested for the third and fourth chapters, and only one was handed in on the second. This came from Mullen of Erie, who wanted a statement to the effect that not everything which could be revealed actually had been revealed. A similar request by Bishop Amat at the thirty-fourth general congregation had been refused, and the Bishop of Erie's petition fared no better.[90]

The canons appended to the constitution came under particularly strong fire from the United States bishops. The most succinct criticism was that of Bishop McQuaid, who made a four-word request: "Omittantur omnes canones, etc."—"Let all the canons be omitted, etc."[91] Archbishop Kenrick was more specific, and he expressed his displeasure with the canons because he opposed multiplication of anathemas.[92] Fitzgerald of Little Rock had the same objection, pointing out that good Catholics had no need of threats and that others made a joke of them. He felt that excessive use of the anathema would only drive away those whom the Church was trying to win to itself.[93] Bishop Elder likewise preferred a positive approach to non-Catholics. He declared himself convinced that there were a great number of people in the United States who followed false doctrines not from any evil intent, but out of either culpable or inculpable ignorance. These people, he protested, were well disposed to listen to the truth if it were proposed to them in a kindly and sympathetic fashion, but they would not listen to words which were calculated to injure their sensibilities. The Bishop of Natchez was not opposed to a strong and vital preaching of

[89] Mansi, LI, 396.
[90] Mansi, LI, 400.
[91] Mansi, LI, 402.
[92] Mansi, LI, 403.
[93] Mansi, LI, 402–3.

truth, but he could see no point in rousing unnecessary antagonism. He also raised a point of order by asking who was the object of the anathemas. They seemed to be directed at those outside the Church and even at the non-baptized. This he declared to be against traditional conciliar practice. In any event, he thought that most of those who were teaching the errors proscribed—especially the professors in European universities—had little reverence for the Church or fear of its condemnations, and so the whole approach was pointless. It would be much better, he felt, to stress a positive exposition of the Church's doctrine than to spend time proscribing and condemning without tangible results.[94]

Elder demonstrated his dislike for a proliferation of canons by declaring himself dissatisfied with seven of those which had been proposed to go with the first three chapters of the constitution. However, he gave no reason for his objections, and so it is impossible to make any further analysis of his thought on such subjects as materialism, ontologism, and so on. The fifth canon of Chapter III was another question. Three American bishops had comments to make on it.

Canon Five read: "If anyone say that the assent of Christian faith is not free, but is produced necessarily by arguments of human reason; or that the grace of God is necessary to living faith alone, which works through charity, let him be anathema."[95] The condemnation was directed at two interconnected errors of the German theologian Georg Hermes (1775–1831). The first of these was Hermes' denial that the act of faith was a free, nonnecessitated act. In other words, Hermes had declared that rational evidence could compel an act of supernatural faith. His second error was to claim that the help of divine grace was necessary only for living faith, that is, for faith informed by charity. He had denied that it was necessary for faith which was not informed by charity. In formulating Canon Five, the deputa-

94 Mansi, LI, 403.
95 Mansi, LI, 37–8.

tion wished to assert: (1) that the act of faith was free, that is, it could not be compelled by rational arguments; and (2) that grace was necessary even for dead faith. Martin of Paderborn pointed out the necessary connection between these two assertions when he told the fathers that the freedom of the act of faith was a necessary condition for the need of grace. If the act of faith could be compelled by rational evidence, then grace was unnecessary.[96]

The entire canon was framed in the context of a refutation of Hermes' errors. His doctrine was scarcely intelligible, even to Germans, and it was not therefore surprising that many of the fathers misunderstood the purpose of the condemnation.[97] A number of them interpreted it as simply an affirmation of the necessity of grace for the act of faith and neglected the correlative affirmation of the freedom of that act.[98] Among those who did so was Bishop Elder, who wanted the adverb "always" to modify the phrase "produce necessarily," because, he explained, arguments can sometimes be such as to produce conviction.[99] Had Elder's amendment been adopted, Hermes would not have been condemned. The bishop did not universalize the necessary production of faith by rational arguments, as did Hermes, but he obviously considered it a not abnormal possibility.

Bishop Vérot would have turned both parts of the canon into a statement of the necessity of grace. He suggested that the first part read as follows: "If anyone say that the assent of Christian faith is not free, but is produced necessarily by arguments of human reason *without the supernatural help of God* ... let him be anathema." Vérot gave as his reasons a desire for greater clarity and the fear that the canon seemed to concede that the usual apologetic arguments for the faith were not con-

[96] Mansi, LI, 330. For this whole section, see Roger Aubert, *Le Problème de l'acte de foi* (Louvain: 1950), pp. 181–5.

[97] Aubert, *ibid.*, pp. 103, n. 2.

[98] *Ibid.*, p. 182.

[99] Mansi, LI, 406.

vincing.[100] In saying this, he missed the point. The first part of the canon did not intend to deny the validity and effectiveness, in their own sphere, of rational arguments. It did intend to assert that a faith which was specifically supernatural ("the assent of Christian faith") could not be the inevitable result of an inexorable chain of human reasoning. Even after rational arguments had been proposed and accepted, the mind remained free to make or not to make an act of supernatural faith. The assent, if made, was therefore free. It was not necessitated by rational arguments. Once this freedom had been established, the second part of the canon went on to determine the role and influence of divine grace in a concrete act of faith. By introducing this latter question into the first part of the canon, Vérot was confusing the issue. His amendment was therefore rejected, as had been that of Bishop Elder.

Bishops Elder and Whelan also had suggestions for the second part of Canon Five. This clause ("If anyone say . . . that the grace of God is necessary to living faith alone, which works through charity, let him be anathema") denied directly Hermes' assertion that grace was necessary only for faith informed by charity. If the German theologian were wrong, then it followed that grace was also necessary for faith not informed by charity. Whelan proposed that the section read: "If anyone say . . . that the grace of God is not necessary to initial faith, not yet informed by charity, let him be anathema." Gasser rejected the change, since it did not hit Hermes' error directly.[101] Elder felt that the phrase "to living faith alone" was ambiguous, and preferred to say "only to living faith." The wording expressed the intended condemnation, and was in fact employed by Gasser in his rejection of Whelan's amendment, but it was not incorporated in the text.[102]

There is one final amendment that should be mentioned. The

[100] Mansi, LI, 406. Vérot's addition to the text is italicized.
[101] Mansi, LI, 407.
[102] Mansi, LI, 406.

fifth canon of Chapter I condemned another of Georg Hermes' errors, namely, his denial that the world had been created for God's glory. Bishop Whelan asked that the proposition be altered to read: "If anyone assert that the world, which was created for God's glory, was also created to increase His happiness, let him be anathema." He felt that this change would make clear the difference between God's glory and His happiness.[103] Once more, the objection failed to take into account the fact that the canon was written in a specific context, that of the Hermesian errors, and that it was intended to refute them. Answering for the deputation, Gasser rejected Whelan's emendation on the grounds that it would say only indirectly that which the deputation wanted to say directly, namely that God had created the world for His own glory. It is interesting to note in this connection, and indicative of the difficulty in achieving a proper understanding of the abstruse thought of Hermes, that Eberhard of Trier contended that the deputation itself had misconstrued the views of the Hermesians. They did not, he said, deny that the world was created for God's glory, but for them this was a secondary purpose of creation, with the primary purpose being the happiness of man.[104]

On this note of confusion, we can leave the debates on the constitution *Dei Filius,* the official name of this set of decrees on Catholic faith. The bishops of the United States had shown an active interest in many phases of the discussion. Their best achievement was the forcing of a compromise on the word *Romana.* When they came to trade metaphysical subtleties with the fathers of the deputation, they were less successful. Nevertheless, there was a certain unity in their approach. In both these cases, their preoccupation was chiefly pastoral and apologetic. The same bent explained their reluctance over the nu-

[103] Mansi, LI, 404.
[104] Mansi, LI, 107. See also Marcel Viller, S.J., *Cours Viller; étude historique et doctrinale des documents de l'Eglise contenus dans L'Enchiridion de Denzinger* (San Miguel, Argentina: 1956), p. 534.

merous anathemas in the constitution. As Peter Kenrick had put it, they had not come to the council to compose a theological treatise, but they were very much concerned with the relation of the Church to those outside its ranks and with their apostolic mission in the world. For this they had no apologies to make.

The constitution *Dei Filius* was approved unanimously, 667 to 0, at the third public session of the council on Low Sunday, April 24. Thirty-nine American prelates were present, and Bayley of Newark was the lone absentee.[105] As has been mentioned previously, Archbishop Kenrick was one of seven fathers who voted affirmatively after having signed a letter declaring that their vote was given under protest.[106] American reaction to the constitution was predictably varied. McMaster printed it in Latin in the *Freeman's Journal* for May 14, as a "welcome treat" for his 2,000 priest-subscribers and for educated laymen. He added that the decree would give some of the American bishops the opportunity to make an act of faith, and commented: "it will do them good."[107] Bernard McQuaid's report was somewhat more sober. He wrote to Father Early: "There are some obtruse [*sic*] metaphysical points which few can fathom and certainly will never trouble the brains of any but a German Philosopher for whose especial benefit they seem to have been made. The rest is quite simple Theology. Yet it was wonderful the care that was needed and the pains taken to make everything just as it ought to be."[108]

After the public session, the fathers were allowed four days to recoup their forces before the next topic for debate was proposed to them. There had been some uncertainty as to what would happen once the constitution on faith was adopted. On April 20, Bishop Miége told his correspondent, Canon Alliaudi:

We shall have a public session on Quasimodo Day: this will be for the first four chapters of the *Schema de fide*. If you are very anxious

105 Mansi, LI, 437–50.
106 Mansi, LI, 425–6.
107 *Freeman's Journal,* May 14, 1870.
108 McQuaid to Early, Rome, April 24, 1870, in Browne, pp. 423–4.

to know what will happen when we re-commence the meetings: if we will deal with infallibility, or simply with faith, or with the Church, or with discipline, I will tell you with all my accustomed simplicity that I know nothing. The rumors are so contradictory that it is not worth the trouble to talk about them.[109]

McQuaid was able, however, to inform Early on April 25 that the next point for discussion would be the "old one of the 'little Catechism.' " He thought it a useless project, since, while it was supposed to be a move towards uniformity, bishops would still be allowed to have larger catechisms according to the needs of their dioceses.[110]

Debate on the proposal to adopt a universal, elementary catechism was resumed at the forty-seventh general congregation on April 29. The first speaker was Archbishop Franciszek Wierchleyski of Lemberg, who appeared on behalf of the deputation on discipline. He was followed by Cardinal François Donnet of Bordeaux, who supported the project, and then by Bishop Hefele, who read a speech by Cardinal Rauscher who was against it. During Hefele's reading, there was murmuring in the hall. When he had finished, Cardinal de Angelis broke in to announce that a *schema* on the primacy and infallibility of the Roman Pontiff would be considered next. He said that comments on the chapter dealing with the primacy were being distributed, and that the same would be done for infallibility on the day following. The president gave two reasons for this move. One was that many fathers had requested it. The second was that great anxiety about the matter had been aroused among the faithful, with a consequent disturbance of the peace and tranquility of the Church.[111] Debate on the catechism project then continued, with a speech in which Bishop Pietro Rota of Guastalla exhorted the council to hasten its work so that it would not be forced to adjourn without having completed it.

Bishop Vérot was the only American orator. His speech was

[109] Miége to Alliaudi, Rome, April 20, 1870, in Garin, p. 150.
[110] McQuaid to Early, Rome, April 25, 1870, in Browne, p. 425.
[111] Mansi, LI, 467.

restrained and brief, and he began by saying that he had an amendment to offer, which he would leave with the presidents, "according to the mind of the rules which have been given to us." At this point, de Angelis cut him off brusquely with the remark, "We are dealing with the *schema* in general, and not in particular, Most Reverend Father. Therefore either speak in general or give place to another." As it appears in the minutes, the interruption seems to have been completely uncalled for. Vérot assured the president that his amendment dealt with the general import of the *schema,* and then proceeded to suggest that the vote which they were to take be only provisory until an actual catechism had been produced for inspection. He wanted a common catechism, he said, with all his heart, but unless it were satisfactory to the bishops, it would be useless. The hierarchy of the United States, he concluded, had been trying for years to agree on a common catechism and had appointed a committee to do the work of preparing one at a plenary council fifteen years previously, but the book had not yet been written.[112] This speech of Vérot stood in marked contrast to his other appearances in the pulpit. He had started out in a conciliatory vein, only to be rebuked immediately by the chair. Perhaps his reference to the rules of February 22 was considered sarcastic. If so, this is not clear from the printed text. At any rate, he had nearly as much difficulty when he rose to speak in favor of this *schema* as he had had when he objected to those which had preceded it. His suggestion was certainly eminently sensible, but it touched upon a delicate point. No actual catechism had been proposed to the fathers. Two spokesmen for the deputation on discipline later made it plain that there had never been any idea of having the council plan the catechism. What was wanted was that the fathers commit the entire project to the Holy See for implementation. This was all that was asked of them.[113]

[112] Mansi, LI, 469–70.
[113] These statements were made by Bishop Johann Zwerger (Mansi, LI, 493–500) and by Bishop Étienne Marilley (Mansi, LI, 535–8).

The preliminary vote on the *schema* took place on May 4, after a discussion that had lasted through three general congregations. The results were as follows: *placet,* 491; *placet juxta modum,* 44; *non placet,* 56. Nineteen American bishops voted *placet,* four voted *non placet,* and five *placet juxta modum.* At least one more American bishop had left Rome since the public session of April 24 (Patrick N. Lynch of Charleston), while others did not participate in the balloting on May 4.[114]

The entire second debate on the elementary catechism is a strange one. On the very first day of the debate had come the long-expected announcement that the question of papal infallibility would be discussed in the council. This was bound to cause a considerable diminution of interest in the matter at hand. The catechism *schema* itself was peculiar. In effect, the fathers were asked to give the Roman authorities *carte blanche,* and both spokesmen for the deputation persisted in treating objections as professions of disloyalty to the Holy See. In his final summation for the deputation, Bishop Étienne Marilley of Lausanne and Geneva put the charge very baldly. He declared that those who demanded that the catechism be the work of the council were saying equivalently that they did not trust the pope, and that they were affording journals hostile to the Church the opportunity of claiming that there was a division between the pontiff and

---

114 Mansi, LI, 510–12. Those who voted *placet* were Archbishops Alemany, Blanchet, and John McCloskey, and the following bishops: Dubuis, Elder, de Goesbriand, Heiss, Henni, Lootens, Miége, O'Connell, O'Hara, Persico, Rappe, Ryan, St.-Palais, Shanahan, and Williams, and Abbot Wimmer. Voting *placet juxta modum* were Bishops Amat, Gibbons, Hennessy, Loughlin, and Vérot. Archbishop Purcell and Bishops Domenec, McQuaid and Whelan voted *non placet.* The absentees were Archbishops Spalding and Kenrick, and Bishops Bayley, Fitzgerald, Martin, William McCloskey, McFarland, McGill, Mrak, and Mullen. It is probable that several of the absentees had already quitted Rome permanently, but there is no way of determining their exact date of departure. Bishop Martin, for example, had been officially excused from the council on March 18, and had written to Bishop Perché on March 12 that he would be leaving within the week, but he was present at the public session on April 24. A similar uncertainty exists with regard to other bishops.

the bishops.[115] It is very difficult, to say the least, to find substantiation for these accusations in the remarks of those prelates who questioned the advisability of the *schema,* either in speeches from the rostrum or in written observations. In the case of the Americans, there is nothing in the record to cast the slightest doubt on the sincerity of their motives. In any event, nothing more came of the project. It was given tentative approval on May 4, but was never voted upon in public session.

By sheer statistics, the contributions of the American bishops to the abortive *schemata* on the Church and on the catechism, and to the dogmatic constitution on the Catholic faith, cannot be considered very impressive. Prelates from the United States delivered five speeches at the twenty-one congregations which were held between March 18 and May 13. Two of these were by Bishop Amat. A grand total of twenty-three bishops—just over half of those present at the council—took some part in the discussion by submitting written emendations or protests. As has been pointed out, the single greatest example of united endeavor, and the most successful, was the campaign which resulted in adoption of a compromise on the use of the word *Romana.* This in itself was a minor accomplishment, yet it was to some extent symbolic and indicative of a clearly traceable pattern in the thought of most of the twenty-three bishops whose activities form part of the official record.

The Americans represented a relatively new and different branch of the universal Church, with its own peculiar problems and hopes. When various questions came up in the council—whether it was the catechism or Church and State or the good faith of non-Catholics—they tried to form their judgments on the basis of a practical awareness of the needs of the Church which they knew best. If they did not seek to impose their own system and approach on others, they were no less unwilling to accept procedural arrangements which were unsuited to their situation. Their approach was less juridical, and it was certainly

[115] Mansi, LI, 535–8.

less speculative, than that of many of their fellow bishops. They did not claim for it an absolute validity which excluded all other opinion, but they were concerned that the American experience should have its day. Cardinal de Angelis' announcement of April 29 focused the complete attention of the fathers on the subject of papal infallibility. We shall see that some of the same concerns manifested during the debates of March and April appeared again in the speeches and other activities of the bishops from the United States during the debates which led eventually to the definition of infallibility.

V

Preparations For the Debate on Infallibility

ALTHOUGH the question of papal infallibility had not been mentioned in the *schema* on the Church submitted to the fathers on January 21, we have seen that it was a very live issue in extra-conciliar discussions, and that a number of petitions for and against its introduction had been handed in during the first month of the new year. According to the rules of the council, these petitions were referred to the congregation on proposals (*Congregatio de postulatis*). Behind the scenes, the councils of the majority were divided on the advisability of bringing matters to a head. As a concession to the minority, one group proposed to let the question lie until treatment of the whole constitution on the Church would logically demand its consideration. Among those who favored this approach were several Italian cardinals, including Bilio, one of the council presidents, Antonelli, the papal Secretary of State, and Pecci, the future Leo XIII. For a time it seemed that Pius IX sided with Bilio, but he eventually yielded to the arguments in favor of an immediate presentation which were presented by Manning, Senestréy, Mermillod, and others, with the support of another of the council presidents Cardinal Annibale Capalti.[1]

Cardinal Manning later recalled that the majority petition for immediate consideration of infallibility came before the congregation on proposals on a Sunday morning. He continued:

[1] Ollivier, II, 257–61.

"We met in the Vatican. Out of 25 all but two or three voted to recommend to the Holy Father that the Definition should be proposed to the Council. This was the first step in advance."[2] The minutes of the congregation report that the meeting on the various proposals occurred on Wednesday, February 9, at 10:00 A.M. in the Vatican Palace. Twenty-four members were present. Eight of them were signers of the majority petitions which were to be discussed, while two, Cardinal Rauscher of Vienna and the Melchite Patriarch of Antioch, had put their names to petitions asking that infallibility not be brought before the council. Archbishop Spalding was absent, as was Archbishop Alessandro Riccardi di Netro of Turin, an opponent of the definition. Some of the committee members suggested that it would be preferable if initiative in the affair were left to the bishops, and others asked that a moderate decree be framed. Archbishop Manning then made a strong plea for immediate consideration of infallibility and listed seven reasons in its favor. Grégoire Jussef, O.S.B.M., the Patriarch of Antioch, stated that he had hesitated on the question because of the difficulties that a definition would cause for the Eastern Orthodox Church, but he announced that he would submit his judgment to that of the pope. When a vote was taken, only Rauscher opposed submission of a decree on papal infallibility to the fathers.[3] On February 28, Spalding told Father Icard that the congregation had completed its work, and that its recommendations had been sent to the Holy Father.[4] The titular Archbishop of Thessalonica Alessandro Franchi acted as agent of the congregation. He was received in audience by the pope, who gave his consent to the decision which had been taken, and this information was communicated to the secretary of the council on March 1.[5]

Chapter XI of the original constitution on the Church had

2 Purcell, II, 453.
3 Mansi, LI, 687–96.
4 ASS, Icard Journal, p. 231.
5 Mansi, LI, 696–7.

dealt with papal primacy. The new chapter on infallibility was designated *caput addendum,* or additional chapter. In a departure from ordinary practice, its text was distributed to the fathers at their residences instead of in the council hall.[6] This was done on March 6, and ten days were allowed for written comments, a deadline which was later extended to March 25. On that same day, observations on Chapter XI were also due.

Distribution of the new *schemata* hastened the crystallization of opinion for and against the definition. On February 26, James A. McMaster's Roman correspondent, Father Eugene M. O'Callaghan, informed him: "I understand that at least half the French and German bishops—and these the men of ability—[are] opposed to at least the opportuneness of any declaration of papal personal infallibility or of infallibility 'ex cathedra' other than the indeterminate belief already existing."[7] Opposition was not, however, limited to French and German bishops. On his way to an afternoon drive in the Villa Borghese, Dupanloup stopped in at the American College on March 4 and found Purcell in an agitated state. In his diary for that day the Bishop of Orléans quoted the archbishop as having exclaimed that the council had been begun with a comedy of invitations and would end with a tragedy of excommunications.[8] Peter Richard Kenrick was more explicit still. He wrote to his vicar-general Henry Muehlsiepen:

The Council appears to have been convoked for the special purpose of defining the Papal Infallibility and enacting the propositions of the Syllabus as general laws of the Church. Both objects are deemed by a minority, of which I am one, inexpedient and dangerous, and are sure to meet with serious resistance. The minds of both parties are seriously excited, and there is every reason to fear that the Council, instead of uniting with the Church those already separated from it, will cause divisions among ourselves most detrimental to Catholic in-

[6] Quirinus, p. 337.

[7] UND, McMaster Papers, O'Callaghan to McMaster, Rome, February 26, 1870.

[8] ASS, Dupanloup Journal, p. 33.

terests. Let us pray that the Providence of God may overrule the passions of men.[9]

Another American who was greatly disturbed by the turn of events was Domenec of Pittsburgh. Father Icard met him, together with Bishop Ryan of Buffalo and another bishop, in the Villa Pamphili on March 8. He found Domenec in the worst possible humor, and the bishop told him that the only explanation he could find for the way the council was going was that divine justice was trying the Church. With apparent reference to the proposed *schema* on Church and State, Domenec declared that the "maxims of intolerance" which were being made to prevail would not go down well in the United States. His remarks on infallibility were even more succinct and vivid. "It will kill us," he told Icard, "we shall have to swallow what we have vomited up." The bishop went on to explain to the Sulpician Superior-General that a standard Protestant reproach was that Catholics made the pope a sort of god who was impeccable, infallibile, and all-powerful. Hitherto, such charges had been met with a straightforward denial. But if the pope were to be proclaimed infallible, the American bishops would have to retract their past teachings on the subject. Icard, who was surprised at the vehemence of the bishop's argument, then suggested to him that he had perhaps been overly influenced by the writings of Dupanloup. Domenec's answer was immediate and clear:

It is nonsense to say that. Monsignor Dupanloup has nothing to do with it. Don't you think we can see what is going on in our own country? They have summoned us from America only for decisions which will do infinite harm to our churches. They do not listen to us. They do all this because they have the majority with them, which makes them more powerful than we. Is that a council?

The discussion then turned to the causes of the situation in which the council found itself. Icard remarked that a good many

[9] Kenrick to Muehlsiepen, Rome, March 6, 1870, in Rothensteiner, *History*, II, 305.

175

inopportunists had changed their views because of the violent attacks being made on the pope, and now favored a definition of his infallibility. But Domenec refused to consider this aspect of the question and laid the entire blame for discussion in the council at the door of *Civiltà Cattolica* and *L'Univers*. On this note the conversation ended.[10]

While the fathers were still considering the two new chapters, Lord Acton was busy trying to mobilize the forces of the opposition. On March 8, he wrote Döllinger on the subject of moral unanimity, without which, he claimed, decisions of the council would not be binding. He reported that this was also the opinion of Archbishop Spalding.[11] A day later Acton wrote once more to Döllinger and urged him to bring out a pamphlet on infallibility which could be distributed among the fathers. He further suggested that autographed copies should be sent to certain friendly bishops. As he put it: "A little attention of this sort, with some appropriate words, in the various languages, or in Latin, would not only do good, but has been deserved by several. I should like particularly to suggest the Rt. Revd. the Bishop of Clifton, the Most Revd. the Archbishop of St. Louis, the Most Revd. the Archbishop of Halifax, Haynald, Archbishop of Calocza, Strossmayer, the Cardinal of Prague [and] Mérode."[12]

The distribution of the *schema* on infallibility had not put an end to petitions on the subject. Proponents of a definition reacted to minority opposition by submitting requests that the topic be scheduled for immediate consideration. One of these memorials bore the signatures of two bishops from the United States, Dubuis of Galveston and Miége of Kansas.[13] Bishop Elder of Natchez did not sign any petition at this time, but in a letter to the Coadjutor Bishop-Elect of New Orleans, he expressed his sympathies clearly as he reported that Döllinger and his French counterpart, Gratry, had been repudiated by bishops from their

---

10 ASS, Icard Journal, pp. 255–6.
11 Conzemius Transcripts, Acton to Döllinger, Rome, March 8, 1870.
12 Conzemius Transcripts, Acton to Döllinger, Rome, March 9, 1870.
13 Mansi, LI, 703–11.

own countries.[14] There was also some talk of an attempt to carry the definition by acclamation, something which *Civiltà Cattolica* had suggested in February of 1869. One of Döllinger's correspondent's informed him of this possibility, and he wrote in the twenty-ninth Quirinus letter on March 15:

> In this connection the answer of a North American Bishop of the Infallibilist party is significant. He said that he remembered having heard, when in the theological class of his seminary, that the condemnation of Pope Honorius by the Sixth Council meant nothing, and now in his old age nobody could require him to study and examine the question for himself.[15]

There is no way of checking the accuracy of Döllinger's quotation, but it was at least true that the question of Pope Honorius was one of the problems being agitated by the minority. On March 11, thirteen fathers, representing Austria, Germany, Hungary, Italy, France, England, and the United States, presented a memorial in which they asked that they be allowed to meet with representatives of the deputation on faith to discuss the cases of Popes Sergius and Honorius. They complained that ten days was too short a time for consideration of such an important matter and they protested that the general congregations did not provide adequate opportunity for full discussion. Archbishop Kenrick's was the sole American signature on this petition, which was rejected by Bishop Fessler.[16]

Members of the minority felt that objections on the score of insufficient time for consideration, the defect of moral unanimity, and the supposed intention of proclaiming infallibility by acclamation were so serious that they brought into question the ecumenicity of the council and, consequently, the validity of its definitions. Continuing rumors that an attempt would be made at definition by acclamation provoked the strongest American protest of the entire council. On March 15 Archbishops Purcell

14 AANO, Perché, Elder to Perché, Rome, March 6, 1870.
15 Quirinus, p. 348.
16 Mansi, LI, 702–3.

and Kenrick joined Bishop Fitzgerald of Little Rock and Bishop Moriarty of Kerry in warning the presidents that if such a maneuver were attempted, they would withdraw from the council and make known the reason for their departure.[17] Acton reported a sequel to this protest to Döllinger on March 17:

> I have warned you that they are again going to make the attempt to proclaim the dogma by surprise. Barnabò came to Kenrick and asked him to make a declaration that he would somehow leave the determination of the teaching to a commission. The story is still not clear to me. Kenrick, who is of the nature of iron, seems to have given a determined answer. I now believe, and so does Strossmayer, that they should let it come to a head once more, and then, in the council itself, denounce the council.[18]

Three days later Acton was still trying to unravel the story. His principal source of information was Connolly of Halifax, who told him that Kenrick was about to publish a tract in which he would sum up the arguments against the ecumenicity of the council. Acton suggested that Döllinger defer any statement of his own until further information was available on Kenrick's plans.[19]

The minority fathers were not the only Americans who were active during the first weeks of March. Spalding had not yet given up hope that his compromise solution might be accepted. On March 15, Cardinal Mathieu of Besançon presented it once more at a meeting of the French opposition bishops, and once more it was rejected. The French decided that they would be inconsistent if they opted for an indirect and implicit definition after having petitioned the pope to remove the question from the agenda entirely. Icard, who recorded the session in his diary, noted also that the bishops really missed the point. The question was no longer whether the issue should be brought up, but what line of action they would take when it came to the floor. He felt that serious consideration should have been given to Spald-

---

[17] Mansi, LI, 714.

[18] Conzemius Transcripts, Acton to Döllinger, Rome, March 16/17, 1870.

[19] Conzemius Transcripts, Acton to Döllinger, Rome, March 20, 1870.

ing's plan as one possible way of conciliating the opposing parties.[20]

Three episcopal letters written during the fourth week of March testified to the sharp division of opinion that existed among the United States bishops. On March 20 Bayley wrote to Father Corrigan at Newark that he was leaving Rome for Paris. He continued enigmatically: "I will tell you the reasons which have induced me to leave Rome, when I see you, or rather why being obliged to go to Paris, I do not intend to return here."[21] However, Bayley did return to Rome and took part in the voting in July. Bishop Wood of Philadelphia, on the other hand, was already on his way home. From Paris he sent a letter of thanks to Spalding for his "kind intervention" in helping him to obtain leave from the council. He ended the letter with "kindest remembrances to all our Rt. Revd. friends, a warm prayer for the conversion of the *recalcitrants* and for the perseverance of the *infallibilists*."[22] The third writer, John Baptist Purcell, was in no such happy mood, as he told two friends in Cincinnati:

Annie is perfectly right in using the phrase 'the bitter end.' The Infallibilists are frenetic. They are are [*sic*] ready for mobbing, as they were at Trent, when beards were plucked. Montalembert, Dupanloup, Maret, Gratry are treated as heretics and abused—so that as Bp. Bayley has often said to me, 'never has the pleasant anticipation of a fraternal union of bishops been so painfully marred as during the last four months'. We here do not disagree, but there is a cloud lowering over our minds and hearts hardly edged by a silverage of light.

I am sorry that [Henri] Ramière [S.J.] is perverting the 'Messenger' [of the Sacred Heart] into an organ of controversy & misrepresentation. Many of our bishops are disgusted with the course he has taken and one of the wisest and saintliest of the French prelates expressed the conviction that the Jesuits are preparing another *cataclysm* for themselves and the Church. But they never learn from experience.[23]

20 ASS, Icard Journal, pp. 202–3.
21 AANY, C-2, Bayley to Corrigan, Rome, March 20, 1870.
22 AAB, 36-T-40, Wood to Spalding, Paris, March 24, 1870.
23 AAC, Purcell Papers, Purcell to "[illegible] and Anna," Rome, March 24, 1870.

The day after he wrote this letter, Purcell translated his feelings into a protest which reiterated the minority's claim that moral unanimity among the fathers was necessary for the validity of a dogmatic definition. He joined Bishops Whelan, Purcell, and Vérot in declaring that it was difficult to put faith in a divided witness and in claiming that Christ had promised that He would be with the Church and would provide the help of the Holy Spirit only when the Church's testimony was unanimous. In a subsidiary point, the protest, which was in Whelan's handwriting, challenged those provisions of the decree of February 22 which allowed cloture to be imposed by a simple majority vote after a petition to that effect had been made by only ten fathers. Finally, the four bishops summed up their objections in a series of lapidary sentences: "Is this how the affairs of God are to be handled? How was it done in the Council of Trent? How in other councils? We speak to those who know. We have done our duty."[24]

Now that the debate over infallibility was obviously approaching a decisive phase, both sides increased their efforts at organization. Until March, the international committee of the minority had been a rather amorphous group. Cardinal Rauscher was one of the first to propose a more tightly knit organization. He suggested that the opposition bishops be paired off by nations against the leading advocates of the definition. In his preliminary listing, Kenrick and Connolly were to answer the arguments of Manning and Spalding.[25] During the latter part of March, the committee was enlarged to nearly three times its original size. The charter members had been Darboy, Dupanloup, Ginoulhiac, Rauscher, Ketteler, Haynald, Strossmayer, Clifford, Moriarty, Kenrick, and Connolly. Connolly withdrew at about this time, under pressure, it was said, from Cardinal Barnabò. He continued, however, to sympathize with the committee's aims and to lend his help when it was possible to do so. No record

[24] Mansi, LI, 716–7.
[25] Conzemius Transcripts, Acton to Döllinger, Rome, March 20, 1870.

180

has been found of the Americans who joined the international committee, but those whose subsequent activity in the council demonstrated most clearly their association with its efforts were— besides Kenrick—Purcell, Domenec, Fitzgerald, McQuaid, Mrak, Vérot, and Whelan.[26]

The first meeting of the enlarged international committee took place on Wednesday afternoon, March 30. Strict secrecy was observed. Strossmayer summarized the history of the first three months of the council and proposed that it be made the basis of a protest at the way in which affairs were being managed. Hefele of Rottenburg, one of the new German recruits, and Clifford seconded Strossmayer's motion, and Dupanloup was commissioned to draw up the document. Hefele and Ginoulhiac were assigned to prepare a study of the question of moral unanimity. Dupanloup's contribution was ready by Friday, April 1, and it was approved at a meeting of the international committee held on that day. Ginoulhiac and Hefele presented separate reports, and the committee set itself to reconciling them. Apparently Clifford had assisted Dupanloup in writing his pro- test, which was handed in over six signatures, including that of Kenrick, on April 3. The document kept in the Vatican Archives File on the council is in the English prelate's handwriting. It was an appeal for greater stress on the role of the fathers in general congregations and for a corresponding de-emphasis of the role of the deputations and their spokesmen. It seems that the committee was not able to arrive at a final formulation of the Ginoulhiac-Hefele treatment of moral unanimity, and no protest was submitted under that heading. As Archbishop Haynald noted sadly in his diary for April 2, the minority bishops still had some way to go before they achieved real unity of action.[27]

---

[26] Conzemius Transcripts, Acton to Döllinger, Rome, March 30, 1870.
[27] Friedrich, *Geschichte*, III, 2, 811–2; Mansi, LI, 717–9. Friedrich quotes as his authority "the unpublished letter of a bishop." Much of his material is, however, taken *verbatim* from Acton's March 30 letter to Döllinger which has just been quoted.

One further petition resulted from the initial minority efforts at collaboration. On April 10, fourteen fathers, including Purcell and Kenrick, recommended that consideration of infallibility be delayed until after the council had completed its work on problems of Church and State. The petitioners pointed out that there were many unresolved areas of dispute in the politico-ecclesiastical field and suggested that a solution should be found for them before the possibility of infallible papal authority was discussed. This approach had the double purpose of recalling to the minds of the council presidents the ever-present threat of intervention by the secular powers, and at the same time expressing the apprehensions of the opposition that once infallibility was defined, the remaining *schemata* on the agenda would be proclaimed by papal decree.[28]

The confusion and fears which beset some of the minority bishops were well expressed by McQuaid of Rochester, who wrote to Father Early on Holy Saturday, April 17:

I have just heard that the Holy Father sent for one of the strongest Infallibilists and told him that he must use his best influence to bring on the question at once, as the state of Europe was such that if not settled now it never would be. Of course if he has said so to one, he has said the same to several. We may therefore expect the all-important question to be placed before us for discussion immediately. As the Holy Father has used all his influence to decide the question his own way, we may expect to have it placed before the Cath. world in some shape or other. If the Council will so limit it that the decisions of Popes dethroning Kings, and setting subjects free from their allegiance, and authorizing the burning of heretics, etc. shall not be declared infallible, we may be able to get along. It seems to me that we are destined to encounter great difficulties and troubles in America in the next few years. What the Almighty has in store for us is past my comprehension.[29]

Just a week later, the Bishop of Rochester returned to the same theme in another letter to the rector of his cathedral:

[28] Mansi, LI, 719–22. For an explanation of the minority's motivation, see Quirinus, p. 489.
[29] McQuaid to Early, Rome, April 16, 1870, in Browne, p. 423.

Several American Bishops leave this week, although some will not go home directly. I stay to fight the great battle if it should come up. We ourselves know little of what we shall have to do next. We may take up the second part of the first *Schema de Fide,* or we may pass on at once to the *Schema de Ecclesia,* taking the question of Infallibility first of all and out of its place. Some Bishops are urging the Holy Father to have this done; on the other hand, the difficulties in the way of such a definition are so many and so serious that there is some hesitation. Opposed to the definition are so many Bishops of unquestionable devotion to the Holy See, who will vote a *non-placet* if it should come before them that men stop to think. Besides the governments of Europe are alarmed. They remember that Popes in the past absolved subjects from their allegiance and in many ways interfered with governments. Even in our country there will arise more or less difficulty on this head. At least politicians will try to use the difficulty against us.

Yet with all these reasons weighing against the definition, I am inclined to think it will pass in some modified form. The Holy Father wishes it, and lets everyone see that he does, the Jesuits are as busy as bees of late and the French Bishops of that way of thinking are as enthusiastic and excitable over the subject as they well can be.

My hope is that in the definition the Pope will in some [way] be connected with the Church. I cannot conceive of a living head without a body. However, I must not enter into the vexed question, which has been such a disturbance to my mind since I came to Rome that once it is disposed of in one way or another I will never want to hear of its controversy again.[30]

These two letters make it clear that McQuaid's reason for opposition to the definition was a threefold one. He believed that it was politically inexpedient, and he was disturbed by the tendency of the majority to demand a formula that was vague and indeterminate in its scope and which could therefore be extended beyond due limits by subsequent broad interpretations. Finally, he felt that the chief stress should be laid on the infallibility of the Church, and he did not see how the papal prerogative could be defined outside that context. He was, therefore, more than a mere inopportunist. There were doctrinal problems connected

[30] McQuaid to Early, Rome, April 24, 1870, in Browne, pp. 424–5.

with the definition to which he thought the majority owed an answer before the proposed dogma could be proclaimed.

Another who took a pessimistic view of the opposition's chances of preventing the definition was Bishop Richard V. Whelan. On April 24, he wrote to Dupanloup:

> I am convinced that all the arguments which can be accumulated will have no effect with those who favor this doctrine. In one way or another they reject everything. Reasons mean nothing. Facts count for nothing. Difficulties for the future do not trouble them. They are not alarmed by the effect which the definition may produce among the faithful, nor of the outside opposition which it may arouse. We must, they say, decide the question—the matter has gone too far—in the present state of affairs the authority of the Pope will be shaken unless there is a definition. They want it; they have decided on it; nothing can prevent it (humanly).

In this hypothesis, Whelan told the French prelate, the only prudent course was to accept the facts and to work for a moderate formula which would spell out exactly the limits of pontifical infallibility and which would emphasize that the pope spoke infallibly only when he functioned as "the mouth of the Church." He enclosed a copy of the formula which he had designed to meet these specifications, and which he had already handed in as an observation on Chapter XII. It will be seen again when we come to survey the various amendments which were suggested by the fathers for the chapters on the primacy and infallibility.[31]

An outside observer, Father Sherwood Healy, who had accompanied Bishop Williams of Boston to the council, gave the following summation of the situation at the end of April to a correspondent in the United States, James F. Edwards: "I think it no indiscretion nor exaggeration to say that the preponderance of talent is decidedly on the side of the non-definitionists, but the preponderance of numbers is all on the side of the definition . . . . The Pope is avowedly for the definition. I go with the Church, willingly and cheerfully, if a definition is made. I know

[31] ASS, Dupanloup Papers, Whelan to Dupanloup, Rome, April 24, 1870.

others than I are not so willing. God help them and give them a docile heart."[32]

Their numerical superiority and the assurance of papal support made the task of the proponents of the definition an easier one than that of their opponents. Nevertheless they encouraged petitions on the subject, and two of these were signed by American bishops. The first was submitted on April 22 and it urged that the question be proposed to the council. Miége signed together with a group of fellow Jesuit vicars apostolic, while Dubuis, de Goesbriand, and Rappe added their names to a page which was headed by the signature of Archbishop Manning.[33] After the *schema* had actually been laid before the fathers, Dubuis joined other prelates in a rather ornate letter of thanks for the action.[34]

Minority bishops were not the only ones who relayed their views on the issues to correspondents elsewhere. Bishop Augustus Martin's lengthy March 12 report to Napoleon J. Perché has already been quoted. The latter was also a strong infallibilist, and he answered the Bishop of Natchitoches in a letter which was released to *Le Monde* of Paris and was then carried in the London *Vatican* and the New York *Freeman's Journal:*

> I am deeply astonished, My Lord, by what you tell me with respect to the Council. It is easy to understand that the Supreme Pontiff should be grieved by it. But I do not see any reason why the Cardinals and Bishops, who form the vast majority of the Council, should be discouraged. The only thing I fear is lest the Sovereign Pontiff, from his love of peace, should be willing to withdraw the question of infallibility on account of this violent opposition. If it is permitted to me, the least among my brethren, to express my opinion, I should say that it is absolutely essential to represent clearly to the Sovereign Pontiff that the withdrawal of this question would be an irreparable calamity, and a step backwards of which the results are incalculable.
>
> For all good priests and good Catholics, the decision of the infallibility is the principal affair of the Council. All other questions,

---

[32] UND, Edwards Papers, Healy to Edwards, Rome, April 30, 1870.
[33] Mansi, LI, 722–4.
[34] Mansi, LI, 722–6.

however serious they may be, have only a secondary importance in the judgment of the Catholic world. At a moment when the fundamental principle of authority is so violently attacked, it is in my opinion the duty of the Church to affirm it with greater solemnity than ever by the definition of the infallible authority of the representative of Jesus Christ. *Such is the sentiment of all true Catholics.* If the question were set aside it would be a triumph for all the enemies of the Church and the Holy See, both within and without; and it would be a cause of discouragement to all Catholics worthy of the name. However you form the majority, and it seems to me, My Lord, that with firmness and union the vote is in your hands. I know that it is God who does everything; but since he deigns to make use of men it is their part so to act that they may be, not only humble and docile, but also active and intelligent instruments in his hand.[35]

Perché's argument underlines one of the most painful trials to which the members of the minority were subjected. Whatever may be said of the motivation of bishops from other countries—and that is not our concern here—it is abundantly clear that prelates like Whelan and McQuaid, whose letters have just been quoted, and others from the United States honestly believed that a definition of papal infallibility would be harmful to the Church. They had, besides, doctrinal difficulties for which they felt themselves obliged in conscience to demand convincing explanation. To assume that such men were not "true Catholics" and to lump them together as "enemies of the Church and the Holy See" was nothing short of the rankest injustice. Allowance must be made for the highly charged polemical atmosphere of the time and cognizance taken of the fact that genuine enemies of the Church did indeed seize upon the arguments of the minority for their own purposes, but this scarcely excuses the tone of the criticism leveled at bishops whose only fault was that they took as seriously as did the members of the majority their role as judges of the faith.

The letters of Bishop Eugene O'Connell of Grass Valley were not much more tolerant of the minority position than were the

[35] The *Vatican* (London), April 1, 1870. See also *Freeman's Journal*, May 21, 1870.

comments exchanged by Martin and Perché, but at least they were more humorous and imaginative. He sent two messages during April to Father William Fortune, the rector of All Hallows College in Dublin. The first was dated Spy Wednesday, April 13:

Pardon me for having delayed so long a reply to your esteemed favor and excuse this hurried scroll, which is penned during the short interval between the grand function of Tenebrae in St. Peter's and Dr. Moriarty's dissertation, as usual, *De Infallibilitate Summi Pontificis.* Whether it be owing to my dullness or not, I cannot be persuaded that the "Venerable Doctor" and Bishop of Kerry treats his subject as ably and *omni exceptione major* as the Papal Choir treated the Lamentations and Miserere. Is it not strange that the Doctor's views have undergone such a change since he taught the Doctrine *ex cathedra* for fifteen years that the Pope was infallible when addressing the Church *de fide aut moribus?* But age and experience mellow the fairest fruit—just as happened to Osius of Cordova.

After giving this vignette of life at the Dominican convent of St. Clement, where both he and the Bishop of Kerry were lodged, O'Connell went on to ask Fortune if there were any substance to Moriarty's fears that the definition would provoke a schism, or if talk of it were in any way responsible for efforts to push a convent inspection bill through the British Parliament.[36] His remarks also provide a not too flattering commentary on the success of the campaign which Dr. Moriarty had described to John Henry Newman when he wrote on February 3: "My mission is to talk to every man I meet—cardinal, bishop or monsignore. I try to frighten our opponents and to encourage our friends, for there are many timid. I am the voice of one crying out, not in the wilderness, nor in the Council, but in the streets and salons."[37]

Two weeks later O'Connell addressed Fortune again, and this time his tone was a little sharper:

[36] AAHC, Marysville Papers, O'Connell to Fortune, Rome, April 13, 1870. See also Henry L. Walsh, S.J., *Hallowed Were the Gold Dust Trails* (Santa Clara: 1946), p. 424.

[37] Moriarty to Newman, Rome, February 3, 1870, in Butler, II, 29.

Were I in any other place but Rome, I'd feel my absence from All Hallows, as the pain of loss. But Rome is more my home than even green Erin.—of course it is so with every *Roman* Catholic. But all Catholics are not, in a certain sense, Roman Catholics; there are German & Bosnian & Gallican, aye American Catholics—not to speak of English *Cawtholics* who seem to be of old Cobbet's way of thinking, viz.: that every man is suppos'd to be a rogue until he is proved to be honest man. So certain Catholics suspect every utterance of the Sovereign Pontiff apart from the Bishops assembled in Council or Dispersed as arbitrary, if not despotic and trenching upon Episcopal Privilege. Such Croakers are perpetually upbraiding the advocates of Papal Infallibility with Honorius & Vigilius & I know not how many others, as if the acts of these Pontiffs were definitions ex Cathedra, or a second edition of Original Sin which must have necessarily descended to their successors. They are quite silent about the Council of Rimini & such assemblies as had to be called to order & rectified by the Sovereign Pontiff. However we must make great allowance for the Gallican Catholics on account of their National Saint Dionysius who, you know, walk'd a long way without his head: little blame then to his spiritual children who imagine that they can 'get along' (as Americans say) without a Head that they haven't a right to *reform*. For my part however & fere omnis Jerosolyma mecum—we are satisfied with the old 'Pontifex anni illius' whose utterances require no more Gallican or German *Reformation* than refin'd gold needs gilding or the violet fresh perfume. The Unanimity—nemine dissentiente, on Low Sunday amongst the 667 Prelates assembled around the Sovereign Pontiff De Doctrina Catholica in the 4 primis Capitulis Schematis Dogmatici was a most cheering & consoling spectacle. Fiat! Fiat! usque ad finem. Won't you have the Review & Record regularly sent to me & continue to pray that we may all be united in this Grand Council like the various tints of the rainbow & form in Heaven's sight one arch of peace?[38]

As May and the debate on infallibility drew near, the bishops from the United States were beginning to adopt firm positions, either for or against the definition, but there was still a certain amount of doubt about the stand which many of them would take. Manning, who wanted a text framed in the broadest possible terms, told the American scholar Charles Eliot Norton that

[38] AAHC, Marysville Papers, O'Connell to Fortune, Rome, April 27, 1870. See also Walsh, p. 425.

there were no more than ten "enemies of the dogma" in the council. This estimate would seem to be optimistic, especially if by "the dogma" was meant Manning's expression of it. The archbishop also told Norton that "almost all the Americans are sound."[39] No doubt they were, but whether this was so in Manning's understanding of the phrase is another question.

The recess in the council which extended from February 22 to March 18 had afforded ample leisure for study of the *schemata* on papal primacy and infallibility which were distributed on March 6. By March 25 a considerable number of written observations were in the hands of the presidents. Bilio had these bound in separate volumes, one for the primacy and the other for infallibility. Bishop Senestréy of Regensburg then persuaded him that a résumé should be made of the episcopal comments, and the Bavarian prelate was commissioned to do the work, with the help of his own theologian Canon Willibald Maier and of Clemens Schrader. This was the origin of the *Synopsis Animadversionum* which is reprinted in Mansi.[40] The work of editing the observations was therefore entrusted to three of the most prominent advocates of a definition. In the copies of the *Synopsis* distributed to the fathers all contributions were anonymous, a fact which annoyed some of the minority bishops who protested that they wanted to know the authorship of the various recommendations. The authors have since been identified by the editors of the Mansi collection.[41]

---

[39] Conzemius Transcripts, Acton to Döllinger, Rome, April 20, 1870. Norton himself elaborated on his April 19 conversation with Manning in a letter to his mother, Mrs. Andrews Norton. He quoted the archbishop as having said: "There are not ten men in the Council who would deny the truth of the doctrine. The whole opposition to it is based on what is called 'opportunity'. And now, as the Civilita Cattolica well said the other day, the word opportunity is found but three times in the Gospel, and the passages are parallel, namely, 'And Judas sought an *opportunity* to betray Him'. That's it; opportunity means personal interest of one sort or another." (Norton to Norton, Rome, April 20, 1870, in Norton and Howe, I, 382.)

[40] Granderath, III, 1, 13. The Senestréy diary is in *Collectio Lacensis*, VII, 1695–1703.

[41] Mansi, LI, 929–1070.

Two bishops from the United States had remarks to make on Chapter XI of the proposed constitution on the Church, which treated the primacy of the Roman Pontiff. Whelan was one of many commentators who discussed the use of citations from the Second Council of Lyons and from the Council of Florence. While a considerable number of the minority bishops wanted these citations either omitted or else, in the case of Florence, quoted in full and not piecemeal, the Bishop of Wheeling found himself in the company of Senestréy in proposing that the text be retained as it stood. Whelan, however, had a reason of his own for making the suggestion. He went on to recommend that the passage which referred to the pope as "supreme father, teacher and judge of all Christians" be deleted, and he also called for omission of any reference to the questions of papal inerrancy and appeal from papal judgments to a general council. His purpose was to dissociate the notions of jurisdictional and magisterial primacy, which the *schema* had taken care to combine. For this he felt that a general reaffirmation of the decrees of Lyons and Florence would suffice.[42]

The second American contributor was Thaddeus Amat of Monterey-Los Angeles. Like Whelan, he was opposed to an explicit definition of papal infallibility, but he adopted a tactic which was exactly the reverse of that proposed by the eastern bishop. In an amendment which paralleled that submitted by his fellow Vincentian, Edmond Guierry, the Vicar Apostolic of Tche-kiang, China, Amat asked that two canons be added to the chapter on the primacy. In the first of these, he condemned the opinion which held that the ordinary jurisdiction of diocesan bishops was not subordinate to that of the pope. Secondly he called down an anathema on those who claimed that assent was not due to papal judgments which proscribed errors in matters of faith and morals, or else declared that it was licit to appeal from the pope to a future council or to the civil powers.[43]

[42] Mansi, LI, 949. See Umberto Betti, O.F.M., *La Costituzione dommatica "Pastor Aeternus" del Concilio Vaticano I* (Rome: 1961), p. 76.

[43] Mansi, LI, 965; 972. Betti, pp. 99–100.

190

These recommendations echoed the terms of the Spalding compromise plan, which, as has been seen, had evoked no very great response from either the majority or the minority. Amat's version was to be no more successful.

When it came to the "added chapter" on infallibility, the United States bishops were considerably more articulate. The first American observation listed in the *Synopsis Animadversionum* was that of Augustin Vérot. As usual, his remarks were vivid and direct. They can be subsumed under five headings: (1) the definition would be unnecessary, unfair, and scandalous; (2) it represented a departure from traditional conciliar practice in that it condemned an opinion that Catholics had been free to hold; (3) if a definition had to be made, it should be severely circumscribed; (4) the arguments alleged in the *schema* were not probative; and, (5) the rules of procedure of the council were such that grave doubts could be cast on its ecumenicity.

Under the first heading, the Bishop of St. Augustine asked that the subject be stricken from the agenda. He saw no need for a definition, since all Catholic bishops obeyed the pope, whether he spoke *ex cathedra* or not. In a thinly veiled reference to men like Louis Veuillot, the bishop stated that the dogma was being proposed only to satisfy the vanity of "the editors of certain journals." He recalled that infallibility had not been mentioned in the bull convoking the council and complained that he had therefore not brought along the books and other materials which would enable him to form a scholarly judgment on the question. He feared, moreover, that scandal would arise, since, he said, the definition would amount to a contradiction of the decree of the Third Council of Constantinople which had censured Pope Honorius. Lastly, he predicted that relations with Protestants would be harmed. Until the present, Catholics had been able to defend themselves with regard to "criminal popes" by answering that they were neither impeccable nor infallible. If the definition were made, Vérot declared, the charge would be made that

Catholics worshiped the pope as a god, "like the blind pagans of the Indies."

Vérot's second point was a spirited defense of the Gallican Church and its doctrine, the merits of which, he said, were demonstrated by the distinguished record of the French clergy, both at home and in the foreign missions. He declared that the Gallican school was a staunch defender of the need for unity with the pope and of the indefectibility of the apostolic see, although it did admit the possibility that one or the other pope might make a mistake, which would then be corrected either by himself or by a successor. As examples of pontiffs who had erred he cited Honorius, Vigilius, John XXII, and Nicholas I. To deny these instances of papal error, Vérot said, was to subvert historical certitude and to play into the hands of unbelievers like Renan. With regard to the obedience of bishops to the Holy Father, the bishop stated that Gallicans acknowledged the pope as their superior. For this infallibility was not needed. As he put it, the man who would demand infallibility in a superior before obeying him did not deserve an answer, but a blow.

Despite his own clearly expressed doctrinal hesitations, Vérot was a realist, and he was under no illusion that the question of infallibility could be avoided. He therefore suggested that the prospective definition be carefully hedged about with restrictions. First, there must be no thought of accepting as an infallible papal decree a declaration made under physical or moral pressure. Secondly, it should be made plain that the pope was not himself the source of revealed doctrine, nor did he receive special inspiration in the matter. Rather, the bishop suggested, he must determine the faith which springs from the consent of the churches and to this end he must employ advice, reading, prayer, and other means, both natural and supernatural. Finally, Vérot asked that the Vatican Council make no decree which could be interpreted as prejudicial to the condemnation of Pope Honorius, and that it explicitly disavow the notion that popes had direct or indirect power in temporal affairs.

192

Turning his attention to the proofs alleged in the *schema,* the bishop noted first that, while opinion for infallibility now seemed to be predominant, this had not always been true. He felt that the texts from Scripture and from the Second Council of Lyons proved nothing except papal primacy. He added that St. Augustine seemed never to have heard of the doctrine, and that Bossuet and even the catechism of Cardinal Patrizi, which was in use at Rome, mentioned only the infallibility of the pope when he spoke in union with the other bishops of the Church. "A bishop," he concluded, "would sin mortally if he were to give his vote only out of pious affection for the Holy See." His last point was a protest to the effect that if freedom of expression were denied to the minority, the authority of the council could afterwards be rejected. But he was sure, he said, that this was impossible in a council directed by the Holy Spirit.[44]

One American supporter of the definition who proposed modifications in the text was Claude Dubuis, the Bishop of Galveston. He joined three other bishops of French origin in suggesting a slightly altered version of the definition, and he also put his name to a petition of eight French prelates who asked that the citation of Luke 22:32 be made fully and in context.[45] Bishop Tobias Mullen of Erie was another who wanted a complete citation of the Lucan text. He also proposed what he thought might be a way of conciliating the differences among the fathers. In the original version of the definition, the pope was said to pronounce infallibly when he spoke in the exercise of his office as supreme teacher of all Christians. Mullen proposed that this be amplified to include the notion that the pontiff, in his infallible declarations, was only confirming the doctrine of the bishops.[46] This was, of course, one of the main

[44] Mansi, LI, 1006–8. Betti, p. 107, analyzes Vérot's observations, and, pp. 108–10, lists the fathers who agreed with one or another of the points which he made.

[45] Mansi, LI, 1014–5; Betti, pp. 126, 137.

[46] Mansi, LI, 1018–9; Betti, pp. 138–9.

points at issue between the parties, and it was an addition that the majority could not accept.

We have already seen that Bishop Amat hoped to avoid controversy by including a substantial affirmation of infallibility in the chapter on the primacy. Two other efforts at a compromise were made by Americans. Archbishops Spalding and Alemany suggested that a paragraph be added to Chapter XI which would demand "internal and external assent of the heart, with the full obedience of faith" to judgments in matters of faith and morals which were made by the pope as "universal teacher and mouth of the Church." They were joined in this petition by five bishops: St.-Palais, Quinlan, Conroy, Williams, and Elder.[47] Alemany and O'Connell of Grass Valley were associated with the second compromise attempt. They signed an observation submitted by a group of Dominican and other bishops headed by Cardinal Filippo Guidi, O.P., of Bologna. There were five points in this memorial. The petitioners asked that the object of papal infallibility be restricted to those cases where the pope "defined something to be held or rejected on faith by the universal Church." They asked for the omission of the term "inerrancy" on the ground that it sounded badly in Latin, and of "infallibility" because St. Thomas did not use it. The Angelic Doctor had instead spoken of the pope as "immune from all error," and this was recommended in place of the words to be omitted. Lastly, they proposed an explicit condemnation of those who held that apostolic constitutions derived their force from the consent of the churches, and that they commanded only respectful silence and not internal and absolute assent. As a corollary of this, they declared that appeal from the judgments of a pope to a future council should be condemned.[48]

Four more Americans submitted observations. They were Domenec, Whelan, McQuaid, and Kenrick; and, all of them opposed the definition. The Bishop of Pittsburgh declared that

[47] Mansi, LI, 1049.
[48] Mansi, LI, 1028; Betti, pp. 130-1.

there was no need for it, and that it would put an end to the conversion of Protestants in the United States. Until now, he said, we have been telling non-Catholics that the question was a free one. If it is proclaimed to be a dogma of faith, they will reply that either we have been lying or else our doctrine has changed. The Spanish-born Vincentian could foresee no good results from the project. He pointed out that good Catholics would obey the pope in any case, and he was of the opinion that bad ones would only become worse. Heretics, the bishop declared, were hard put to accept the infallibility of the Church. The infallibility of the pope would erect an impenetrable wall between them and Catholics, and it would be but another occasion of scorn for unbelievers. After this recitation of the reasons why he thought the definition would be inopportune, Domenec continued. "I add that the doctrine of the infallibility of the supreme pontiff is not altogether certain, and moreover, many of the authorities on which it rests have been found, in the course of time and with critical examination, to be false and spurious, while others of them have not been correctly interpreted."[49]

Both Bishop Whelan and Bishop McQuaid were concerned about the historical evidence for the dogma. The former proposed a text of his own which would avoid the word "infallibility" and speak instead of "inerrancy." He stated that this would be more consistent with past conciliar pronouncements and that it would help to avoid unnecessary controversies.[50] McQuaid began his comments with a rapid survey of the evidence of tradition. He had been unable to find a patristic text in which the doctrine of the *schema* was clearly expressed, and he remarked that it was strange that the fathers of the Church had never explained the pertinent Scripture texts in the sense now assigned to them. He then mentioned the case of Pope Honorius and, after admitting that many theologians had come

[49] Mansi, LI, 1034; Betti, p. 102.
[50] Mansi, LI, 1050–1.

195

to accept the doctrine after the twelfth century, said that even so it was not clear that it had become common teaching. Certainly, he continued, there was no lack of contemporary authors in Germany, France, England, and America who declared that the doctrine was not of faith. The Irish bishops had made a statement to that effect to a committee of the British Parliament, and in the United States the common Catholic teaching was that the question was a disputed one.

With these doctrinal doubts on record, the Bishop of Rochester proceeded to an enumeration of the reasons why he thought the definition would be inopportune. He repeated the same points with regard to Protestants which were made by Domenec, and added that unfortunate political consequences might also follow. There was, he added, no need for the dogma. If the Italians be excluded, he said, there were no Catholics who rejected papal authority. In fact, devotion to the apostolic see had never been greater, and he did not want to see any action taken which would diminish either the universal compassion felt for the pope in his temporal difficulties or the subsidies which were offered to him from all sides. The definition, said the bishop, would be the cause of disputes. As matters stood, all papal pronouncements without exception were accorded a respectful reception, but if some of them were to be infallible, all would be subjected to intense scrutiny. He also regretted that the controversy was hindering the work of the council, which had been called to remedy the ills of society. For all these reasons, he concluded, the subject should be removed from the agenda.[51]

The last American commentator was Peter Richard Kenrick. He prefaced his critique with the statement that the opinion which held that the Roman pontiff alone, without the consent of the bishops, was infallible was not certain enough to be defined as a dogma, and that even if it were certain, it was not expedient that it be defined by the Vatican Council. On the

[51] Mansi, LI, 1051–2; Betti, p. 103.

doctrinal question, he argued that the proposed dogma was insufficiently grounded in Scripture and Tradition. The Petrine texts proved nothing beyond the primacy, he declared, and the evidence of Tradition seemed to be that the consent of the churches was the tessera of faith. Kenrick further challenged the possibility of making a distinction between the pope as a non-infallible private teacher and as the infallible doctor when he spoke *ex cathedra*. He declared that the distinction was an *ad hoc* arrangement, with no foundation in fact, and stated that it would inevitably lead to misunderstandings and disputes. The archbishop had no difficulty in admitting the infallibility of the Church, which he said sprang from its very constitution. Instead of proclaiming the pope infallible, he asked for the more frequent convocation of general councils and he blamed many of the evils of the past four centuries on the fact that no council had been held. He declared that it was playing with words to try to deduce papal infallibility from the pontiff's acknowledged primacy of jurisdiction and of honor. Supreme authority in this area did not bring with it infallibility in matters of doctrine. Rather, this latter prerogative belonged properly to a council presided over by the pope.

Having committed himself to forthright opposition to the *schema,* Kenrick turned next to an analysis of the contemporary state of theology on the question. He conceded that the infallibility of the pope had been taught for four hundred years, and by saints, and that it was defended by the greater number of theologians. It was, he admitted, common teaching, but he emphasized that there was a difference between common teaching and dogma, which could only be defined by a council. At one time, he recalled, the doctrine of the "two swords" had been commonly held, but he declared that in the nineteenth century there was scarcely anyone who would uphold the right of papal interference in secular matters to the extent that they allowed popes the right to depose kings and bestow their kingdoms on others. As a final fillip to his argument on the distinction between common teaching and dogma, he remarked that infallibility itself had been unknown for ten centuries, which made the possibility of its definition questionable at best.

Kenrick realized that the definition of the Immaculate Conception by Pius IX in 1854 was a strong argument against the position which he was taking. He approached this delicate question in two stages. First, he pointed out that the definition of 1854 was not quite in the same category as that of papal infallibility. Its intention was to do honor to God and to Our Lady, and it did not in itself prejudice any episcopal rights. Nevertheless, he admitted, it was a departure from traditional practice and was contrary to the rule of faith of Vincent of Lérins, which demanded for a dogma that it be doctrine which was accepted everywhere and at all times by everyone. The definition of the Immaculate Conception was also unique, Kenrick continued, in that it was motivated by piety rather than necessity, while the practice in former times had been to make definitions only in order to proscribe errors. In any case, he felt that the problem of a definition made by the pope alone was not completely solved by Pius IX's action, since he had in fact taken care to canvass the opinion of the bishops before issuing the bull *Ineffabilis Deus*.

Like Domenec and McQuaid, Kenrick attacked the opportuneness of the definition on the score that it would work harm in the area of Catholic-Protestant relations. This was his only excursion into the argument of inexpediency, and he returned immediately to doctrinal issues with a series of comments questioning the ecumenical character of the council. He argued that the present controversy was one between the pope and residential bishops, and he thought that it should be decided by the litigants, but instead he found that the council counted among its members a considerable number of fathers who did not represent actual dioceses, and who in some cases were not even bishops. The archbishop contended that the presence of these prelates, who were presumed to side with the central authority of the Church, weighted the scales heavily against the residential bishops, and he feared that their vote for infallibility would reduce the latter to the status of mere counselors of the pope. He completed his challenge of the validity of the council by enumerating some of the standard complaints of the minority, namely, that procurators of residential bishops had been excluded from the sessions on the sole authority of the pope, that the freedom of the fathers to propose subjects for discussion was severely circumscribed, and that the composition of the deputations left much to be desired from the point of view of the opposition.[52]

Archbishop Kenrick's far-ranging criticism of the *schema* established him as one of the leaders of the opposition. As Spalding had discovered at the Second Plenary Council of Baltimore in 1866, the St. Louis prelate was not a man to mince words or to disguise his true feelings. In the question of infallibility, he had sincere doubts, and he was genuinely concerned by what he saw as the attempted erosion of episcopal prerogatives. He expressed these doubts and this concern in the memorandum which he submitted to the council presidents and which eventually found its way into the *Synopsis Animadversionum*. This was not, however, his only effort during the final weeks before the all-important debate on the *schema* began. As April drew to a close, he engaged, as will be seen, in a controversy with Archbishop Spalding, and he also had an elaboration of his observations on infallibility published anonymously at Naples. This brochure, which ran to forty-two pages in Latin, was distributed to all the fathers of the council and covered all the subject headings which have just been enumerated; it concluded with a plea for the decentralization of the Church. The archbishop felt that this could be achieved without prejudice to the unity of pope and bishops, and he declared that it would

[52] Mansi, LI, 1059–70; Betti, p. 111.

199

be well received by many Catholics and also by many outside the Church who wished to return to it.[53]

The most startling evidence of the deep rift which had occurred among the bishops of the United States because of their disagreements over papal infallibility is to be found in the exchange between Archbishop Spalding on the one hand and Dupanloup, Kenrick, and Purcell on the other. The American aspect of the controversy began when Dupanloup, in the course of a literary debate with Archbishop Dechamps of Malines, used arguments against a definition of infallibility drawn from Spalding's January petitions on the subject. The French prelate's pamphlet quoting Spalding appeared on March 1. Among other things he used the January petitions to buttress his argument that a conciliar definition demanded the morally unanimous consent of the fathers.[54] The Archbishop of Baltimore spent a full month preparing his answer, which appeared in Louis Veuillot's *Univers* on April 4. He expressed his regret that Dupanloup had brought his name into the debate with Dechamps and pointed out that the petitions had been written when the council was much younger and the question not yet fully matured. He and his cosigners, he said, were neither enemies of the dogma nor inopportunists. Instead they saw papal infallibility as intimately united with the infallibility of the Church and a logical corollary of the pope's primacy. Spalding also challenged the French bishop's attempt to use texts from the works of his predecessor in the See of Baltimore, Francis Patrick Kenrick, as arguments against the papal prerogative. He concluded by saying that a definition was inevitable and that the only question was whether the individual bishop would stand with or against the Holy Father.[55]

[53] Kenrick's brochure (the first of two which he published) was entitled *De pontificia infallibilitate qualis in Concilio Vaticano definienda proponitur dissertatio theologica* (Naples: 1870).

[54] Felix Dupanloup, *Résponse de Mgr l'évêque d'Orléans à Mgr Dechamps, archevêque de Malines* (Naples: 1870). See Granderath II, 1, 379–409. For the Spalding petitions, see Mansi, LI, 663–6.

[55] *Collectio Lacensis,* VII, 1362–6. Spalding, pp. 397–403.

The debate with Dupanloup marked Spalding's debut as a confirmed supporter of the definition. The few notes which he left concerning the controversy testify to his efforts to meet all the objections of the opposition and to evolve his own notions more clearly.[56] He also kept a file of newspaper clippings on the subject.[57] One point irked him immediately, and it was that his letter to Dupanloup first saw the light of day in *L'Univers.* Even though Veuillot was the outstanding lay advocate of the definition, the archbishop disapproved of the French editor's methods, and, in a second letter to the Bishop of Orléans (which may or may not have been sent), he said explicitly that he had given his original rebuttal to M. Ravelot of *Le Monde.*[58] Veuillot himself confirmed this, and later wrote that he had never met Spalding. The letter had been circulation in Rome for twenty-four hours before he obtained a copy of it and dispatched it to France for publication.[59] Spalding subsequently asked at least two French papers to print his letter, since they had published Dupanloup's March 1 response to Dechamps.[60]

The opening of the controversy with the Bishop of Orléans also occasioned a few uncomfortable moments for the Superior-General of St.-Sulpice, whose community was charged with the direction of St. Mary's Seminary in Baltimore. On April 4, the same day on which Spalding's letter was published in *l'Univers,* the archbishop, who was riding in his carriage with two other American bishops, noticed Icard walking on the street in Rome and invited him into the carriage. They drove out to the gardens of the Villa Borghese, and Spalding inquired if Dupanloup had studied at St.-Sulpice. Icard answered that he had and added that Bishop Pie of Poitiers, a leading infallibilist, was also an alumnus of the seminary. Spalding then went on to speak in a

---

[56] A twenty-point guide sheet on infallibility is in AAB, 39-N-5.

[57] These clippings are in AAB, 39-K-2-13.

[58] A rough draft of this letter is in AAB, 39-N-10.

[59] Veuillot, II, 76–7.

[60] AAB, 39-K-6, 7. The papers were *Le Monde* and *L'Union de l'Ouest* of Angers.

kindly way of the Sulpicians and assured the Superior-General that he had no reproaches to make against them. Icard noted in his diary that he seized the opportunity to indicate that former Sulpician students were to be found on both sides in the council. He said that their orientation depended on what had happened to them after they had left the seminary. It was true, he admitted, that Gallicanism had been taught when everyone in France was teaching it, but he insisted that his community had always been careful to stress respect and obedience for the Holy See at the same time. Spalding and his companions professed themselves satisfied with this explanation, and the remainder of the drive was considerably more comfortable for Father Icard.[61]

The Archbishop of Baltimore's letter provoked a spate of comments, both friendly and hostile. The first support which he received was indirect. *L'Univers* had published a letter attacking Dupanloup which had been sent by Christophe Bonjean, the Vicar Apostolic of Jaffna. On April 5, Veuillot was able to follow this up with a second letter from a group of missionary prelates who declared that they deplored the scandal which the French bishop's opposition to the dogma was causing in their mission territories. The Americans who signed this protest were Archbishop Blanchet and Bishops Heiss, Martin, Miége, Dubuis, O'Connell and de Goesbriand.[62] Spalding received more direct commendation from Francesco Nardi, an official of the Roman Curia, who wrote to him on April 12: "I read with extreme pleasure your splendid letter to Mgr. d'Orléans, written with Christian and *American* courage, and frankness. It is a tremendous blow! The wrong quotation from your glorious predecessor's works, this poaching [?] with your, and your venerable fellow-Bishops' adhesion, got what they deserved." Nardi asked the archbishop to send him extra copies of the letter "for my Italian and German newspapers."[63] A shorter, but equally

[61] ASS, Icard Journal, pp. 335–7.
[62] *Freeman's Journal,* April 23, 1870, quoting *L'Univers,* April 5, 1870.
[63] AAB, 39-K-8, Nardi to Spalding, Rome, April 12, 1870.

positive note of congratulations came from Angelo Paresce, the Jesuit rector of Woodstock College: "I have rec'd your Grace's letter to the Bishop of Orléans with great pleasure. It is worthy of the Archbishop of Baltimore!"[64]

As usual, news from Europe took some time to reach the United States. The *Freeman's Journal* printed the first news of the Spalding letter in its April 30 issue. Editor McMaster was exultant and commented: "There is an end put to the indecent lucubrations of the incompetent Roman correspondents of Catholic journals—*organs* or *fiddles*—in these States, about the *adherence* of our American prelates to the singular and untenable position of Bishop Dupanloup"[65] A week later, the editorial columns of the journal carried a translation by McMaster of the letter to Dupanloup, and this was followed by a statement of gratitude to the archbishop for his defense of orthodoxy and the remark that opposition by some of the bishops only proved their fallibility. This last was apropos of the text of the January petition against infallibility which had been signed by a number of Americans and which had been printed in the New York *Herald* for April 27.[66]

Spalding's intervention on the side of the infallibilists was received with joy by the European editors who advocated the definition. On April 27, the London *Vatican* published the following praise in its correspondence columns: "Nothing which I have yet seen or heard proves so irrefragably the *absolute necessity* of a clear, unflinching, black and white definition of Papal Infallibility as that letter."[67] Louis Veuillot was also extremely pleased, and wrote to a correspondent in France:

Here is a very fine letter of the Archbishop of Baltimore to the Bishop of Orléans, on his last pamphlet. That pamphlet, it must be admitted, was not a happy one. The refutation which I send you, frank, sharp and eloquent, really has something terrible about it. Like that of

---

[64] AAB, 35-O-1, Paresce to Spalding, Woodstock, May 4, 1870.
[65] *Freeman's Journal,* April 30, 1870.
[66] *Ibid.,* May 7, 1870.
[67] The *Vatican,* April 27, 1870. The letter is signed "M.F.H."

Monsignor Bonjean, the Bishop of Jaffna, it touches only one point, but the point which it touches, it annihilates. From the point of view of skill, it is a masterpiece of polemic. What firmness! What precision! What triumphant moderation!

I have no need to add any commentary to demonstrate for you the more and more frank and decided attitude of the council. The letter of the eminent Archbishop of Baltimore is a sufficiently clear manifestation of it.[68]

This enthusiastic response to the letter of Archbishop Spalding was, of course, not a universally shared emotion. The New York *Herald* was particularly unfriendly. On May 11 it berated the archbishop for what it called his childish desire to break into print, and it claimed editorially that his effort was generally laughed at because of its "general appearance and general aspect of 'hard times.' "[69] Two weeks later, the *Herald* quoted Dupanloup as having charged that Spalding had been against the definition until his appointment to two commissions of the council, and it attributed his attack on the French bishop to the influence of Manning. However, the New York newspaper's correspondent continued, the English prelate could not "humbug" the other Americans, since they were men who liked "converts who say their prayers and give alms to the poor, but they cannot stomach them when they run around Rome like one-horse politicians on the eve of a local election, asking for signatures in favor of a dogma which . . . is only an *opinion theologique.*"[70]

Among the European commentators, Johann Döllinger's critique was a sober one, and he specified two weak points which Spalding would have to explain further. In the forty-third Quirinus letter, the German historian remarked that the archbishop had made two changes in his position. Previously, he had wanted an indirect definition; now he called for one which was open and explicit. Secondly, he had formerly declared that

[68] Veuillot, I, 460–61.
[69] New York *Herald,* May 11, 1870, in Beiser, p. 100.
[70] New York *Herald,* May 22, 1870, in Beiser, pp. 98–9, 100.

moral unanimity was necessary, but he was now satisfied with "a mere majority of votes."[71] More emotional and chauvinistic was a report cited with disapproval by the *Vatican*. It came from the Roman correspondent of the London *Standard,* who complained of "the insolent letter addressed by the Archbishop of Baltimore to the Bishop of Orléans, in which this ignorant trans-Atlantic prelate takes the accomplished Mgr Dupanloup to task for his Latin and his French, accusing him of presenting doctrines under a form remote from the truth, and refusing to be associated with his struggles." He concluded: "There is something shocking to one's sense of the fitness of things that the Bishop of Orléans should have such a correspondent at all."[72]

The English reporter's remarks are scarcely worth recording, except insofar as they indicated the attitude towards the United States bishops which existed in certain quarters, but a more serious storm was building up. In mid-May, the Cincinnati *Catholic Telegraph* told its readers that a bishop from one of the southern dioceses had written that Spalding was pretending to speak in the name of the American hierarchy in his dispute with Dupanloup. "The American bishops of both parties," wrote the prelate, "are displeased that he should speak as their representative without their consent or even knowledge." He went on to say that a reply was being prepared that would set the record straight.[73] By the time this news had reached the American Catholic public, the attack on Spalding by Archbishops Purcell and Kenrick was history. It was launched during Easter week and continued into the early part of May.

The first round was fired by Kenrick, in a printed circular addressed to Spalding, which bore the date, "Tuesday of Easter Week." This was April 19. The Archbishop of St. Louis concentrated on a single issue, namely, Spalding's use of citations from the writings of his late brother, Archbishop Francis P. Ken-

---

[71] Quirinus, p. 503.
[72] The *Vatican,* April 29, 1870, quoting the *Standard,* April 24, 1870.
[73] *Catholic Telegraph,* May 19, 1870.

rick of Baltimore, in support of the infallibilist position. Peter Kenrick admitted freely that his brother had been ardently devoted to the Holy See. But he quoted a passage from the latter's *Theologia Dogmatica* which seemed to him to make it clear that the author demanded the consent of the bishops before any pontifical decree could be considered irrevocable.[74] On April 21, Archbishop Kenrick sent this document to Spalding with a covering letter in which he expressed both his regret that he had been obliged to take public issue with him and his hope that they would always remain friends. The Baltimore prelate's answer was equally courteous. He thanked Kenrick and promised a reply in due time, but told him that he could not consent to a public controversy in the matter.[75]

While this preliminary exchange was taking place, two other documents were being prepared. Bishop Dupanloup's diary for Easter Sunday and the days following has these cryptic notations: "Sunday, April 17, 1870 . . . answer to Baltimore; Monday, April 18, 1870 . . . work on Baltimore; Thursday, April 21, 1870 . . . revised Baltimore and finished; Tuesday, April 26, 1870 . . . revised answer to Baltimore."[76] The references were to his *Réponse de Mgr l'évêque d'Orléans à Mgr Spalding, archevêque de Baltimore,* which was published at Paris. It contained the French prelate's answer to Spalding, a copy of the arguments which the latter had used in urging his compromise petition during January, the April 19 letter of Kenrick to Spald-

[74] *Ibid.,* May 26, 1870. The passage cited by Peter Kenrick occurred in Francis Patrick Kenrick, *Theologiae dogmaticae tractatus tres: de revelatione, de ecclesia, et de Verbo Dei* (Philadelphia: 1839), pp. 283–4. It reads as follows: "Non tamen placet ea loquendi ratio qua Pontifex se solo infallibilis praedicatur, nam de eo tamquam privato doctore, privilegium inerrantiae nemo fere ex Theologis Catholicis noscitur propugnasse; nec tamquam Pontifex solus est, ei quippe docenti adhaeret Episcoporum collegium, uti semper contigisse ex Ecclesiastica historia liquet. Pontificias autem definitiones ab Episcoporum collegio exceptas, sive in Concilio, sive in sedibus suis, vel subscribendo decretis, vel haud renitendo, vim habere et auctoritatem nemo orthodoxus negaverit."

[75] AAB, 36A-L-10, Kenrick to Spalding, Rome, April 21, 1870. A rough draft of Spalding's reply is on the inside flap of this letter.

[76] ASS, Dupanloup Journal, pp. 45, 46, 48.

ing, and a new letter "of several archbishops and bishops of North America," who supported Dupanloup against the Archbishop of Baltimore.[77] It is with this last letter—the second of the two documents mentioned above—that we are principally concerned. It was addressed to the Bishop of Orléans, and the original is in the handwriting of Michael Domenec of Pittsburgh. The other signers were Purcell, Kenrick, McQuaid, and Fitzgerald. All but Kenrick's signature were crossed out, and another hand has added the words "in the name of several bishops of North America."[78] As finally published, the letter bore this last legend and the names of Purcell and Kenrick.[79] Some explanation for the alterations was contained in a note from Bishop Vérot to Dupanloup:

As I have had the honor to tell you, the names which are found on the letter are for your personal satisfaction, and the prelates would not like to see their names figure publicly, either in the newspapers or otherwise, but in case of need, you can prove your assertion, if it becomes necessary to do so.

P.S. There are other prelates who would sign, but they do not want to expose themselves to the publicity.[80]

As will be seen, Archbishop Spalding had another explanation for the absence of more signatures on the letter, which was printed in the *Gazette de France* on April 28, 1870, a Thursday. On the next Monday, the *Gazette* added the remaining items from Dupanloup's pamphlet, that is, his own letter to Spalding, the Kenrick letter of April 19, and Spalding's January arguments for an indirect definition.[81] The Kenrick-Purcell letter was first published in English by the *Vatican* on May 6, and it did not become known in the United States until James A. McMaster translated it in the *Freeman's Journal* of May 21.

[77] The Dupanloup-Spalding letter is reprinted in *Collectio Lacensis*, VII, 1366–73, with only minor variations.

[78] The original is in ASS, Dupanloup Papers, and is undated.

[79] *Collectio Lacensis*, VII, 1373–6; *Gazette de France* (Paris), April 25, 1870; *Freeman's Journal*, May 21, 1870.

[80] ASS, Dupanloup Papers, Vérot to Dupanloup, Rome, April 21, 1870.

[81] *Gazette de France*, April 28 and May 2, 1870.

The first point which the objectors made was that Spalding's letter seemed to speak in the name of the American hierarchy. They denied that, and asserted that at best he spoke for a party among the bishops who agreed with him. Secondly, they declared that the Spalding letter had been sent without prior consultation, an action which they said was contrary to custom in the United States, where matters affecting the general interest were first thrashed out in a meeting of the individuals concerned. Therefore they not only dissociated themselves from the archbishop's sentiments, but also consented that their views be made public, "considering that there is a question of strict duty toward the Catholic Church, in which we are established by Our Lord Himself, judges of the faith; and that we are well convinced that it is an assault made on the faith to agitate for the erection of a theological opinion into a dogma of Catholic faith."

The letter to Dupanloup continued with a direct attack on Spalding:

You have believed, Monseigneur, that it was the clearly enunciated opinion of the author of the Postulatum of which this letter treats that it was not opportune to define the Pontifical Infallibility. According to the present declarations of the author himself, it would seem that you are mistaken. But, we think we can assure you, you are not the only one that has been mistaken on this subject. Those who have the honor to enjoy the company of the amiable Archbishop are mistaken about the matter as well as your Lordship—and they have not well and clearly perceived the change that has taken place till since [sic] the honorable Prelate has found himself a member of two Deputations of the Council.

Several of us could, at need, declare having heard him, more than once, exhort and induce his colleagues in the Episcopate to oppose a definition supremely inopportune. We think, even, that the mere reading of the Postulatum puts sufficiently in evidence the real desires of the author. We have not the least doubt, or suspicion, but that the change of opinion that has happened since has been accomplished under the influence of solid intrinsic reasons. But these reasons are unknown to us as much as to you; and so it is easy to explain the unfortunate mistakes that have occurred on the subject. It seems to us, however, that the blame, if any, ought not to weigh entirely and exclusively on your Lordship.

After this negative section of their letter, the bishops went on to discuss the issues which had come up in the course of the Dupanloup-Spalding dispute. They claimed that the declarations made by the Second Plenary Council of Baltimore in 1866 and by the prelates assembled in Rome in 1867 had been expressions of respectful obedience to the supreme pontiff, but not professions of faith in his infallibility. Another difficulty was Spalding's use in January of the Latin verb *deberet* to express the need of moral unanimity. Dupanloup had translated this into French as *il faut,* while Spalding said that he had meant *il serait désirable.* The latest American entrants into the debate did not pretend to be experts in French philology, but they referred instead to the history of the Council of Trent and to the Dominican theologian Melchior Cano as authorities for the validity of their stand on the need for moral unanimity.

Turning to the American scene, the authors granted that the "great majority" of the bishops of the United States admitted papal infallibility, but they insisted that they admitted it only as a theological opinion. Even though it was extrinsically more probable, and was upheld particularly by those prelates who had made their studies in Rome, they did not feel that this was sufficient for the proclamation of a dogma. They also alleged the difficulties that would follow in the wake of a definition because of past papal claims in the matter of deposing power and freedom of worship. A special problem would arise, they stated, with regard to the Irish, who could never be brought to accept Pope Adrian IV's gift of their homeland to King Henry II of England. The letter closed with a statement which reflected both the practical and the doctrinal doubts of the signers: "For several of us believe that ecclesiastical history: the history of the Popes, the history of the Councils, and the tradition of the Church are not in harmony with the new dogma; and it is for this that we believe that it is very inopportune to

209

wish to define, as of faith, an opinion that appears to us a novelty in the faith, that seems to us without solid foundation in scripture and tradition; while it appears to us contradicted by irrefragable monuments."[82]

Archbishop Spalding held fast to his resolution not to engage in public controversy with other American bishops, but he did draw up two statements of his views. One of these was the draft of a letter to Dupanloup. The second document was an explanation of the opinion on infallibility of Archbishop Francis Patrick Kenrick which was printed on May 9 and mailed to the fathers of the council on the twelfth.[83] Spalding set the crucial passage from his predecessor's *Theologia Dogmatica* in context and pointed out that it referred to the pope as private teacher. No one, he indicated, claimed infallibility for a pontiff acting in his private capacity. He felt that the other passages which he adduced proved sufficiently that Francis Kenrick could not be counted among the adversaries of the dogma, and he rested his case on this evidence.

In the draft letter to Dupanloup, the archbishop prefaced his remarks with several comments on the provenance of the Kenrick-Purcell letter. He declared, accurately enough, that he had reason to believe that the "several" prelates on whose behalf the two metropolitans had written meant in fact four or five bishops. They had said that the great majority of the American hierarchy admitted infallibility only as an opinion, and Spalding said that he had to agree with them on that point, since it had not yet been defined as a dogma. He then repeated his intention of not entering into controversy with Kenrick and Purcell, since, he asserted, the bishops of the United States had always been a moral unit and would remain that way. The archbishop seems to have hesitated over the absolute character of

[82] *Freeman's Journal*, May 21, 1870. The comment that the dogma would be "a novelty in the faith" is omitted in the text published in Dupanloup's brochure referred to above.
[83] It was published in the *Vatican*, May 20, 1870. Dupanloup's copy is in ASS, Dupanloup Papers.

this last statement. He had at first written "almost always," but then crossed out the qualifying adverb.

With this preface done, Spalding turned to the issues. He denied strongly that his basic position had shifted, and referred Dupanloup to the letter which he had addressed to the Holy See in the summer of 1869, in which he professed his belief in the doctrine of infallibility, but questioned the advisability of a definition. This, he said, had been written before he came to Europe, and when he was under the impression that Gallicanism was a dead issue. However, the reading of pamphlets by Döllinger and by the Bishop of Orléans himself had convinced him of the error of his ways. He had then, he went on, proposed a compromise solution, but Dupanloup would have nothing to do with it. The archbishop was obviously still persuaded that an indirect definition would have been preferable, and he told his correspondent that the minority would now get for its intransigence a formally defined dogma, with all the results which he had predicted in his August letter. In other passages he denied that he had given his first letter to Veuillot, whose methods he disapproved, and he charged Dupanloup with mistranslation of the word *deberet* of the January petition. He repeated his defense of the orthodoxy of Francis P. Kenrick and promised his prayers for the French bishop's speedy conversion to the side of the infallibilists. The letter closed with an apology for the straightforward manner in which he had spoken, and the archbishop remarked that this was due to his "American republican education," and to the fact that he had not had the advantages of the refined politeness of French society or of membership in the French Academy. This last jibe at Dupanloup, who was a member of the Academy, was crossed out.[84] No copy of this letter has been found among the papers of Dupanloup, but at least its essential outline was released to *Le Monde* of Paris, which on

[84] AAB, 39-N-10. Preliminary notes for the draft are in 39-N-5 and 9. In the latter notes, there is a long section on Gallicanism, which Spalding described as "conceived in schism, brought forth in despotism and resurrected in modern liberalism—so called."

May 11 printed a summary of the letter's main points, together with a copy of Spalding's August, 1869 letter to Barnabò.[85]

Reaction to the dispute was not long in coming, and it was predictably varied. On May 3, Louis Veuillot wrote that the combined attack of Dupanloup, Purcell, and Kenrick on Spalding was a tactical move, designed to take advantage of the archbishop's well-known abhorrence of controversy. The Kenrick-Purcell letter he criticized for its rashness and for what he saw as a lack of sufficient reflection behind it.[86] Ten days later, the *Vatican* reported that "the attempt to divide the American Bishops has signally failed." The report continued: "Of the sixty members of the hierarchy of the United States, more than fifty, mindful of the solemn decisions of their own provincial councils, are of one mind and heart with the Archbishop of Baltimore, who will leave his five or six dissentient colleagues to their own pious reflection, confident of the restoration of that perfect unity which they have been the first to disturb, but which will again be the glory of the American Church."[87]

Diocesan newspapers in the sees of three of the most prominent minority bishops handled the dispute cautiously. On May 21, the Pittsburgh *Catholic* published a moderate editorial which said that the editors did not feel that they were in any position to judge the actions of distinguished bishops who were on the scene in Rome. A letter signed "Veritas" in the May 28 issue of the *Catholic* was less pacific. The author, a priest, castigated McMaster for what he considered his vicious attack on the archbishops, accused him of an incredible egotism, and ended by saying that if he were his confessor he would not give the editor absolution unless he apologized publicly for what he had written. The item in the *Catholic Telegraph* which had aroused McMaster's ire was along the same lines. Father Callaghan declared that nothing could excuse the scurrility of Mc-

85 *Le Monde*, May 11, 1870.
86 Veuillot, II, 74–5.
87 The *Vatican*, May 13, 1870.

Master's pen, and he added: "The great scandal in connection with this correspondence is of the *Journal's* own making."

The *Western Watchman* of St. Louis followed the same pattern as the *Catholic Telegraph*. On May 21, it reported: "The Archbishop of this diocese is undoubtedly laboring to defeat the promulgation of the new dogma of the Papal personal infallibility . . . . Compared with him, Dupanloup is but an essayist." But the editor, Father David Phelan, was not quite sure of his ground and surmised that Kenrick had perhaps been deputed, in the scholastic tradition, to marshal opposing arguments so that the question would receive full discussion. Phelan likewise chided the "false zeal" of Spalding, whom he accused of misrepresenting the opinion of Archbishop Francis Kenrick.

Comment on the controversy by the secular press in the United States was not particularly profound or enlightening. The New York *Herald,* which kept up a steady stream of fire on Spalding, was loud in its praise of Kenrick's scholarly attainments, and it found the position which he and Purcell had adopted a "noble and unselfish" one. Their letter was, the paper said, "one of the boldest documents that has ever been seen in Rome from the pen of an ecclesiastic."[88] Another metropolitan daily, the *Post,* could not quite bring itself to credit the sincerity of the opposition, and dismissed the Archbishop of St. Louis as a disappointed office-seeker who had been refused the cardinal's hat and was now "showing his teeth."[89]

More important than all the journalistic chaff was the fact that the sharp agitation of the last few weeks before the debate on infallibility stimulated thought in higher American ecclesiastical circles and made prelates explicitate their convictions. One indication of this result was the letter sent to *Le Monde* by an anonymous bishop who described himself as a veteran of thirty years in the American mission field. It was not a commentary on the Kenrick-Purcell dispute with Spalding, but it paralleled it

[88] New York *Herald,* May 11 and May 22, 1870, in Beiser, pp. 95–6.
[89] The *Evening Post* (New York), June 18, 1870, in Beiser, p. 96.

and was directed at Dupanloup. The bishop denounced com-
promisers, whom he termed "dumb dogs who knew not how to
bark," and declared that the "liberal Catholics" made no converts despite the praise heaped on them by Protestants. He saw
the definition as a great boon to conversion work, because non-
Catholics approached the Church looking for clear and definite
truth, and not for opinions or theories. This truth was to be
found in an infallible pope. The author of the letter rejected
the notion that it resided in the council and remarked: "Six
hundred Bishops assembled in Council are only six hundred
fallibilities. How can these six hundred fallibilities constitute
an infallibility?" He then explained his own position:

> The true solution is this. The infallibility of the decisions and
> judgments of a Council derives all its force from the union of the
> body of Bishops with the Supreme Head of the Church, to whom alone
> it belongs, by divine right, to give to the judgments of his brethren
> the irreformable sanction of his own judgment. But then, in fact, it is
> in this Supreme Head that infallibility resides? In one sense, yes. But
> nevertheless, when convoked by him, and judging with him, the
> Bishops, considered collectively, become an infallible body. Separated,
> they are no longer so. But, independently of a Council, this infallibility
> of judgment which the Bishops do not possess, does the Pope possess
> it? Undoubtedly. Otherwise it would be from them he would receive
> it. Himself fallible, he would receive from other fallible men the
> infallibility which they do not possess: which is absurd.[90]

The letter just quoted is the best exposition by an American
of the majority point of view. Although he did not enter into
any of the historical difficulties alleged by the minority, the
author challenged the assumption that an infallible pope would
make the Church less attractive to non-Catholics and declared
that, on the contrary, a reaffirmation of papal authority was the
principal remedy demanded by the needs of the times. This need,
he felt, was in itself sufficient warrant for proclamation of the
dogma. Another United States prelate who shared the same
sentiments was Bishop Thomas Foley, the Administrator of

[90] The *Vatican*, April 15, 1870.

Chicago, who wrote to express his agreement with Spalding on June 13. The recently consecrated bishop deplored the divisive effect of the stand taken by Purcell and Kenrick and reported that Protestants were gloating over their letter to Dupanloup. He asserted that all Catholics believed the dogma, and concluded by saying: "A fair definition of it will silence cavils & quibbles forever—or drive the Gallican element to its proper place."[91]

The situation of the council at the beginning of May was not a happy one. With all compromise efforts practically at a standstill, positions had hardened and the fathers were divided into two camps of unequal size. The larger majority party realized that victory was within its grasp and was impatient of the success which was felt to be inevitable. Among the minority, a sense of frustration was evident. As for the hierarchy of the United States, the dominant motive of the American opposition was the fear that a definition would hinder conversions and embarrass the progress of the Church in Protestant countries. The American anti-definitionists turned for support to the evidence of Scripture and Tradition, and what they found there made many of them also question the validity of the dogma itself. A third facet of their thinking was the emphasis which they placed on individual episcopal responsibility, both in matters of church government and in the affairs of an ecumenical council. The bishops of the majority, while they sought to provide answers for historical difficulties, took a stand that was essentially less complicated than that of the minority bishops. For many of the more zealous proponents of the definition, the question was simply one of loyalty to the Holy See, and they were unable to understand how any Catholic bishop could reconcile such loyalty with opposition in the council. Examples of this type of thinking have been seen in the letters exchanged by Bishops Martin and Perché. With all the good will in the world they could not fathom the mentality which was well described in a letter which Richard Gilmour, the future Bishop

[91] AAB, 34-A-4, Foley to Spalding, Chicago, June 13, 1870.

of Cleveland, wrote to Archbishop Purcell after the latter's return from Rome:

> To many of us here it is a gratifying satisfaction to see that at least there are some of the great and venerable prelates who are not afraid to proclaim their disapprobation on questions of grave moment to the Church, while at the same time they are ready to acquiesce in the final decision of the Church. To us raised in America, freedom of discussion is a sacred right. And when men hold convictions, at the proper time and in the proper place, they should calmly and respectfully declare them, salva auctoritate. The world is watching the action of this great council and all hail to the men who are laboring so ably and so fearlessly in the grand cause of religion.[92]

As the event proved, Purcell, Kenrick, and the rest did acquiesce in the final decision of the Church. They did not believe that their willingness to do so forbade them to argue their case before that decision had been made.

The attitude of Archbishop Spalding must be distinguished from that of the outright infallibilists, and it was sufficiently nuanced to create some confusion as to his true feelings in the matter. Like many of his colleagues from the United States, he feared the possible consequences of the definition. Cardinal Gibbons later stated that this "seemed to be the consensus of the opinion of the majority of the American bishops at the Council."[93] There can be no doubt that Spalding left Baltimore an inopportunist. In his January petition he did, as his critics claimed, advocate the strong desirability, if not the necessity, of moral unanimity among the fathers. Events in the spring of 1870 persuaded him to submerge his fears in the interest of what he had come to feel was the greater good of the Church. The aspersions cast upon his motives for this change were unworthy of the bishops who uttered them. Nevertheless, although Spalding became a supporter of the formal definition in the closing months of the council, he did not do so without regret that a compromise had proved unworkable, as his second

[92] ADCL, Gilmour Papers, Gilmour to Purcell, Dayton, July 19, 1870.
[93] AANY, A-34, Gibbons to John M. Farley, Baltimore, May 9, 1910.

letter to Dupanloup indicated. When the formal debate on infallibility began, there were, then, three discernible groups among the United States bishops. Two of these were deeply committed, one for and one against the proposed dogma. The third group, which was symbolized, if not represented by, Spalding, held to a middle ground. The story of the further evolution of these groups belongs to the next chapter.

VI

Primacy and Infallibility

ON April 2, 1870, the New York *Tribune* rhapsodized that the bishops opposed to a definition of papal infallibility represented "the Teutonic race, the contemplative and profound German—the acute, however versatile French—and the practical, hard-thinking, resolute men of England and America."[1] The *Tribune's* analysis of the situation was an oversimplification prompted by wishful thinking. The fact was that Germans, Frenchmen, Englishmen, and Americans were to be found on both sides of the question, and it was those who belonged to the majority who were the most active in displaying their national characteristics during the month of April. Members of the minority party were, if anything, disheartened. In a letter to Father Early dated April 25, Bishop McQuaid wrote that Archbishop Purcell, who had shared with Kenrick titular leadership of the American opposition group, was leaving for home, "worried almost to death by the trouble of the Infallibility question." James Roosevelt Bayley was also supposed to be returning to the United States, and McQuaid reported that the Bishop of Newark was "only too glad to get away from the fight." "In fact," he added, "some of the strongest opponents of the Infallibility are leaving. The Americans, of course, cannot return should the question come up, whilst the Europeans will be back in time."[2]

[1] New York *Tribune,* April 2, 1870, in Beiser, p. 93.
[2] McQuaid to Early, Rome, April 25, 1870, in Browne, pp. 425–6. Neither Purcell nor Bayley actually returned to the United States at this time.

While McQuaid was sending out his gloomy news, a German and an Englishman were busy setting in motion the forces that would eventually bring about the definition of the pope's primacy and infallibility. They were Ignaz von Senestréy, Bishop of Regensburg, and Henry Edward Manning, Archbishop of Westminster, both of whom had taken a vow two years previously to do their utmost to secure the definition of papal infallibility.[3] We have already seen that the observations of the fathers on the *schema* of March 6 had been given to an editing committee composed of Senestréy and the theologians Maier and Schrader. The committee had been appointed by Cardinal Bilio, president of the deputation on faith, and should normally have reported back to him. However, the more vigorous proponents of a definition were not completely satisfied with the cardinal's enthusiasm for the project, and the initial report of the committee was actually made to a rump session of the deputation which was held in Manning's apartments during Holy Week (April 10–16).[4]

Nine of the twenty-four members of the deputation on faith attended the Holy Week meetings. Besides Manning and Senestréy, they were Mieczislaw von Ledóchowski, Archbishop of Gniezno and Primate of Poland; Patrick Leahy, Archbishop of Cashel; Archbishop Walter Steins, S.J., Vicar Apostolic of Calcutta; Bartolomeo d'Avanzo, Bishop of Calvi and Teano in southern Italy; Bishop Conrad Martin of Paderborn; Pierre de Preux, Bishop of Sion in Switzerland; and Bishop Federico Zinelli of Treviso. Neither of the two American members of the deputation, Archbishops Alemany and Spalding, were present. The self-appointed, nine-man commission heard a report from Maier and Schrader in which it was suggested that the

3 Purcell, II, 420. Manning declared that he and Senestréy had made this vow while assisting at the papal throne on the feast of Saints Peter and Paul, 1868.

4 Details of the meetings in Manning's apartments and of the subsequent activity of the Manning-Senestréy group are from the diary of Senestréy, which has been published in Mansi, LIII, 276–86 and in *Collectio Lacensis*, VII, 1695–1703. See also Granderath, III, 1, 14–8.

chapter on the primacy and the *caput addendum* on infallibility of the *schema* on the Church should be divided into four chapters, which would form a separate constitution on the Roman pontiff. This proposal was accepted, and it was further decided to call for an opening of debate on the new constitution on Easter Monday or Tuesday.

Toward the end of Holy Week, Senestréy presented the demands of his group to Bilio. The cardinal was reluctant to press matters with such haste, and he told the German bishop that he was so worried about the possibility of provoking a schism that he was unable to sleep. He wanted the council to finish its consideration of the second part of the constitution on faith first, and then go on to that on the Church. Infallibility and primacy, he thought, should be discussed in their proper place within the framework of the latter constitution. Having failed to persuade Bilio, the committee's next step was an appeal to Cardinal de Angelis, the first president of the council. A delegation called on de Angelis on Easter Monday, April 18, but the results of the interview were not entirely satisfactory. Senestréy noted in his diary that the first president had "lost courage." Of the other four presidents, Bilio and Cardinal Antonio de Luca were opposed to immediate consideration of the new constitution, while Cardinals Annibale Capalti and Giuseppe Bizzarri were favorable to its introduction. There was but one further court of appeal, and Senestréy determined to take his case to it. After his failure to convince de Angelis of the need for quick action, he sent the Vicars-General of Quimper and Nîmes, who had accompanied him to the meeting with the first president, to invite four French prelates and Auxiliary Bishop Gaspard Mermillod of Geneva to go with him the next morning to the Vatican and seek an audience with the pope. Pius IX received the six bishops before nine o'clock, the hour at which the council was scheduled to convene, and promised that he would take whatever action seemed appropriate. He gave the impression that he would send orders to the cardinal presidents that same day for introduction of the constitution on the Roman pontiff.

When three days had passed since the papal audience and there was still no sign of action, the Manning-Senestréy group met again, this time at the residence of Bishop François Roullet de la Bouillerie of Carcassonne, and decided to send a formal petition to the pope, requesting that he order the discussion of primacy and infallibility to be begun. The petition was circulated among the fathers on Saturday, April 23, and by the time that it was presented to the Holy Father on the evening of that same day 150 bishops had signed it. Four bishops from the United States were represented: Miége, de Goesbriand, Dubuis, and Rappe. This *démarche* was finally successful, and on Wednesday, April 27, at the thirty-fourth meeting of the deputation on faith, Bilio submitted for consideration the four-chapter constitution which had been prepared by Maier and Schrader.

Archbishop Manning and Bishop Senestréy had achieved the first part of their purpose in getting the questions of primacy and infallibility brought before the deputation on faith, but this was only the beginning of the struggle. According to Senestréy's diary, the one objector to the introduction of the new constitution was Archbishop Janos Simor, the Primate of Hungary, who was also the one minority member of the deputation. But in spite of this practical unanimity on basic issues, the course of the debate did not run smoothly. The first few days were taken up with reports by Maier and Schrader, who analyzed the observations which had been submitted by the fathers of the council on the pertinent passages in the original constitution on the Church. These reports, and a discussion on the formulation of the text, occupied three sessions, from April 27 to May 1.[5] The text of the constitution, called *Pastor Aeternus,* was distributed on the morning of May 2, and at the thirty-seventh meeting of the deputation, which was held on that day, Archbishops Spalding and Alemany were among those who sug-

[5] Mansi, LIII, 238–9.

gested several changes in wording, none of which were accepted.[6] On the following day, both American prelates had substantial contributions to make. Alemany suggested use of the citation from the Council of Ephesus which in the finished text of the constitution formed the heart of the argument for the perpetuity of the primacy in Peter's successors. He also asked that the universal nature of papal authority in the Church be made explicit. Spalding and Alemany were among the members of the deputation who supported a proposal by Archbishop Dechamps of Malines and Bishop Pie of Poitiers, who felt that it was superfluous to state that the pope's universal jurisdiction was episcopal in nature, and therefore asked for omission of the phrase as a concession to the sensibilities of the minority. Thirteen of those present, including Manning, voted for omission of the phrase, while only five, among them Senestréy, favored its retention, but the chair refused to entertain the motion, and the statement that the Roman pontiff's power of jurisdiction was "truly episcopal" remained in the text. The problem was an important one, since many feared that affirmation of universal papal episcopal jurisdiction implied that other residential bishops were mere vicars of the pope. To resolve the dilemma, Spalding proposed adding a statement to the effect that the papal jurisdiction which was being defined in no way conflicted with the ordinary and immediate jurisdiction of each residential bishop in his own diocese. This declaration, and the quotation from St. Gregory the Great as authority for it, were incorporated substantially in the final version of *Pastor Aeternus*.[7]

[6] Mansi, LIII, 244–5.

[7] Mansi, LIII, 245–7. The seeming conflict between the jurisdiction of pope and bishops, both of which were declared to be ordinary and immediate in *Pastor Aeternus,* is something which must be explained in the course of the development of a theology of the episcopate. It is also of capital importance in the matter of Christian reunion. Many non-Catholics, especially in the Eastern Churches and among episcopally minded Protestants, find that the primacy, as defined in the first three chapters of *Pastor Aeternus,* is a more serious stumbling block for them than is the infallibility defined in Chapter IV. See Betti, p. 164; Jean-Pierre Torrell, O.P., *La Théologie de l'épiscopat au premier concile du Vatican* (Paris: 1961),

The disagreement over the word "episcopal" was the first major problem which proponents of the new definition had to face. The second objection of a really serious nature was raised by Cardinal Bilio on the morning of May 5. He contended that the proposed *schema* allowed too wide an ambit to the exercise of papal infallibility. The cardinal protested that he did not deny that the pope was infallible in pronouncing on dogmatic facts, in canonizations, and in like matters, but he pointed out that it would scarcely be proper to attribute to the pontiff an infallibility wider than that which had been defined of the Church itself. With a delicate thrust at those who had forced the issue, he remarked that the difficulty had arisen because the *schema* on the Roman pontiff had been taken from its natural context in the integral constitution on the Church.

All that had ever been defined of the Church was that its infallibility extended to definitions of dogma strictly so-called. Bilio could not see how more than this could be defined of the pope until a proper foundation had been laid by determining exactly the extent and object of the Church's infallibility. In the debate which followed upon this speech, Spalding was one of those who urged that great care be taken to make it clear that the infallibility of pope and Church were one and that they embraced the same object. Partisans of the new *schema* protested that Bilio had set up a false problem, and that the infallibility of the Church was so fundamental that it did not need formal definition, but the cardinal was adamant and refused to retreat from his position. He adjourned the meeting and announced that an extraordinary session of the deputation would take place that same evening.[8]

---

pp. 91–2, and Wilfrid F. Dewan, C.S.P., "Preparation of the Vatican Council's Schema on the Power and Nature of the Primacy," *Ephemerides Theologicae Lovanienses*, XXXVI (1960), 55. Dewan comments that Spalding stated, but did not explain the compatibility of the two jurisdictions. It is nevertheless due to the archbishop's foresight that the theological groundwork has been laid for further fruitful discussion of the problem.

[8] Mansi, LIII, 247–50, and, from the Senestréy diary, *ibid.*, 281–2.

At the special meeting on the evening of May 5, Cardinal Bilio reiterated his stand and claimed for it the support of all the great theologians of the past. He was seconded by Dechamps, Spalding, Steins, and Martin. Alemany had already submitted an amendment which would have restricted papal infallible pronouncements to instances where the pope condemned errors in faith and morals as heretical. Senestréy commented that all these prelates were motivated by their desire to conciliate the opposition. Manning's memories of the session were a bit more tart. Speaking of Bilio, he wrote: "In the *deputatio de fide* he was overborne by Malines and Paderborn, and had a fear of French Bishops, who beset him in private."[9] The supporters of the *schema* countered Bilio's argument from theological tradition by a distinction. It was true, they conceded, that theologians had generally assigned the note *de fide* only to the assertion that the pope was infallible when he defined a dogma, but they declared that the same theologians had always considered it theologically certain that papal infallibility extended also to dogmatic facts and to censures less than heresy. It was precisely this discrepancy that the proponents of the definition wanted to clear up with their new formula. They wanted, in other words, to raise the qualification "theologically certain," as applied to papal declarations on dogmatic facts and lesser censures, to the level of *de fide,* so that there would be no difference in force and authority between this latter class of statements and papal definitions of dogmas strictly so-called.[10]

The May 5 evening session served to clarify the positions of the opposing schools of thought within the deputation, but it did nothing to achieve agreement. Another meeting was called for the morning of May 6, at which Bilio proposed a new formula for the definition of infallibility which had been drawn up by Martin of Paderborn. The Jesuit theologians Franzelin and Schrader were on hand to explain its import to the members.

[9] Purcell, II, 454.
[10] Mansi, LIII, 250–51, and, from the Senestréy diary, *ibid.*, 282.

The Martin formula as finally accepted by the deputation incorporated notions which had been suggested previously by Alemany and Spalding. It restricted the exercise of papal infallibility to those occasions when the pope "defines with his apostolic authority what in faith and morals is to be held by the universal Church as of faith, or is to be rejected as contrary to faith," and it identified the pope's infallibility with that of the Church. When a vote was taken, only two negative ballots were cast, although some of those who voted for the new formula did so with reservations.[11] Further modifications in the text to take care of these last objections were made on May 7 and 8. The only American contribution was an unsuccessful request by Alemany that a *monitum* be added to the definition which would call for obedience to all commands of the Roman pontiff, even if they were not phrased as infallible pronouncements.[12]

The constitution on the Roman pontiff was distributed to the fathers on May 9, and debate began on May 13. Subsequent discussions in the deputation belong properly to the history of that debate. However, it may be noted here that the advocates of the original formula did not give up the fight easily, and they continued to hold private meetings at the apartments of Archbishop Charles de La Tour d'Auvergne-Lauraguais of Bourges and of Bishop Roullet de la Bouillerie of Carcassonne until the beginning of June.[13] Their persistence was rewarded when, on May 22, Bilio summoned the members of the deputation to their first meeting since May 8. He had been the target of considerable criticism on the score of the Martin formula and he now wanted to know if it should be redrafted. Whereas all but two of the members had approved the formula before its submission to the fathers on May 9, only Martin himself, Dechamps,

[11] Mansi, LIII, 251–2, and, from the Senestréy diary, *ibid.*, 282. Three successive texts of the definition are presented by Butler (II, 134) in parallel columns.

[12] Mansi, LIII, 252.

[13] Mansi, LIII, 283.

Spalding, and Steins held out for it on May 22.[14] As Manning later reminisced, he and Senestréy had been rebuked for their obstinacy and obstructionism, but they had gradually been able to win the support of an increasing number of the fathers for their position.[15] No immediate action to revise the definition was taken at the May 22 meeting, but the Martin formula was not the definitive redaction of the text on infallibility, as will be seen in the history of the debates in the council. For now, we may take leave of the deputation on faith with a quotation from a letter of Archbishop Alemany which tells something of the pressure to which its members had been subjected. On May 9 he wrote to Father William Fortune of All Hallows College that he hoped to be able to return to San Francisco in June, and he commented: "Since Feb. we have been exceedingly engaged, at least those bishops who compose our committee. We had one or two sittings a day (Sundays included), each of 4 or 5 hours, and much study was required to prepare the lesson."[16]

While Manning, Senestréy, and their colleagues were taking steps to bring the question of papal infallibility before the fathers, the bishops of the opposition were doing their best to organize a countercampaign. Lord Acton reported to Döllinger that when word was first received that infallibility would be placed at the head of the council's calendar, the international committee of the minority hastily formed a delegation of nine prelates headed by Archbishop Purcell which was to make an appeal "in the most direct fashion" to the pope. However, to the distress of the English lord, they allowed themselves to be distracted from their purpose by the distribution of the *Synopsis Animadversionum* which had been prepared by Senestréy and the two German theologians. Acton felt that this had been a tactical blunder, and he remarked that the minority had, "as so

14 *Ibid.*
15 Purcell, II, 417.
16 AAHC, San Francisco Papers, Alemany to Fortune, Rome, May 9, 1870.

often before," let itself be outmaneuvered by the infallibilist party.[17]

Bernard McQuaid wrote to Father Early about the *Synopsis* on May 1:

I have now on my desk 106 pages quarto of printed remarks on the schema on the Primacy and 242 pages on that of the Infallibility. The discussion in the Council will bring out the most learned and able men in the body on both sides. It will be a great discussion and a long one, I fear, unless it should be brought to a close arbitrarily. I cannot leave until this matter is settled, and I cannot tell when that happy moment will come although I hope that it will be over by the end of June.

In another portion of the same letter, the Bishop of Rochester declared: "Some one will have a terrible account to render for having stirred up this question for many a soul will be lost no matter how it is disposed of, even if put to one side which is now impossible." He was, however, not entirely pessimistic in his estimate of the situation. "I believe," he said, "that the extreme men like Manning and some of the French Bishops and the Jesuits will not carry their point, but whether the dogma will be so defined as to prevent a schism in Germany and Hungary is more than I know."[18]

Acton told Döllinger in this letter that the project of the constitution on the Roman pontiff was known in the city on May 1, and this knowledge prompted still one more futile protest on the part of the minority. On May 8, a petition was addressed to the presidents of the council by a long list of signatories headed by Cardinal Schwarzenberg. Archbishops Kenrick and Purcell and Bishops Domenec, Mrak, and Vérot represented the United States in the list. The first argument which the petitioners employed was that which had been urged in the deputation meetings by Cardinal Bilio. They declared that primacy and infallibility had been taken out of context by forming them into

[17] Conzemius Transcripts, Acton to Döllinger, Rome, May 13, 1870.
[18] McQuaid to Early, Rome, May 1, 1870, in Browne, pp. 428–9.

a separate constitution, and they asked how they could be expected to decide upon the papal prerogatives before they had had an opportunity to study the nature of the Church. They further inquired how the object of papal infallibility could be said to be the same as that of the Church when no definition about this last had been made. Shifting their ground to apologetic arguments, they asserted that a complete tract on the Church would provide solid food for instruction, but they feared that a restricted declaration on just the prerogatives of the pope would alienate rather than attract non-Catholics. Finally they protested that it was their loyalty to the Holy Father which prompted them to present the petition. They had, they declared, defended Pius IX against the calumnious charge that he had summoned the council simply to increase his own power, but they were afraid that such charges would be renewed if the council, after six or seven months work, had to show for its efforts only a brief decree of four chapters on faith and a still briefer one on papal primacy and infallibility. The petitioners concluded by assuring the presidents that they were confident that, if questions which were liable to stir up discord were excluded from their deliberations, the fathers would be able to complete the entire constitution on the Church by Pentecost Sunday. The protest was received by Bilio, who gave it to Cardinal de Angelis. It was read to the other presidents, but no answer was given.[19]

Another letter from Bishop McQuaid portrayed the state of mind of the minority when they realized that their best efforts had been unavailing and that they would, after all, have to face up to the debate on infallibility. Once more, his correspondent was Father James Early. The bishop wrote to the latter sometime in May:

The damage to the Church will be immense. In some countries there will be large schisms, and great losses to the Church in all countries except Italy, Spain and Ireland and among our poor people at home. I find that some Bishops who were unwilling to join in trying

[19] Mansi, LI, 727–32.

to avert the discussion are now frightened when they see it impending over them. My head is fairly splitting with pain and anxiety. I have just come from seeing a friend who has been prostrated by the news, only received today, of a determination to force the matter through the Council in spite of all remonstrances. God help the Church is my constant prayer. If some decrees are passed as they have been presented to us, we can look out for hard times in all countries in which Catholics and protestants are expected to live together. In fact we furnish them with good reasons to drive us out of the country.[20]

Even if they were discouraged, the bishops of the minority had not given up all hope of averting the definition, and efforts were made on the eve of the debate to organize the opposition for maximum effectiveness. Thus, Domenec was named to represent the United States in a set scheme of speeches against the proposed dogma.[21] Lists were also gathered which categorized the fathers according to nationality and then according to the attitude when they were presumed to have toward the program of the minority. Bishop Dupanloup's copies of the American list counted ten United States bishops as definitely "for us." They were Kenrick, Purcell, Domenec, Whelan, Vérot, Mrak, Bayley, McQuaid, Fitzgerald, and Amat. Another nine were called doubtful. The first of these was McCloskey of New York, who was termed "a man of great authority, uncertain about the truth of the question." Archbishop Alemany's stand was also in doubt. He was classed as an independent, and it was suggested that the former Coadjutor Archbishop of Westminster, George Errington, might be able to influence him. Nothing was known of the position of McCloskey of Louisville who had arrived in Rome only in early April. Bishops Henni and O'Hara were listed as doubtful without further comment. Eugene O'Connell of Grass Valley was another whom it was hoped Errington might influence, but he had to be classified as doubtful, as did Loughlin of Brooklyn, who was called "uncertain" in one redaction of the list and "timid" in another. Hennessy of Dubuque was

---

[20] McQuaid to Early, Rome, [May, 1870], in Browne, pp. 430–31.
[21] ASS, Dupanloup Papers, Minority—Notes and Letters.

considered doubtful, but it was noted that he was a suffragan of Archbishop Kenrick. The final question mark was Patrick Lynch, but he was reported to be returning to America.

Eight Americans were listed in the minority calculations as "against us," and another six were termed "vehement against us." Spalding was the only one whose name was put into the first category without further remark. Williams, Conroy, and Ryan were all called "moderates," while Shanahan of Harrisburg was "moderate and independent." One of Dupanloup's informants reported that Bishop Rappe of Cleveland was a friend of the infallibilist Bishop of Marseilles, Charles Place, but this information was crossed out in a second list. Two of the eight more or less moderate opponents of the minority view were thought to be borderline cases. James Gibbons was variously listed as "for us" and "against us," and was in any event considered to be "moderate and independent," while Maurice de St.-Palais was classified as hesitant. No qualifications were appended to the judgment "vehement against us" which was applied to Archbishop Blanchet and to Bishops Dubuis, Elder, de Goesbriand, Heiss, and Augustus Martin.

A final section of the Dupanloup lists categorized eleven prelates who were said to have already left Rome. Three of them, McFarland, Melcher, and Feehan, were believed to favor the minority, while three others were for the definition. These were McGill, Quinlan, and Lootens. Miége was also recorded as having gone home, and he was listed as a strong infallibilist. Actually, Miége and Lootens were present at the council at least until the final vote on infallibility, and they both supported the definition. Nothing was known of the views of Archbishop Odin or of those of Bishops Bacon, Mullen, or O'Gorman, although the last three had signed the minority petition of January 15. Four bishops and Abbot Wimmer were not mentioned at all in any of the lists found among Dupanloup's papers. Of the five, Wimmer and Persico should have been classed as infallibilists, and they remained to vote for the definition in July. Lamy,

230

Hogan, and Wood, the remaining three, had in fact returned to the United States. Lamy had never committed himself one way or the other. Hogan signed the minority petition in January, but later retracted his signature, and Wood, who was an ally of Spalding, would probably have fallen into the "moderate" category.[22]

These estimates of relative strength revealed that the minority was losing ground. Acton confirmed this when he wrote to Döllinger on May 20 that Kenrick and Connolly could marshal only twenty-three Anglo-American prelates for the opposition. Even this count was optimistic, since Acton included in his totals fifteen unnamed bishops from the United States.[23] Dupanloup's reporter was more accurate in placing the size of the hard-core United States opposition at about ten. One reason for the decline in the fortunes of the minority was obvious: The question of infallibility had actually been brought to the floor of the council. Once this had been done, the most compelling arguments for a resistance that was based solely on the inexpediency of defining the doctrine lost their force. A given bishop might still feel that it would have been better for the Church if the question had never been raised. He had now to ask himself if the effects of a negative vote might not be worse still, since such a vote would seem to many observers to be tantamount to a rebuke delivered to the pope by the council. After May 9 the only genuine opposition in the council would come from fathers who had what they felt were serious intellectual and historical difficulties about the doctrine of papal infallibility itself. They might still urge the old inopportunist arguments, but, among the Americans at least, those who continued their opposition to the end were all men who had real, conscientious scruples about some aspect of the dogma, and who, for this fundamental reason, did not want to see it defined.

The first prelate from the United States to address the council

[22] ASS, Dupanloup Papers.
[23] Conzemius Transcripts, Acton to Döllinger, Rome, May 20, 1870.

on the subject of the new constitution on the Roman pontiff was Archbishop Alemany, who spoke at the fifty-first general congregation on May 14, the second day of debate. He indicated that he favored the definition, although with certain reservations as to its extension and terminology, and he scouted the fears of the minority that it would be inopportune. The only question before the fathers, the archbishop continued, was to determine whether in fact Christ had given His Church an infallible pope. Their discussion, he said, should be carried on with moderation, kindness, and charity. It should be an interchange of questions, arguments, and answers, all with the sole object of finding truth and all carried on in a spirit that was signalized by a unity of mind and heart among the participants.[24]

Not until two weeks after Alemany's speech did the next American, Bishop Vérot, mount the pulpit, but in the interim the name of Peter Richard Kenrick came twice to the notice of the fathers. On May 19, Cardinal Cullen of Dublin challenged from the rostrum the textual criticism of the "Feed my sheep, feed my lambs" text from John 21: 16–17 which the St. Louis archbishop had offered in his observations on the *schema* on the Church, and on the following day Kenrick himself made it a point to congratulate publicly Archbishop John MacHale of Tuam after the latter had delivered an attack on the proposed definition.[25] When word of this latter action reached James A. McMaster, he managed to make a comment on it which condemned both archbishops in one sentence: "That clammy grip given him [MacHale], as he came down from the steps of the *ambon* or pulpit, in the Council, and the flattering hail: 'bene vindicasti Hiberniam,' were thrown away on him."[26]

Two other bishops left letters that told something of the opposing mentalities as the council ended its second week of general discussion on the *schema*. On May 25, O'Connell wrote

[24] Mansi, LI, 42–5; Betti, pp. 222–3.
[25] Mansi, LI, 122. MacHale's speech is *ibid.*, 144–51.
[26] *Freeman's Journal*, August 27, 1870.

to Fortune the suggestion that the All Hallows faculty of theology imitate the Dominicans, the Franciscans, and the Louvain faculty by petitioning for the definition. "The Gallicans," he went on, "are doing their utmost to prevent the definition and are insisting upon the *moral unanimity* necessary to define this long disputed question; they say that the witnesses are not so much *numerandi quam ponderandi,* and that the very few may be the most learned. This is Archbishop Kenrick's theory put forth in an anonymous pamphlet."[27] The day before O'Connell's letter, McQuaid had brought Early up to date on developments. His sincerity of purpose and intelligent approach to the problems of the council appear clearly in his letter. Beyond that it serves as its own commentary. He wrote:

We have entered upon the discussion of the great question, and when that discussion may end no man can say. Already we have listened to 38 discourses on that *schema in genere,* and there remain about 70 more to be heard not to speak of the fresh crop brought forth at each meeting. Then comes the discussion in particular, which will not fall behind the first. If there be not a greater number of speeches, they will make up for the deficiency in number by greater length. In fact, unless a short cut is found for ending the discussion in some way, we cannot get through in less than six months. Some of the discourses thus far delivered have been master pieces of oratory. Such were the speeches of Schwartzenbergh [*sic*], Paris, Cashel, Prague, Mayence and Grenoble. The Archbishop of Cashel threw Cardinal Cullen into the shade. Tuam did well considering his age. There has been nothing from the Italians or Spaniards thus far worth listening to. The Italians put me in mind of professors of Theology who have never left their class-room, or had met opponents able and disposed to contend seriously with them. The Spaniards look to me like men who want to put everyone who differs with them in the Inquisition.

After this analysis of the early stages of the debate, McQuaid set down his predictions as to the probable future course of the discussion. The letter continued:

Neither extreme in the Council is likely to carry their point. It is already evident that the definition that will be presented to the faithful

[27] O'Connell to Fortune, Rome, May 25, 1870, in Walsh, p. 426.

233

for their belief will be such a definition as they will have no difficulty in accepting. The Jesuits who are responsible for forcing this question on the Church are sure to be defeated. To use commercial language, 'their stock is below par.' The definition that will pass will state that this Infallibility is not *personal,* not *absolute,* not *separate* or *independent,* not *inspired,* not *miraculous,* does not means *impeccability.* Furthermore all those bulls of Popes in the past open to so much fault-finding will be recognized as not infallible. Such a definition will be a heavy blow to some who have been working heaven and earth to bring about one almost the opposite of this. The schema now before [us] does not contain all this, but the real leaders say it means this. We want to compel them to put its equivalent in the schema. In the end we shall succeed. We could succeed in quick time but for the Holy Father himself who is the strongest on his own side. God, however, rules the Church, and the truth will come out in the end. Ten thousand times would I rather be one of those who have quietly to await the promulgation of the truth, rather than where I am to be at the bringing out of it.

With his doctrinal position set in perspective, the bishop then proceeded to defend his right to hold that position by commenting on a suggestion that he had just received:

I have been quite annoyed today at receiving a letter from a Priest, not of our Diocese, urging me to sacrifice my convictions, and yielding to the judgment of others, vote for the Infallibility, unconditional and absolute, as he understands it. Just as though I could dare to do such a criminal act. Thank God so far every vote of mine has been according to my judgment and not according to the judgment of anyone else. My convictions on the Infallibility question are very clear and decided; I bought Perrone and Bellarmine and Guerin's history of the Councils, all good Infallibilist authorities; I offer my objections and doubts right and left; I am open to a change of mind, but it must be upon proofs and facts, and not upon what someone else may happen to think or vote, that my vote shall be given. Besides of my way of thinking are some of the holiest, most clear-headed, learned and disinterested Bishops in the Council; Bishops of whose loyalty and devotion to the Holy See, no one would presume to raise a doubt.[28]

Augustin Vérot, speaking during the general discussion of the schema on primacy and infallibility, developed the biblical and

[28] McQuaid to Early, Rome, May 24, 1870, in Browne, pp. 432–4.

patristic evidence which he thought militated against acceptance of the latter as a dogma of the Church, and he treated the fathers to a lengthy discourse which covered the whole of church history from the Council of Jerusalem down to modern times. He prefaced his remarks by declaring that he had made a thorough study of the problem from learned sources, not from the newspapers. His conclusion from this study was that there was lacking the element which was essential to any doctrine which was proposed for solemn definition, namely a constant tradition of the Church in its favor.

The Bishop of St. Augustine was not very far into his speech, when he was interrupted by murmuring from the floor. The first time this happened was when he referred to the "personal, separate infallibility" which he claimed was the deputation's interpretation of the doctrine contained in the *schema*. A more understandable protest was registered when the bishop announced that he intended to prove that infallibility had no foundation in tradition by means of a survey that would take in all church history, beginning with the first century, but it is a little difficult to see what was so humorous in Vérot's citation of Acts 2: 2 that it provoked laughter in the hall. The passage tells of the way in which the first Christians disputed with Peter, and the speaker proposed it as evidence that infallibility was an unknown concept in the early Church. Similar laughter greeted a quotation which the bishop offered from Galatians 2: 1. In the first incident, he had dismissed the interruption with the remark that it was "easier to laugh than to find an answer," but on the second occasion he reminded his hearers that he was citing Scripture and said that this gave him confidence despite the obvious opposition of many of the fathers.

As a preface to his promised survey of the history of the Church, Vérot delivered a little eulogy of the Gallican Church and some of its leading figures. He warned the fathers that they should not be hasty in taking an action that would brand as heretics men like Bossuet, and he suggested that they consider the possible consequences to the missionary work of the Church if a definition of papal infallibility should cause France to denounce its concordat with the Holy See. Without the French Society for the Propagation of the Faith, he said, the foreign missions would be hard put to find means for subsistence. There was nothing new in the historical difficulties of which Vérot then gave a long catalogue, and, in fact, he had used the works of the infallibilist Cardinal Bellarmine as a source, but his speech did have the merit of bringing the problems forcefully to the attention of the council. His own conclusion from the evidence was that infallibility resided in the teaching Church, that is, in the pope and bishops united. He had, he declared, always preached on the necessity of communion with Rome, but he could not see how such communion demanded an infallible pope.

The bishop then turned to the arguments which had been advanced by the majority up until that time. Archbishop Leahy of Cashel had spoken, he recalled, about the faith of the Irish in the pope's infallibility. The French-born Sulpician said that he found nothing strange in this, since the Irish also believed that their parish priests were infallible and were always ready to strike anyone who contradicted them. He suggested, however, that the Irish be quizzed on the infallible nature of Adrian IV's gift of their island to the King of England, and he remarked that all the armed might of Britain had not been able to force the Fenians to accept that gift as an accomplished fact.

In a more serious vein, Vérot asserted that none of the arguments thus far alleged had done more than prove the necessity of communion with Rome. As for the moral homilies which some speakers had delivered about the need for embracing the truth, he dismissed them with the comment that they begged the question. He then loosed a final shaft at the ultramontane journalists who had been promoting the definition. An editor, he said, had once criticized the Roman practice of blessing animals on the feast of St. Anthony. Vérot told the critic that he would be sure to let him know the date of the blessing, so that he could be on hand, "for the greatest beasts I know are the editors of religious newspapers, especially the laymen."[29]

Until this point, Vérot's speech had dealt with generalities. He intended to go on with a discussion of particular points in the constitution, but was interrupted and forced to leave the pulpit by Cardinal Capalti. The occasion for this dismissal was the final sentence in his summation of his initial remarks. After declaring that he did not find papal infallibility in the apostolic tradition, the bishop stated that it had been introduced into the council "by a piety which does not seem to be sufficiently understood, by a zeal which is not according to knowledge." "Therefore," he declared, "I cannot in conscience give my vote for this opinion, because that would seem to me to be a sacrilege; it would be a sacrilege." Capalti broke in and rebuked him for this statement, and told him that if he had nothing but jokes to add, he should leave the rostrum. Many of the fathers began to shout, "Come down." Vérot tried to answer above the tumult that he had meant that it would be a sacrilege for him to vote for infallibility, and that he was not passing judgment on the opinions of others, but Capalti ordered him peremptorily from the pulpit, and he bowed to the command.[30]

As in so many of Vérot's other appearances at the council, the strong points in his argument were obscured by the humorous touches he was unable to resist. This caused many of the fathers to discount what he had to say. Bishop James Goold of Melbourne, for example, dismissed the May 28 performance with the following notation in his diary: "Another French prelate from the United States spoke absurdly on the same [Gallican] side. He had to quit the pulpit. He had outraged the patience of

[29] A pun is involved here. In Latin Vérot used the word *bestiae* of the editors. He would seem to have been thinking of the French *bête*, which means both "beast" and "fool." George G. Coulton, *Papal Infallibility* (London: 1932), p. 163, points this out.

[30] Mansi, LII, 289–302. Coulton, p. 164, rightly points out that neither Capalti, nor Butler, in his treatment of this episode (II, 53), acknowledged Vérot's disclaimer that he was not reproaching others, but was only expressing his personal conscientious conviction.

all."[31] Archbishop Giulio Arrigoni of Lucca was not quite as severe as Goold, but he expressed similar sentiments when he wrote of Vérot that he had made "one of his accustomed serio-comic discourses which held the attention of the fathers for an hour and a half."[32] Criticism was not limited to majority sources, as we learn from the memoirs of Albert du Boÿs, a French lay-man and confidant of Dupanloup, who remarked that Vérot was "full of boldness . . . , but of a boldness that was not always happy and which sometimes went beyond bounds."[33]

A reply to Bishop Vérot and others of the minority was made by Archbishop Spalding on May 30. Speaking without a manu-script,[34] and in the name of the deputation on faith, the Arch-bishop of Baltimore denied that anyone intended to declare the pope infallible except when he exercised his apostolic authority as head of the Church. He then proceeded to rebut Vérot's historical arguments and, in an aside, commented that he was surprised to hear "even holy bishops" using the same weapons against infallibility that Protestants used against the primacy. In a more positive vein, the archbishop traced a pattern of deference to the finality of Rome's judgment beginning with the time of Augustine and Cyprian, but he was unable to resist another jibe at the opposition and added that he hoped the "Gallicans" would not follow the Protestant exegesis of Cyprian's text on the primacy. He argued that it was impractical to demand the consent of the Church before a pope could make an infallible pronouncement, and declared that the Gallican articles which proposed this theory had long since been condemned. Spalding referred to a pamphlet which had recently been circulated in Rome, which asked bishops to consider whether they could with safe conscience vote for infallibility and stated that his own conscience would not permit him to vote against the dogma, in

[31] Patrick Francis Moran, *History of the Catholic Church in Australasia* (Sydney and Wellington, n.d.), p. 806.
[32] Betti, p. 200.
[33] ASMP, Du Boÿs Papers, Memoirs of the Council.
[34] Gibbons, I, 156.

favor of the absurd Gallican theories. He concluded: "Either the Roman pontiff, when he teaches the whole Church as pontiff in a solemn judgment, is infallible; or Christ's Church itself is not infallible. They stand and fall together; they will stand because the gates of hell will not prevail."[35]

Bishop Goold of Melbourne continued to be unimpressed by the performance of the Americans. Of Spalding's effort he wrote: "The speaker on behalf of the deputation *de fide* was the Archbishop of Baltimore, Monsignor Spalding. He did not impress me favorably." The next United States prelate to ascend the rostrum fared no better in Goold's estimation, and his diary for May 31 contained the comment: "Dr. Purcell, Archbishop of Cincinnati, addressed the Council feebly and incoherently against, but concluded in favor."[36] Purcell's actual words were not quite so contradictory. He began by protesting the comparison which had been drawn by the titular Patriarch of Jerusalem Giuseppe Valerga between the opposition at the Vatican Council and the Monothelite heretics of an earlier age—a comparison that had gone unrebuked by the chair. He went on to tell the fathers of his fifty-one years as a priest and bishop in the United States and declared that he had always upheld the rights and prerogatives of the Holy See, sometimes disputing with Protestant ministers five times a day and seven days a week. No one, he asserted, could challenge his record of loyalty to the pope.

Having established his orthodoxy, Purcell declared that he could vote neither for the expediency of the present discussion, nor for the definition itself. His reason was a simple one, namely, that no clear explanation had been given of the meaning of the term *ex cathedra*. Some partisans of the definition said that every papal utterance was to be taken as infallible. If this were true, asked Purcell, what was to be said of the thirty or forty popes whose errors were recorded by Bellarmine? Another problem which he felt particularly vexing was the onetime papal

[35] Mansi, LII, 313–9; Betti, p. 230.
[36] Moran, p. 807.

claim to supreme dominion over kings and peoples. He was afraid of the consequences in the United States if a pope were to make an infallible pronouncement against democratic government. As for himself, the archbishop declared, "I believe that kings are nothing but representatives of the people; I believe that the king is established for the people, and not the people for the king."

Murmurs in the hall greeted this last republican affirmation, but Purcell continued and finally summed up this portion of his speech by asking for information on two points. One was the meaning of the phrase *ex cathedra.* The second was an explanation—or preferably a renunciation—of papal claims to temporal dominion. He then stated his own position on papal infallibility: He was willing to acknowledge it provided that it was understood as a prerogative of the Church which belonged to the bishops dispersed throughout the world and acting in union with the Roman pontiff, or to the same bishops and pope joined in general council, or, finally, to the pope acting as head and teacher of the whole Church, and in union with it, as the interpreter and custodian of doctrine in matters of faith and morals.[37]

Purcell's speech indicated the extent of the confusion that reigned in many minds as to the exact import of the proposed definition. The explanation which had been given by Spalding on the previous day should have helped to allay some of the fears expressed by the Archbishop of Cincinnati, but unfortunately the highly charged atmosphere of the debate was not conducive to the best communication of ideas between the opposing groups. Another feature of Purcell's speech which attracted attention was his defense of popular sovereignty. Writing to Döllinger on June 2, Acton reported that he found the archbishop's point of view "interesting," and suggested that there was in it a parallel which could be applied to the Church. If kings were for the people, and not *vice versa,* he commented,

[37] Mansi, LII, 365–70; Betti, pp. 200–201.

perhaps the same could be said of the Church, so that popes were for the Church, and not the other way around.[38] The Toledo *Blade* drew another conclusion which was scarcely flattering to Purcell when it editorialized that if the pope were to live in the United States, the Church would probably soon be "in the hands of men like Döllinger, Hyacinthe and Purcell."[39]

Before the next American contribution to the debate, Bishop O'Connell summed up the situation at the end of May in a letter to Father Fortune. His attitude revealed that the minority were making little headway with their arguments. The letter read as follows:

> The Vatican Council is progressing slowly, altho' we have Congregations on every available day. So many have ask'd and obtain'd leave to speak & as many more no doubt mean to apply for leave, that there is no telling how long the 'torrens dicendi copia' will continue to flow. Really: I'm pretty much of Professor Neville's way of thinking that the Pope ought to walk into the Council Hall & discharge us in globo. I believe that the great majority of us would be serving the interests of religion as effectually; & a small minority far more effectually *dispersed* throughout their respective Dioceses than here in Concilio coadunati & a reliquiis Gallicanorum provocati: really Gallicanism is more provoking than the Judaism which was forc'd on Xians in the first Century, because the latter deserv'd and obtain'd a decent burial, but we owe nothing to the former save our reprobation. The old Synagogue was a stately tree and no fungus like the offspring of Louis the 14th & the precious Harlay yclept Archbishop of Paris. Quales patres talis proles. Atqui Patres Gallicanorum &c. Ergo.[40]

On the same day that O'Connell wrote to Fortune, it was announced to the council that Archbishop Odin of New Orleans had died in France on Ascension Thursday, May 25.[41] He was the only prelate from the United States to die during the course of the council.

---

[38] Conzemius Transcripts, Acton to Döllinger, Rome, June 2, 1870.

[39] Toledo *Blade,* June 23, 1870, in Beiser, p. 243. Hyacinthe Loyson was a French Carmelite who had left the Church shortly before the council began.

[40] AAHC, Marysville Papers, O'Connell to Fortune, Rome, May 31, 1870.

[41] Mansi, LII, 379.

The next American speaker was Michael Domenec, who addressed the fathers on June 3. He restricted himself to the argument that the definition was inopportune and spoke only as an interpreter of the religious situation in the United States. He was not, he said, sufficiently well versed in the circumstances of other countries to pass judgment for them, but he was sure that the proposed dogma would spell nothing but disaster in the land where he had labored for over thirty years. Bishops like John England, John Hughes, and Francis Patrick Kenrick had always silenced Protestant attacks by declaring that the Roman pontiff, as a man, could both sin and make mistakes. They had stressed the fact that papal infallibility was not a Catholic dogma, and that no Catholic was bound to hold it. Now, continued Domenec, if infallibility is proclaimed to be a dogma, the bishops would have to return to their pulpits and retract the charge of calumny that they had made against the Protestants. The definition, he said, would make liars out of them.

Domenec claimed that nearly all the bishops of the United States agreed with him when he said that there would be no hope of progress for the Catholic religion in their country if the definition were made. He therefore begged the fathers to give serious consideration to the question, especially since there was good hope that within the space of thirty or forty years there would be more Catholics in North America than in the whole of Italy, and, he added, "with this consolation, however, that our Catholics are Catholics not only in name, but in fact, I mean in the practice of their religion." The speaker had already been interrupted several times by murmuring among the fathers, but this last sally was too much for the presidents, and de Angelis called the bishop to order with the admonition that he should speak more reverently of the faithful of Italy. Domenec made no reply, but finished his summation and ended with a plea that the council remove the definition from its agenda.[42]

[42] Mansi, LII, 425–9. Purcell later remarked of Domenec's evaluation of the Italian Catholics that the Bishop of Pittsburgh had been called to order "after he had uttered a great truth." (*Catholic Telegraph*, August 25, 1870).

Domenec's speech was the last but one in the general discussion of the *schema*. The titular Bishop of Sura, Henri Maret, attempted to speak after him, but was interrupted frequently by disturbances on the floor and by adverse rulings from the chair. When Maret had sat down, the subsecretary of the council announced that a motion for cloture had been made by more than 150 fathers. A vote was taken, and an end put to the general discussion. The great majority of those present voted for the cloture resolution, although some manifested audible signs of displeasure. The Americans who signed the petition for an end to the debate were Spalding, Dubuis, Rappe, and de Goesbriand.[43] On the next day, June 4, a protest against the action was registered by the international committee of the minority. The signers of this counterpetition from the United States were Kenrick, Purcell, Domenec, Fitzgerald, McQuaid, Mrak, Vérot, and Whelan.[44] According to Acton, this protest was the outcome of the largest meeting of the opposition that had yet taken place. He told Döllinger that eighty bishops had met on June 4 at Cardinal Rauscher's apartments. The Anglo-Americans, most of the Hungarians, and the leaders of the French opposition had wanted to abstain from further participation in the council on the ground that they were no longer free to speak, and to appear again only at the end, to vote against the definition. However, the majority of the Germans and many of the French argued that a single protest should be made, and that the minority should then continue to participate in the debate.[45] It was the latter strategy which prevailed. Four days

[43] Mansi, LII, 440.
[44] Mansi, LII, 444–6.
[45] Conzemius Transcripts, Acton to Döllinger, Rome, June 4, 1870. According to Odo Russell, Strossmayer, Dupanloup, Darboy, Clifford, Kenrick, Connolly, Haynald, and others wanted to make a protest against the rules of procedure and the cloture and to follow this with a mass withdrawal of the opposition bishops from Rome. Hefele and Ketteler opposed them and persuaded the majority of those present that they should not take this drastic step. The Hungarians then suggested that the opposition continue to attend the sessions, but not speak at them. Cardinal Rauscher disapproved

later, Acton reported that Kenrick had decided that he would not speak again in the council, so as to indicate that he did not recognize it. The Englishman also told Döllinger that he had delivered a parcel to the railroad station for the archbishop, a thick manuscript which Kenrick was sending to be printed at Naples.[46]

This manuscript was a brochure which Archbishop Kenrick entitled *Concio in Concilio Vaticano habenda at non habita*. It was the speech which he had intended for the general discussion and had been prevented from making because of the imposition of cloture. Dupanloup's friend, Albert du Boÿs, gave the following somber estimate of its effect: "What also perhaps stood in the way of conciliation [between the opposing parties at the council] was a Latin brochure of Monsignor Kenrick, Archbishop of St. Louis, wherein that prelate said his piece to the majority with a crudeness that was quite American."[47] Bernard McQuaid also reported on the pamphlet when he wrote to James Early:

> The latest sensation here is a pamphlet of 100 pages by the Archbp. of St. Louis. In it he makes some very bold assertions and pays his respects to the Archbps. of Dublin, Westminster and Baltimore who had attacked him in the Council. As Dr. Kenrick had been cut off [from] his right of reply in the Council by the abrupt closing of the discussion in which he was attacked, and had been refused five minutes of personal explanation, he has published his pamphlet in which he goes over many things likely to make a stir.[48]

A less sympathetic commentator was Bishop Modeste Demers of Vancouver, who told James A. McMaster:

---

this on the ground that a bishop had the obligation to express the truth according to his conscience. A further proposal of Bishop Dupanloup that the minority address pastoral letters explaining their stand to their respective dioceses was also rejected. The meeting than decided on the protest mentioned by Acton. (Russell to Clarendon, Rome, June 8, 1870, in Blakiston, p. 440.)

[46] Conzemius Transcripts, Acton to Döllinger, Rome, June 8, 1870.

[47] ASMP, Du Boÿs Papers, Memoirs of the Council.

[48] McQuaid to Early, Rome, June 30, 1870, in Browne, p. 439.

The discussion was put a stop to, by which he [Kenrick] was prevented from delivering his discourse; he was very much vexed at that, but determined the world should know his mind and thoughts on the subject, he had it published at Naples, and, for the sake of the Irish name and the cause of the American Church, would to God he had not. I forbear to say more about it; it will reach you sooner or later, and you will judge for yourself.

Demers also had some general remarks to make on Kenrick and others of the American opposition. His letter continued:

And his financial difficulties! They are known here in all their details, even among a certain class of people! And the unfortunate Chicago affair! For a whole month he kept away from the sessions of the Council, living alone by himself in part of the city; he came the other day to give his vote! We thought he had left for Paris some time ago . . . now, between us, the question is among ourselves, what shall become of him? You could see in his very countenance, in his face, the trouble, the agony of his mind! We pray hard for him. . . . Bps. Purcell and Whelan will soon be home. I should like to know the reception they are going to meet with . . . the Bps. of Pittsburg, Harrisburg, Little-Rock will soon be going too, both [*sic*] against. Bp. McCloskey of Louisville is also against—a poor augur at the beginning of their episcopal career![49]

Archbishop Kenrick was not nearly as distraught over his situation as was the Canadian bishop, but he was quite annoyed at statements by Cullen, Spalding, and Manning, and the first section of his *concio* was an attempt to refute their arguments and to vindicate his own honor. Against Cullen he argued that the most that could be established from the standard Petrine texts was that St. Peter had a primacy of jurisdiction and honor, although he confessed that if the norm of unanimous consent of the fathers were to be applied to those texts, it was difficult to establish even this. In any event, he found nothing in Scripture which proved papal infallibility. The archbishop laid great stress on the opinions of the fathers of the Church and concluded from his study of them that the pope could indeed be said to be infallible, but only on the condition that he use the

[49] UND, McMaster Papers, Demers to McMaster, n.d. [June, 1870.]

counsel of his brethren, the bishops, and speak in their name. He was very concerned at what he saw as a growing tendency to absolute rule in the Church, a tendency that would be fostered by the definitions of primacy and infallibility under discussion, and he wondered if the next logical step would not be to declare the pope impeccable. In the final section addressed to Cullen, Kenrick took exception to the Irish prelate's interpretation of the thought of his late brother, Francis Patrick Kenrick. The Archbishop of St. Louis was aware that his brother, a graduate of the Urban College of the Propaganda, was far more ultramontane than he was himself, but he repeated his claim that he had, nevertheless, not held the doctrine proposed in the *schema.* As for his own opinion, it was simple and straightforward: "I believe that for this [the definition of a new dogma of Catholic faith] a council which truly represents the universal Church is demanded."[50]

Kenrick's remarks on Spalding were much shorter. He attempted to refute him out of his own mouth. It was being claimed, he declared, that the letter which was sent to the Holy Father by the bishops assembled at the Second Plenary Council of Baltimore in 1866 constituted an affirmation of their belief in the dogma of papal infallibility. The archbishop recalled that the letter had been composed by Spalding, and, as evidence of what was then the view of the Archbishop of Baltimore on the infallibility of the pope, he quoted at length from the fifth edition of Spalding's *History of the Reformation,* which had appeared in the year of the Baltimore council. Commenting on some remarks made by the Protestant historian D'Aubigné, the Archbishop of Baltimore had written:

[50] Peter Richard Kenrick, *Concio in Concilio Vaticano habenda at non habita* (Naples: 1870). The preceding section occupies pp. 1–37. The whole *Concio* is also in Mansi, LII, 453–81, and, in English translation, in Leonard W. Bacon (ed.), *An Inside View of the Vatican Council in the Speech of the Most Reverend Archbishop Kenrick of St. Louis* (New York, n.d.), and in Clancy, pp. 93–131.

We learn for the first time that the Roman Chancery decided on articles of faith: We had always thought that this was the exclusive province of General Councils, and when they were not in session, of the Roman Pontiffs with the consent or acquiescence of the body of bishops dispersed over the world. We had also in our simplicity believed, that even these did not always decide on controverted points, but only in cases where the teaching of revelation was clear and explicit; and that in other matters, they wisely allowed a reasonable latitude of opinion.

Kenrick felt that the quotation proved his thesis sufficiently, and he went on to make a few comments on Archbishop Manning before taking up the arguments which the latter had advanced.[51]

The archbishop told of the great thrill which Manning's eloquence had given him. He did not know, he said, which to admire more—the eloquence of the man or his perfervid zeal in promoting, or rather commanding, the new definition. The many fine qualities of the Archbishop of Westminster's presentation had made him wish that he could have been recruited for the opposition. And yet, Kenrick continued, it all put him in mind of what used to be said of the English settlers in Ireland, that they were more Irish than the Irish. "The Most Reverend Archbishop" he found to be "certainly more Catholic than any Catholic whom I have ever known." Manning, he declared, had no doubt about the personal, separate, and absolute infallibility of the pope, and he did not intend to allow anyone else to have any doubts about it. Rather he was like a prophet who took care to see to it that his predictions came true. His own views, based on nearly sixty years of education in the faith and on some forty years in the clerical life, were quite different from those put forth by the English prelate. He set down his credo in these words:

I boldly declare that the opinion, as set down in the *schema,* is not a doctrine of faith, and that it cannot become such by any definition whatsoever, even of a council. We are custodians of the deposit of

51 Kenrick (Naples edition), pp. 37–9.

faith, not its masters. We are teachers of the faithful entrusted to our care just insofar as we are witnesses.[52]

The next part of the *Concio* distinguished the science of theology from its object, the deposit of faith. It was in confusion of the two that Kenrick found the root of discord in the council. Theology's function was to systematize the truths of faith and to deduce theological conclusions from explicitly or implicitly revealed data, but theological conclusions, the archbishop insisted, could never be elevated to the status of dogmas of faith. Everyone, he declared, admitted that the pope, united with the bishops was infallible. This he took to be the doctrine of faith. All the rest was theological speculation, which might be right or wrong, but which in any event could not be proposed to the faithful as part of the revealed deposit.[53]

Archbishop Kenrick concluded his argumentation with a survey of the ecclesiastical tradition of the English-speaking world. He pointed out that for some two centuries a book called *Roman Catholic Principles in Reference to God and King* had been a standard authority, and he quoted the following passage from it:

It is no matter of faith to believe that the Pope is in himself infallible, separated from the Church, even in expounding the faith: by consequence Papal definitions or decrees, in whatever form pronounced, taken exclusively from a General Council, or universal acceptance of the Church, oblige none, under pain of heresy, to an interior assent.[54]

[52] Kenrick (Naples edition), p. 40. In his reminiscences of the council, Manning quoted Kenrick's passage of appreciation for his abilities and added the laconic comment: "No doubt." (Purcell, II, 456-7.)

[53] *Ibid.*, pp. 41-3.

[54] *Ibid.*, p. 46. The work is attributed to James Maurus Corker, O.S.B. (1639-1715) and is supposed to have been written while Corker was in Newgate after the Titus Oates plot. There were numerous subsequent editions, and *Roman Catholic Principles* seems to have been the basis of Stephen Badin's *The Real Principles of Roman Catholics in Reference to God and Country* (Bardstown: 1805), the first Catholic book published in the western United States. (Robert Gorman, *Catholic Apologetical Literature in the United States, 1784-1858* [Washington: 1939]), pp. 17-8.

Kenrick's next authority was the incumbent Archbishop of Baltimore, who, as Bishop of Louisville, had delivered a sermon in which he stated that the notion of the pope's infallibility was no more than an opinion and warned his hearers that it would be rash to impugn the orthodoxy of men like Bossuet who held a contrary view.[55] Finally, Kenrick launched into a lengthy treatment of the tradition of the Irish Church. It was true, he admitted, that the majority of the Irish bishops now seemed to favor the *schema,* but this had not always been the opinion of either the hierarchy or clergy in Ireland, and it had not been the doctrine taught at Maynooth until Father John O'Hanlon proposed it on a tentative basis in 1831. Kenrick had been in O'Hanlon's class at the time, and he was ready to admit that the thesis appealed to him as a theological opinion.[56]

By way of apparent afterthought, the archbishop next challenged Manning on three points. One was the case of conscience, which had already been mentioned in the council by Spalding. Kenrick was satisfied that no evidence had yet been alleged which would justify a bishop voting for the definition, and, with regard to the Gallican Assembly of 1682 which had been attacked in the general congregations, he claimed that its records had been deliberately falsified. He could not agree with the Archbishop of Westminster that a bishop would be without serious fault if he voted for the *schema* without having made a careful examination of the evidence.[57] Kenrick's next point of disagreement with Manning was on the latter's insistence that infallibility was a charism. The Archbishop of St. Louis preferred to drop the word altogether, and to speak of the divinely guaranteed inerrancy of the Church, and he was particularly disturbed by the English prelate's refusal to discuss possible limitations on the exercise of the charismatic gift which he claimed for the pope.[58] Finally he professed himself astounded

[55] Kenrick, pp. 47–8.
[56] *Ibid.,* pp. 49–56.
[57] *Ibid.,* pp. 56–63.
[58] *Ibid.,* pp. 63–5.

by Manning's claim that the final clause of the constitution on faith amounted to an implicit acceptance of papal infallibility. The representative of the deputation had stated the exact opposite when queried on the point. Either he was wrong, if Manning were right, or else he had deliberately led the council into error, which could scarcely be believed.[59]

The peroration of the *Concio* consisted in an enumeration of the grievances of the minority—beginning with the deputation elections in December—and an appeal to drop the whole question of infallibility. The last sentence read: "The salvation of the world is more important than that of the city." There were six appendices, including complete documentation on statements of the Irish bishops to the British Parliament on the eve of Catholic Emancipation, and a record of Kenrick's own protest at Spalding's management of the Second Plenary Council of Baltimore. The whole brochure, in Latin with occasional English footnotes, came to 100 pages.[60]

We have already seen something of the episcopal reaction to the *Concio.* Other commentators were not far behind the bishops. On June 11, the *Freeman's Journal* printed a letter from the Roman correspondent of the *Vatican* which characterized Kenrick as having "imbibed the Gallican principles of Delahogue in his "youth" at Maynooth, and said of the pamphlet itself that it contained "propositions which are accounted scandalous, proximate to heresy and absolutely heretical."[61] The New York *Herald* took the opposite side, and reported on June 19: "It caused a great deal of excitement here. His brother bishops from America are anxious to hear what he has to say in opposition. He is considered the most intense of the bishops in his opposition to the dogma and will enter a solemn protest against it that will cause many Italians to pause before the vote."[62]

Three Americans addressed the council on June 6, when

[59] *Ibid.,* pp. 65–6.
[60] The main text ends with p. 68. The appendices take up the rest of the pages.
[61] *Freeman's Journal,* June 11, 1870.
[62] New York *Herald,* June 19, 1870, in Beiser, p. 96.

the debate resumed. This time the subject was the proëmium, or introduction, to the constitution. The speakers from the United States were Bishops Amat, Vérot, and Whelan, all of the minority. Of Amat, Bishop Bernard Ullathorne later wrote:

> In my estimation the shrewdest man in the Council is a young Bishop from California, a native of Spain, but brought up in America, a little man, with broad shoulders, and a broad compact head, like that of the first Napoleon, and he never speaks above a few minutes, but he hits the nail on the head invariably. He neither argues, nor talks, but simply proposes amendments on the text and comes down again.[63]

The June 6 speech of the Bishop of Monterey-Los Angeles was a good example of what Ullathorne meant. He proposed three amendments. In the first instance, the priestly prayer of Christ (John 17:20 *ff.*) had been cited so as to make its object seem to be the unity of the faithful. Amat asked that the true sense of the passage be brought out, that is, that Christ had prayed for the apostles and for those who would believe because of their preaching. This emendation was accepted by the deputation and incorporated in the final text of *Pastor Aeternus.* Secondly, Amat objected to the phrase which styled Peter the "principle" of the Church's unity. He proposed that the word "center" be substituted as more expressive of the real role of the apostle. This change was rejected on the ground that, while Christ was the primary principle of unity, He had placed in the Church a secondary principle, namely, Peter. The bishop's third amendment was more successful and it was included almost verbatim in the final text. He suggested that it be made clear that the principal target of the Church's enemies was the Church itself, and not the primacy, and also that the primacy be referred to as a bulwark of the Church, but not, as the text had it, as its "salvation." Having said this, he left the pulpit.[64]

---

[63] Butler, II, 113.

[64] Mansi, LII, 496–7; Betti, pp. 244–5; 252–4; Georges Dejaifve, S.J., "Etudes sur le premier Concile du Vatican," *Nouvelle Revue Théologique,* LXXXIV (February, 1962), 565–6. The replies on behalf of the deputation were made by Archbishop Leahy of Cashel. (Mansi, LII, 637–9.)

Augustin Vérot's June 6 appearance on the rostrum was a comparatively brief one. He began by remarking that after the cloture resolution of June 4 some opponents of the *schema* had decided to abstain from further participation in the debate, but he declared that he himself thought it more worthy of a Christian and a bishop to defend the truth as he saw it whenever the occasion arose. This was apparently the first publicity given to the discussion of the international committee which had taken place at Rauscher's apartments on June 4, and Acton reported to Döllinger that Vérot had broken the veil of secrecy that had been cast over those proceedings.[65] León Dehon, one of the French stenographers at the council, entered a less sympathetic notation in his diary when he wrote: "Playing the role of *enfant terrible*, he betrayed the little plots of his friends."[66]

After this introduction, Vérot turned his attention to the *schema* at hand. His first objection was to the statement that the age was marked by increasing hatred of the Holy See. On the contrary he had found the religious climate in the United States appreciably better in recent years. It was true that there had been troubles in the past, but the odium was principally directed at the temporal dominion of the pope and not at his spiritual prerogatives. In fact, the bishop asserted, he had had great hopes of a rapprochement with Protestants when the council was announced, because he thought that it might produce a moderate and mild exposition of certain controverted points which would open the door to many conversions in America. As for Catholics, Vérot stated that there had never been a time when they were more devoted to the Roman pontiff. It was true that certain Catholics—who were also Freemasons or Carbonari—had invaded the temporal domain of the pope, but even this the bishop thought was inspired more by political motives than by a desire to attack the primacy on theological or moral grounds.

[65] Conzemius Transcripts, Acton to Döllinger, Rome, June 8, 1870.
[66] Dehon, p. 159.

The speaker's second point was that it was not in accord with the facts to say that the doctrine of the *schema* represented the "ancient and constant tradition of the universal Church." Rather it explained papal prerogatives as they were understood by ultramontanes. The use of this last word set off a chorus of "noes" from the floor. Vérot was not deterred, and asked leave to use the term. He said that he had heard the opposite epithet, "Gallicanism," employed often enough from the rostrum. All knew what he meant by an ultramontane, and he knew no better word to express the idea. He then attempted to continue by saying: "Everyone knows that there are two Catholic theological systems . . . ," but he was interrupted by Cardinal Bilio, who told him that what he was about to say had no pertinence to the proëmium, and that he should reserve his comments for the appropriate chapters. Vérot yielded to the order from the chair and left the pulpit.[67] His comments had no effect on the wording of the constitution.[68] Acton could only remark to Döllinger of his performance: "He is a very remarkable but strange man."[69]

The third American bishop to speak on June 6 was Richard Whelan. He apologized for his unfamiliarity with Latin because, as he said, he had been laboring for thirty years in "a vast and wild region," but he felt compelled to speak since others had decided not to do so. His first appeal was for a complete revision of the proëmium. It should be replaced, he felt, by an exposition of the nature of the Church, making use of rich Scriptural images like that of the Mystical Body. As matters stood, the fathers were laying themselves open to the charge that they had written a constitution on the Church without explaining what the Church was. This procedure, he declared, was not consonant with the dignity of the Holy Father, who would surely not want himself mentioned before the Church of Christ.

[67] Mansi, LII, 497–9.
[68] Mansi, LIII, 263; LII, 639.
[69] Conzemius Transcripts, Acton to Döllinger, Rome, June 8, 1870.

253

The deputation, Whelan charged, had arranged the *schema* so as to reflect the preoccupations of a certain school, and in doing so they had neglected all that might have been said about the Church which Christ had founded.

Of course Bishop Whelan did not expect that his suggested radical revision would be accepted, and he also had a number of minor amendments to propose. Like Amat he was concerned with what he thought was a misuse of Christ's priestly prayer, and he asked that the text be revised to indicate that its principal object was a petition that men might believe and be saved, while the unity for which Christ prayed was contributory to this primary intention. He also denied the assertion of the *schema* that it was on the "fortitude of Peter" that the indefectibility of the Church depended. What Christ was stressing in the "Thou art Peter" text, declared Whelen, was His own omnipotent power. He also concurred with Vérot's statement that it was untrue that hatred of the Church was increasing everywhere. He was ready to grant the existence of a constant opposition, but he saw no signs that it was worse than usual in the mid-nineteenth century. Another Whelan amendment attacked the notion that "the whole salvation and strength of the Church" depended upon the Holy Father. Lastly, the Bishop of Wheeling pointed out that the final clause of the introduction was ambiguous and should be written more clearly.[70]

This last proposal was the only one of Whelan's suggestions to win acceptance, but he was made the target for two particularly strong rebukes when Leahy of Cashel reported to the council the views of the deputation on suggested amendments. Whelan's sweeping request that the proëmium be revised was dismissed as "a censure, not an emendation," and it was not even submitted to a vote. The second item which irritated Leahy was the claim of Whelan (and of Vérot) that the age was not an era of special hostility to the Holy See. The Archbishop of Cashel delivered an emotional oration on this point, detailing the

[70] Mansi, LII, 514–7.

nefarious activities of contemporary heretics, schismatics, enemies of the temporal power—who he said were also necessarily enemies of the pope's spiritual power—and, finally, of
"liberal Catholics, who are a real calamity to our holy religion . . . who would oppress the pontiff and the Church if they
could, and as much as they could by denying and limiting the
rights of both."[71]

The next topic for discussion was the first chapter on the
primacy, and it drew no speakers from the United States. On
June 7, Bishop Amat was the third and last orator on the
second chapter, which dealt with the perpetuity of the primacy
in the successors of Peter. He had two omissions and two
changes to suggest: first, that the words which claimed that there
had been a constant and universal conviction in the Church
with regard to Peter's primacy be dropped, and also, the attribution to the apostle of the phrase *columna fidei*. Both statements
were taken from the speech of Pope Celestine I's legate to the
Council of Ephesus, and Amat felt that their rhetorical form was
out of place in a dogmatic decree. He also warned against
taking Scriptural phrases out of context and said that this would
weaken the position of the Church in the eyes of non-Catholics.
Secondly, he proposed that the word "legitimately" be included
in the description of the succession of the Roman pontiffs to
Peter and that the final sentences of the chapter be rearranged
to achieve greater clarity.[72] None of Amat's emendations were
accepted.[73]

The first and second chapters of the constitution had been
dispatched in a single day of debate, but on June 9 twenty-one
names were read out as having been put down on the list of
speakers who wished to comment on Chapter III. Among them

[71] For discussion of the amendments in the deputation, see Mansi, LIII,
262–3. Leahy's speech is *ibid.*, LII, 637–641.

[72] Mansi, LII, 538–9.

[73] Mansi, LIII, 263–4 (for the deputation meeting); LII, 720–21 (for
the report of the deputation's representative to the council).

were Amat and Vérot. The basic point made by the former was that the chapter should deal explicitly only with the pope's primacy and jurisdiction. His primacy as teacher belonged, Amat thought, to the chapter on infallibility. He proposed three separate amendments which would make this distinction clear, but all of them were rejected by the deputation. Two other emendations were received favorably. In one of these, the bishop recommended that a phrase which seemed to indicate that the Church was divided into many "churches" be dropped, and in another he requested explicit affirmation of the fact that bishops were successors of the apostles and real pastors.[74]

Something of a contretemps developed over a further suggestion which Amat made in his June 9 speech. In line with his desire to exclude the notion of doctrinal primacy from the treatment in Chapter III, he had asked that the canon which concluded the chapter be revised so as to omit any mention of faith and morals. Amat's reformulation of the canon was turned down in favor of a similar effort by Bishop Louis Regnault of Chartres, and the representative of the deputation, Federico Zinelli of Treviso, declared that he was accepting the Regnault version conditionally. As the text finally came out, it developed that the "condition" was the reintroduction of faith and morals, which defeated the purpose of both Amat and Regnault. On July 9, sixty-two fathers protested this maneuver, but on the same day Cardinal Patrizi informed Bilio that Pius IX wanted the change to stand in the text submitted to the general congregation. It was approved as submitted. Americans who signed the protest of July 9 were Kenrick, Vérot, and Domenec.[75]

The Bishop of St. Augustine's tenure of the rostrum on June

---

[74] Mansi, LII, 567–70; LIII, 266–7 (the deputation); LII, 1101–11 (report of Bishop Zinelli to the council).

[75] Zinelli's original statement accepting Regnault's canon *juxta modum* is in Mansi, LII, 1116. The events of July 9 are documented *ibid.*, LIII, 267–8. The final vote was taken on July 11. (*Ibid.*, LII, 1200–203.)

10 was a typically stormy one. He begged the fathers to give him a patient hearing, but he soon had them murmuring. The initial occasion was provided by his opening remarks, which went as follows:

> I know the position in which I and others are placed. Until the present, certain opinions have been freely discussed among theologians without censure. Now, however, you say to me and to many others, that is, to more than 100 bishops from every nation under heaven, at least equivalently: 'You must abandon your own opinion and embrace ours or you must leave the Church, that is, you must leave the bosom of the Church unless you embrace our opinion.'

Vérot answered the rumblings of disapproval which greeted this declaration by a plea for a fair hearing motivated by justice, charity, and religion, and he called upon his opponents to provide him with solid responses to his difficulties, responses which would convince the minority bishops of the error of their ways.

The Florida bishop had a half-dozen amendments to propose. The first of these charged misuse in the *schema* of a citation from the Council of Florence about the plenitude of papal power. Vérot's research had been thorough. He had consulted the Greek text of the Florentine decrees, the only text which had been signed by the Eastern bishops, and he had studied the explanation of its meaning given by the contemporary Cardinal Bessarion. It was clear to him that when Florence said that plenary papal power was to be understood according to the acts of ecumenical councils and the sacred canons, it intended this clause to be a restrictive one. Vérot therefore suggested that it be stated that supreme papal authority was always to be exercised "according to the sacred canons."[76]

Bishop Vérot's next complaint was one that had been raised before, and had been only partially satisfied through a com-

---

[76] Mansi, LII, 585–91. José Rincón, *La plenitud y supremacía del primado jurisdiccional del Romano Pontífice en el Concilio Vaticano* (Rome: 1943), pp. 53–75, *passim,* discusses Vérot's contribution at this point, and studies the speeches of fathers who agreed with or disputed his interpretation.

promise suggested to the deputation by Spalding. The bishop asked for deletion of the word "episcopal" from the description of papal jurisdiction, and the addition of the word "supreme." He remarked that unless this change were made the pope would be defined to be universal bishop, a dignity to which St. Gregory the Great had said no pope should aspire. Along this same line, Vérot also wanted an explanation of how papal jurisdiction could be called ordinary and immediate. He granted that it was ridiculous to think that the Holy Father would need authorization from the local ordinary before he could preach and administer the sacraments in any given part of the world, but he did not understand clearly why universal papal jurisdiction did not submerge local episcopal authority. With a flourish of humor that was typical, but diverting, he concluded his argument with an invitation: "However, the field in America is vast, and if anyone from Rome wishes to come to us, he will be most welcome." In a more constructive vein he then suggested that matters would be helped if a declaration were subjoined that all bishops derived their power directly from Christ, and that, as St. Paul had said, they, as well as the pope, were the foundation on which the Church was built.[77]

A final series of suggestions concerned the freedom of papal communication with the faithful and the relation of the pope to ecumenical councils. Vérot admitted the general right of the Roman pontiff to communicate freely with the Church, but he felt that there were times when prudence counseled delay in promulgating Roman documents. As an instance of this he mentioned the Syllabus of 1864. To the accompaniment of a now-familiar chorus of "noes" from the floor, he declared that

[77] Gustave Thils, *Primauté pontificale et Prérogatives épiscopales: "Potestas ordinaria" au Concile du Vatican* (Louvain, 1961), pp. 64–5, is one of those who feels that Vérot missed the point of the debate. In pages 63 ff., Thils discusses other contributions to the discussion and stresses the importance attached to it by many bishops who felt that the divinely founded rights of the episcopacy were being challenged. See also Betti, pp. 284; 293–5.

publication of that particular document in the United States would have resulted in a "universal conflagration," in which every Catholic church in the country would have been burned to the ground. With regard to the relation of pope and council, the bishop asked for omission of the clause which implied papal supremacy. He suggested this, he said, out of reverence for the Third Council of Constantinople and that of Constance, both of which had passed judgment on holders of the papal chair. In the written emendations which he handed in, Vérot further recommended that the prohibition of appeal from the decision of a pope to a council be restricted to future councils, but that appeal to a council already in session be allowed.

The only one of these many proposals to find its way into the text of *Pastor Aeternus* was the addition of the adjective "supreme" to describe universal papal jurisdiction.[78] But the final sentence of Vérot's speech was one of his more memorable contributions to the history of the council. On June 9, Archbishop Dechamps, without interruption from the presidents, had called for condemnation of the doctrines of Bossuet, Cardinal Lorraine, and Cardinal de la Luzerne, all luminaries of the Gallican Church. The Bishop of St. Augustine felt obliged to rise to this challenge, and did so with the following canon, which he proposed as a conclusion to the chapters on the primacy: "If anyone say that the authority of the Roman pontiff in the Church is so complete that he may dispose of all things according to his whim, let him be anathema." There was laughter and murmuring in the hall, and Cardinal Capalti broke in with a stern admonition:

We are not in a theatre to listen to buffooneries, but in the church of the living God to transact the serious business of the Church. While we are doing this, nothing contumelious, absurd or erroneous ought to be said. The most reverend father will pardon me if my zeal has

[78] Mansi, LIII, 267–8 (deputation); LII, 1102–14 (report of Zinelli to the council).

259

led me to say these things; for whenever he goes into the pulpit he detains the fathers of the council to listen to his pleasantries.[79]

To which Butler comments: "A not undeserved rebuke."[80] This is true, but it would have been an even stronger rebuke had the chair been more impartial in restraining the attacks to which the minority had been regularly subjected since the beginning of the debate.

Debate on the fourth chapter of *Pastor Aeternus,* the subject of which was papal infallibility, began on June 14. There was a certain amount of irony in the fact that Archbishop Purcell, one of the most outspoken opponents of the definition, celebrated the Mass which opened the session that day.[81] No Americans spoke until June 20, but before that date several interesting letters had been mailed from Rome which told something of American hopes and fears as the long-anticipated discussion commenced.

On the same day that Vérot addressed the council on the primacy, Lord Acton was preparing to leave the city. One of the farewell visits which he paid was to Kenrick, and his final report to Döllinger contained the following evaluation of the Archbishop of St. Louis:

Kenrick is a rock of bronze. . . . He considers the council null and void. The dogmatic decrees will take effect when the council has ended and been confirmed. This day will never come. Nor will he recommend this dogma to his flock or defend it against Protestants, since he considers it quite false and impossible. He and the opposition say: . . .'Time will work for us.' He is indignant at the lack of sincerity and good will; he thinks it is to be explained by confusion of ideas. People confuse theology with faith, more or less correct conclusions with the deposit of faith. . . . I still stick to my earlier judgment: Strossmayer, Kenrick, Darboy, Hefele are the best men.[82]

[79] Mansi, LII, 591.
[80] Butler, II, 80–81.
[81] Mansi, LII, 709.
[82] Conzemius Transcripts, Acton to Döllinger, Rome, June 10, 1870.

A somewhat different estimate of Kenrick and his colleagues was given by Bishop Demers to McMaster on June 13. After stating that prudence had prevented him from writing about certain matters previously, he continued:

But now the veil is removed and I am at liberty to write to a friend, to one, I knew it before, who believes with me, to thank him [who] has had the courage, for the sake of truth, to sacrifice noble feelings towards persons, to expose their wrongs. These wrongs, I call them so, are very great indeed and may cost very dear to their authors; they have already borne very sad and bitter fruits by destroying the prestige attached to the American Episcopacy all over Europe, principally from the time of the last Council of Baltimore. . . .

I could not believe that not [*sic*] one single American Bishop would go against the Pontifical Infallibility, not even against the opportunity of proclaiming it as an article of Faith, but how sadly I have been mistaken! Nothing could equal my astonishment at this but the shocking instance of a brother and a brother Bishop trying to prove a brother Bishop, long cold in the grave, guilty of what there is no doubt he would willingly subscribe to as a revealed truth if he had lived to be better informed on this important question, had he only listened to the learned and convincing arguments of our orators in favor of it; at least it is my conviction he would: why did not his own brother entertain the same charitable intention? But [what] shall I say of the man who has been for the last two years moving heaven and earth to create prejudice all over the world in the mind of his brother Bishops and of the Faithful by means of the Press; and who this man is you know but too well. *Ipse viderit!* . . .

Time will reveal things that will astonish the world and show how deep the evil was, and that the convoking of this council was an inspiration from above, and the only remedy that can cure it, at any cost or loss, you understand me.[83]

Both McQuaid and Bayley wrote to the United States in mid-June. The Bishop of Rochester commented: "I am glad to hear that minds at home are more quiet on the Infallibility question. The loss will be in the East and in Hungary, Bohemia, Germany and France. The amount of Infidelity here in Italy is fearful. The revolution that is coming will make great changes." How-

[83] UND, McMaster Papers, Demers to McMaster, Rome, June 13, 1870.

ever, he had not lost his peace of soul, and he concluded: "Whatever happens in the Council will be God's will, and though great calamities may follow at first, good will eventually come out of it all."[84] Bayley, who had canceled his plans to return home in order to be on hand "for the discussion of 'the great question,'" was cautiously optimistic as he summed up the situation for Father Corrigan: "The question," he wrote, "is in reality one of *form* rather than of *fact*. With the exception of a *very* few we all believe in the Infallibility of the Pope teaching ex Cathedra—and lately there has been a disposition manifested to push the Decree into such a shape as will gain for it a nearly unanimous vote—so that before long I trust you will have good news from us."[85]

The first United States prelate to speak in the debate on infallibility was Archbishop Alemany, at the seventy-fourth general congregation on June 20. He had only one modification to suggest, namely, that an explanation of the nature of the prerogative be included in the constitution to distinguish it clearly from impeccability and inspiration. The main burden of his speech was to quiet fears about a possible hostile reaction to the dogma in the United States. He recalled the affirmation of universal papal jurisdiction and doctrinal authority which had been subscribed by the bishops of the Second Plenary Council of Baltimore, among whom he named specifically Whelan, Domenec, and Vérot. Mention of the Bishop of St. Augustine drew laughter from the fathers. The archbishop pointed out that the president of the United States had been in attendance at the final session of the Baltimore council, and that Catholics, including those in "the regions of Florida and Savannah," had accepted the council's declaration with joy, while Protestant opposition had been minimal. He concluded that the apprehensions expressed by Domenec were unfounded. Alemany then

---

[84] McQuaid to Early, Rome, [Mid-June, 1870], in Browne, p. 436.
[85] AANY, C-2, Bayley to Corrigan, Rome, June 20, 1870.

finished his speech by citing St. Antoninus of Florence, Francis Patrick Kenrick, and Martin J. Spalding in favor of the dogma, and he added a last argument from reason. There was, he said, need of a supreme authority in the Church. Without it the Church could not be one, as the multiplicity of Protestant sects demonstrated.[86]

The Roman summer was beginning, but still the debate went on. McQuaid wrote to Early on June 25 that his greatest regret was that he was not home in Rochester, "instead of being boiled to death in this sweltering atmosphere of Rome." "The perspiration flows from me day and night," he continued, "and if I were to remain here all Summer, my dried bones might be gathered up as all that would be remaining of me." But progress was slow, and the bishop predicted that from three to six months would be needed to do justice to the subject. "We are still at the Infallibility," he told Early "and no more likely to get through by the 29th. than we are of going on an overland trip to the moon."[87]

Three minority bishops from the United States spoke on the chapter on infallibility during the final week of June. First to mount the pulpit was Whelan, on June 25. He began by disputing the contention that a universal belief in papal infallibility existed in the Church. Such, he declared, was not the case in the English-speaking world. On the contrary, educated Catholics in that area were under the impression that it was only the opinion of the ultramontane school, and they believed—wrongly, Whelan conceded— that only Italians were ultramontanes. He reminded the fathers again that bishops in the United States and elsewhere had preached that infallibility was not a dogma, and that in 1825 the Irish hierarchy had confirmed this preaching under oath. While Archbishop Manning was undoubtedly specially qualified to interpret the probable reaction of Protestants, he went on, still in this instance he found that the English prel-

[86] Mansi, LII, 790–97.
[87] McQuaid to Early, Rome, June 25, 1870, in Browne, pp. 436–7.

ate's predictions contradicted the opinion of everyone else he knew who had ever engaged in controversial work. Finally, he asked if the attitude of the English-speaking countries was not echoed in France, in Germany, and in central Europe. His conclusion was that the "universal belief" about which some had been speaking was confined within rather restricted limits, and he suggested that the affirmation of it be accepted only with great care.

There was, however, a formulation of papal infallibility which Whelan thought that everyone could accept, since it represented the traditional belief of the Church. It would be a formulation which stated that the pope's definitions were in fact expressions or declarations of the faith of the Church, which was the guardian and teacher of the revealed word of God. If this nexus were established, and if the pope made his pronouncements as the head and the spokesman of the Church, the Bishop of Wheeling felt that infallibility would be saved without at the same time destroying the rights and office of other bishops. He was convinced that the constant and immutable consent of the episcopal college was needed, at least ordinarily, when there was question of resolving obscure and doubtful points or of promulgating new definitions. Should an extraordinary case arise, where it was necessary for the pontiff to speak out before he had had the opportunity to consult the bishops, Whelan was ready to admit that divine assistance would enable him to do so infallibly. He did not feel that this compromised his basic principle, which was that in every case the pope spoke precisely as "head of the mystical body of Christ and mouth of the Church."[88]

In the written observations he submitted, Whelan asked that all reference to the teaching authority of the pope be stricken from the chapter on infallibility, since he did not believe that infallibility had its source there, but rather in the papal position as head of the Church. He also asked for deletion

[88] Mansi, LII, 870–76.

of the citations from the Councils of Florence and Lyons because he did not think them pertinent. Instead he proposed that infallibility be deduced from the promises made by Christ to Peter and to the other apostles. Finally, he suggested an explicit declaration that the pope was infallible because he was the head of the Church. None of these recommendations was accepted by the deputation on faith, and only the last was even proposed to the fathers, after Bishop Vincenz Gasser of Brixen had characterized it as ambiguous and seeming to demand the consent of the bishops for promulgation of dogmatic decrees.[89]

Bishop Amat was the next American speaker. He did not object to the connection which had been made between the teaching authority of the pope and his infallibility; instead he thought that the title of the chapter should be changed so as to indicate that it was because of his primacy of *magisterium* that the pope could be inerrant. The word "infallibility" he wanted dropped, out of charity and Christian prudence, since it was the occasion of so much disagreement. He distinguished three cases. The first was beyond controversy: The teaching authority of the Church, that is the bishops in union with their head, the pope, was infallible. Secondly, Amat declared that there was no question but that the Roman pontiff, as head of the Church and principal member of the body of Christ, was also infallible, since it was through him that the body was ruled and the unity of faith preserved. However—and the third case was that of the doctrine proposed in the *schema*—the Bishop of Monterey-Los Angeles did not think that it was certain that the pope was infallible when he spoke without any consent, prior, concomitant or subsequent, of the bishops, nor did he believe that papal infallibility extended as far as that of the Church. He did not think that the arguments from Scripture or from ecclesiastical practice which had been presented proved the doctrine of the *schema,* and he associated himself with the opinion of Bishop Ketteler, who had laid that doctrine to a

[89] Mansi, LIII, 270–72 (deputation); LII, 1219–24 (Gasser's report).

confusion between what pertained to the total teaching body of the Church and what pertained to the pope.

Amat was willing to grant that there were occasions on which the Roman pontiff had to resolve controverted questions of faith or morals. This was a function of his primacy in doctrinal matters. Here the pope was infallible, but even so he did not act alone, but in concert with the bishops who had brought the case before his tribunal and with all the other bishops of the world who wanted to see the controversy ended by that bishop whose divinely given task it was to confirm his brethren.

A corollary followed from the preceding argumentation. It was that there was a distinction to be made between the object of the Church's infallibility and that of the pope. The latter was restricted to specific controversies in faith and morals which the pontiff had to settle, in virtue of his magisterial primacy, for the preservation of the unity of the Church. The former had a wider scope. It was, Amat asserted, as wide as the deposit of faith and the preservation of that deposit demanded, and it extended, therefore, not only to what had been directly revealed, but also to those doctrines which, while not revealed, were necessarily connected with divine revelation and necessary for its safekeeping. The bishop ended his speech with a request that Chapter IV of the constitution be rewritten according to a formula which he had prepared. He omitted the word "infallibility," and placed emphasis on the role of the pope as head of the mystical body of Christ, whose task it was to resolve controversies among the members of that body. These conclusions he thought warranted by the evidence and calculated to conciliate divergent views in the council. As he left the pulpit, the shouts of "No, no" from the floor indicated the fallacy of his assumption.[90] All Amat's suggestions were rejected by the deputation and an adverse report on them was later made to the council by Gasser, so that none of them was adopted.[91]

[90] Mansi, LII, 915–20. Betti, pp. 325–6; 336; 357.
[91] Mansi, LIII, 270–72 (deputation); LII, 1220, 1224 (Gasser).

The last orator from the United States to address the council was, fittingly enough, Augustin Vérot, who had been its most prolix representative on the rostrum. He spoke at the seventy-ninth general congregation on June 30. Léon Dehon commented in his diary: "Monsignor Vérot, long discourse: for an hour and a half the speaker repeated all the objections, especially the historical ones."[92] Vérot started out with a promise: he would speak with all due gravity. This provoked laughter in the hall. But the laughter was good-humored, especially when he made the further promise that he would read his speech so that he would not indulge in extemporaneous amplifications or less cautious phraseology. He then explained his position. He was opposed only to the personal and separate infallibility of the Roman pontiff, which he had heard defended from the pulpit, and which he was convinced was intended by the *schema*, despite the disclaimers advanced by speakers for the deputation.

After these introductory remarks, the bishop commented on the June 20 speech of Archbishop Alemany. He denied that there was any contradiction between his present stand and his signature to the letter sent to Pius IX by the Second Council of Baltimore. That council had been rushed through in two weeks, he complained, and there had been no time for study of anything but disciplinary matters. All the documentation was then sent off to theologians in Rome, and, therefore, Vérot concluded: "With them is the whole merit and the whole praise of a definition of papal infallibility if it is to be found there." But it was not, as both he and Spalding well knew. In fact, he told the fathers, Spalding had not long since invited and encouraged him to make a special study of the question of infallibility, and he had done so, using the ultramontane books which were all that were available in the library of the American College. Parenthetically, he added that he was happy to have heard in the council that his opinions and those of Bossuet coincided. He had been unable to find the latter's defense of the Gallican clergy, but it was

[92] Dehon, p. 175.

obvious that their agreement could have come only from the fact that both had found the truth. When this was greeted with renewed laughter, he suggested that the deputation owed it both to truth and to Bossuet to refute him in the council.

Bishop Vérot's catalogue of the scriptural and patristic evidence, and that from church history, was a long one. He began with the Peter and Paul controversy as narrated in *Acts* and carried the argument down through a whole litany of fathers of the Church. His best argument, he felt, was that Pope Liberius had been deposed for heresy and that a Roman synod under Pope Symmachus had declared that a pope could not be deposed except for heresy. He gave other examples and concluded that the Roman Church at least conceived the possibility that a pontiff might become a heretic, which was scarcely compatible with personal and separate infallibility. The case of Pope Honorius still bothered him, too, and he said that only his desire not to be as offensive as Patriarch Valerga, who had compared the Gallicans to the Monothelites, prevented him from suggesting the parallel between the Jansenists and the efforts of the ultramontanes to evade the problem of Honorius' condemnation by three general councils and two popes.

With regard to the doctrine of the *schema,* Vérot was willing to assign it the theological qualification of "most probable," but he stressed that this still left it in the category of opinion, and he reiterated his complaint that no advance warning of its introduction had been given in the bull which convoked the council. Only after he had got to Rome did he—and more than 100 other fathers—find that they had been living in material heresy and were on the verge of being proclaimed formal heretics, and this after they had lived within the Church peacefully for years and had labored most fruitfully in its interests. The so-called "universal and constant faith" was not the faith of France, Germany, Ireland, the United States, or even of part of Italy, to judge from the sources of opposition to the definition, and Vérot could not see how this limited witness could form the basis for a dogma of faith.

The Bishop of St. Augustine concluded his final appearance before the council by proposing an amended form of the definition. He would give the pope, by reason of his primacy, the power to define what must be held in matters of faith or morals, and even in other areas. This supreme papal authority would be exercised as the expression of the collective authority of the episcopal college. It would apply only to the condemnation of heresies. Alternatively, Vérot suggested that his purpose could be achieved by adding a declaration to the effect that the pope made his definitions "after he had in his wisdom ascertained the faith of his brethren in the episcopate." In explaining these amendments, Vérot enunciated an interesting theory of the development of dogma. He asserted that he intended them—and the entire definition—to be prospective only, and not to apply to the past. This he thought would avoid the difficulties which arose from the history of the Church. He then apologized for having kept the fathers so long and left the rostrum for the last time. His apologies were unnecessary. Many of the prelates had already left the hall.[93] Both Vérot's suggestions were turned down by the deputation. One of them would have eliminated the whole concept of a specifically papal infallibility, while the second would have made the pope simply the spokesman of the bishops.[94]

The debate continued for four more days and was then brought to a halt. McQuaid explained the chief reason for this: "The climate is fearful, hot, sultry and enervating . . . . The only way to get along is to exclude outside air, by closing windows and doors."[95] Given this situation, chiefs of both the majority and minority parties agreed to terminate the discussion, and on July 4 this was done. The constitution *Pastor Aeternus* was

[93] Mansi, LII, 955–66. Betti, pp. 325; 351–2.
[94] Mansi, LIII, 270–72 (deputation); LII, 1222–3 (Gasser's report).
[95] McQuaid to Early, Rome, July 8, 1870, in Browne, p. 439.

269

returned to the deputation for final revision. In the July 8 meeting of the deputation Alemany suggested that a *monitum* be added to the definition of infallibility, asking that pastors of souls explain the doctrine carefully to the faithful. This suggestion was disallowed. A similar proposal by Spalding, Dechamps, and Martin was also rejected.[96]

A document which belongs to this period of the council, but which was not submitted to the secretary until July 17, was the undelivered speech of Archbishop Blanchet, who had been one of those who renounced his turn in order to shorten the proceedings. His purpose was to counter the efforts of Whelan, Domenec, and Vérot who had predicted dire results, if the definition were adopted, in the United States. The Archbishop of Oregon City declared that, on the contrary, belief in papal infallibility was general in America, and he believed that a solemn definition would only increase devotion to the Holy Father, whereas if the dogma were not proclaimed, "a huge and unheard of sorrow will pervade the whole new continent, from the North Pole even to the Southern."[97]

Progress in the deputation was slow. McQuaid had already explained something of the situation to Early on June 30 and on July 8 he offered further reasons for the delay. The first of these letters is valuable for the insight it gives into the mind of a bishop who stayed with the opposition until the end. He wrote as follows:

Efforts are being made to draw up a form of definition that will meet with the *placet* of nearly all. Two extremes oppose this: Manning leads those who would put the Bishops to one side, and make the Pope infallible, without a condition of any kind. Unfortunately the Pope himself sides with that party, and has made his influence felt very markedly. Another extreme is made up of Gallicans, or of Bishops whose ideas run towards Gallicanism. Between the two it is to be hoped that a definition will be found that will not give the lie to

96 Mansi, LIII, 272–3.
97 Mansi, LII, 1047–50. An English translation is in Clancy, pp. 89–92.

all the past history of the Church. I have been much amused at some things here. For example a Bishop from our side of the water [Alemany] has passed as a strong infallibilist and has received favors, etc. because he was so sound on the test question; the other day he made a speech on the Infallibility, professing his belief in it, etc. winding up with a definition to which I would be only too happy to say *placet* at any time. He was only one of that large number who claim that the Pope, speaking *ex cathedra* is infallible, without really understanding the meaning of the words. I have met many who wished to convert me, but when I cross-questioned them a bit, found that they were as unsound as myself in the exaggerated sense of the question. An Irish Bishop who is a red hot Infallibilist, in a conversation the other day turned out to hold the same views as myself, with this difference that I insisted on the explanation of the doctrine being put in black & white and he did not. The *formula* that does not contain full explanations and the proper conditions, such as are conceded in the Council by many of the strongest adherents of the doctrine will never meet with my approval, for without those conditions being expressed we should keep alive controversies and wranglings on the subject worse than anything in the past.[98]

A week later, McQuaid had more news, or rather he reported that there was a dearth of any real information:

Rumor has it that we shall not have the public session until the 24th. There is no reason for this long delay that I can see except the fondness of every one in Rome for taking things easy. The definition, it seems to me, might have been got ready for the 17th. The only explanation offered is that the members of the *Deputatio de Fide,* with whom the question now rests, are debating among themselves about the terms of the definition. It is easy to say, the Pope is infallible; it is not so easy to say how, when, under what circumstances, and about what matters he is infallible.

As the majority have assumed the responsibility of the definition, all the others now ask is to get that definition and leave Rome.[99]

As the events of the final week would show, the minority did not give up quite as easily as McQuaid predicted. That last week of the session began on Monday, July 11, with a long report

[98] McQuaid to Early, Rome, June 30, 1870, in Browne, pp. 438–9.
[99] McQuaid to Early, Rome, July 8, 1870, *ibid.*, p. 439.

from Bishop Gasser, who explained the text of the decree as finally decided upon by the deputation. Votes were then taken on the emendations which had been suggested in the course of the debate, and in every instance the recommendation of the deputation was followed.[100] The stage was set for the final balloting on the constitution, which took place in two phases, the first of which was scheduled for Wednesday, July 13.

[100] Butler, II, 134–48.

VII

Close of the Council

IN a letter which was sent on July 10, the British diplomatic agent Odo Russell reported to Archbishop Manning that the French, Hungarian, and German opposition had resolved to stand fast against the definition of papal infallibility, "which they have unanimously declared to be unacceptable."[1] Two days later, the English diplomat had more encouraging news. A preliminary roll call on the constitution *De Romano Pontifice* was scheduled for Wednesday, July 13, and Russell had been informed that unless the minority polled at least eighty votes on that occasion they would absent themselves from the final public session at which the constitution would be promulgated in the presence of the pope. He estimated that no more than fifteen fathers would in any case be "courageous enough to say 'No' " at the public session, and concluded: "I reckon now with certainty on a unanimous *placet*."[2]

The first order of business at the eighty-fifth general congregation on July 13 was the granting of leaves of absence to eighteen bishops, including Domenec, Dubuis, Fitzgerald, and Gibbons. The fathers then voted to accept Chapters IV and V of the constitution. The stage was set for the ballot on the constitution as a whole. When it came to a vote, 451 gave their unqualified

[1] Russell to Manning, Rome, Sunday night [July 10, 1870], in Purcell, II, 443.

[2] Russell to Manning, Rome, Tuesday [July 12, 1870], in Purcell, II, 443-4.

approval, another sixty-two approved conditionally, and eighty-eight voted *non placet*. Twenty-eight prelates from the United States took part in this voting. Eighteen accepted the constitution without comment, three approved it on condition that it be amended in certain particulars, and seven rejected it.[3] All told, the sixty-two fathers who suggested changes in the text submitted some 200 amendments, and these were referred to the deputation on faith.[4]

One of the Americans who proposed an amendment to the constitution felt that the formula of the definition of papal infallibility was not strong enough, and that it still left a loophole through which "the perverse and heretics" might escape. This was Archbishop Blanchet, who recommended that the scope of the object of infallibility be broadened and explicitated.[5] His request was never formally considered by the deputation. In a letter to James A. McMaster on July 12, either Blanchet or his close associate, Bishop Demers of Vancouver, explained the motives behind this petition. It was prompted by the fear that "Febronian" and "Gallican" elements might yet prevail. The letter declared: "They promise everything—agree to everything—if the exact *terms* that, specifically, condemn their heresy, be omitted. If this compromise is made, the Council will not kill these heresies."[6] Some months later, Blanchet paid a personal visit to the New York editor to explain his vote of July 13. As McMaster put it in his own inimitable prose, the archbishop

[3] Mansi, LII, 1241–53. Americans who voted *placet* were: Spalding, Alemany, Bayley, Conroy, Dubuis, de Goesbriand, Elder, Heiss, Henni, Lootens, Loughlin, Miége, O'Hara, Rappe, St.-Palais, Shanahan, Williams, and Wimmer. Voting *placet juxta modum* were: Blanchet, John McCloskey, and Amat. Those who voted *non placet* were Kenrick, Domenec, Fitzgerald, William McCloskey, McQuaid, and Mrak. All the other United States bishops had either left Rome or else absented themselves from the session. One of those who fell into the latter category, Ryan of Buffalo, was prevented from attending by a near-fatal illness. (Ryan to Pius IX, Rome, September 10, 1870, in Mansi, LIII, 1050–51.)

[4] Butler, II, 152.

[5] Mansi, LII, 1297; Betti, p. 494.

[6] *Freeman's Journal*, October 15, 1870. McMaster identified his correspondent only as "a man not young in the episcopate." Demers had written to him on previous occasions, and on July 13 he suggested an amendment similar to Blanchet's. (Mansi, LII, 1297, 1302.)

indicated that he had intended to register a protest that the formula of the definition was not "potent enough to kill the dirty snake of Gallicanism."[7]

A second archbishop from the United States who recorded himself as not completely pleased with the text was John McCloskey. His objection recalled previous American protests, and he was seconded by Ullathorne of Birmingham and others. They wanted the anathema at the end of Chapter IV dropped, and the primitive formulation of the constitution restored, so that those who refused to accept the definition would be solemnly admonished that they were deviating from Catholic truth, but without the threatening overtones of the anathema formula. Like Blanchet's proposal, this recommendation was never considered.[8]

The voting of July 13 provided Bishop Amat with his last opportunity to make some of the concise suggestions which had so impressed Ullathorne, and he availed himself of the occasion by proposing modifications to the introduction and to three of the four chapters of the constitution. His first request was for an explicit statement that the purpose of Peter's primacy was not that the episcopate become one, but that it be preserved in the unity which its Founder had given it.[9] This amendment was declared not germane to the argument by Bishop Bartolomeo d'Avanzo, who spoke on behalf of the deputation at the eighty-sixth general congregation on July 16.[10] Amat's next objection was to the rhetorical language of Chapter II. He restated his earlier opposition to the attribution of the term *fidei columna* to Peter, and he suggested that in a dogmatic decree it ought not be said that no one had ever doubted the primacy of the pope, or that everyone had acknowledged it for centuries, when, as a matter of fact, the contradictory of these assertions was nearer the truth.[11] D'Avanzo disallowed both these emendations.[12] The

[7] *Freeman's Journal,* November 26, 1870.
[8] Mansi, LII, 1301; Betti, p. 499.
[9] Mansi, LII, 1265; Betti, pp. 450, 453.
[10] Mansi, LII, 1305.
[11] Mansi, LII, 1267–8; Betti, p. 461.
[12] Mansi, LII, 1306–07.

Bishop of Monterey-Los Angeles had two changes to propose for Chapter III. He asked, as he had during the debates, for a clearer distinction between matters of faith and morals and those which pertained to discipline, explaining that in the one case there was question of obedience to the pope as guardian of the deposit of faith and in the other of the principle of hierarchical subordination. Secondly, he requested omission of the phrase "in each and every church," which was used to designate the object of the pope's ordinary and immediate supreme power. In the course of the debates it had been suggested that the phrase seemed to reflect on the unity of the Church.[13] Neither of these proposals was accepted, and Bishop Federico Zinelli rejected them for the deputation as unnecessary and so drastic as to demand a completely new vote on the chapter.[14]

Chapter IV contained the definition of papal infallibility, and Amat submitted two revisions to its text. He and several others felt that the phrasing of the chapter implied that the help of the Holy Spirit had been promised only to the successors of St. Peter. They wanted it made clear that the promise had been made to the whole Church.[15] The California prelate also made one last effort to have the actual text of the definition changed to accommodate the views of the minority. Eleven other bishops submitted amendments analogous to his. Their hope was that the definition would state that the pope acted as spokesman for the Church when he pronounced a solemn definition, and that he did so after having ascertained the Church's faith by consultation with the bishops. Amat's specific suggestion was that the object of papal infallibility be designated as "doctrine on faith or morals contained in the deposit committed to the Church."[16] Bishop Vincenz Gasser was the last representative of the deputation on faith to address the council, and in his closing speech on July 16,

13 Mansi, LII, 1275; Betti, pp. 476–7.
14 Mansi, LII, 1313.
15 Mansi, LII, 1282; Betti, p. 486.
16 Mansi, LII, 1294; Betti, p. 492.

he passed over Amat's amendments to Chapter IV in silence.[17]

While the members of the deputation on faith were considering the amendments submitted on July 13, the international committee of the minority met to plan their final strategy. On Thursday, July 14, Russell informed Manning that they were "flushed with their success" of the previous day, and that they hoped to win over forty of those who had voted *placet juxta modum*, so as to ensure 120 *non placets* in the public session. The English agent reported that Bishop Ketteler and others had announced a list of concessions which would be the price of their approval for the constitution, and he told Manning that "Villa Graziola [*sic*] has sent a bulletin to the press announcing a great victory—a moral Sadowa."[18] That same evening, Russell wrote again to Manning, to tell him that Archbishop Darboy, "who now takes the credit of the Minority vote to himself," planned to visit Cardinal Bilio and dictate his terms to him. Darboy, he reported, was confident that the opposition would reach 140 votes.[19] Russell's next despatch was dated Friday night, July 15. He had learned that the international committee was sending a five-man delegation to the pope, headed by Darboy. They were to make two demands. The first of these was for the deletion from Chapter III of the assertion that the pope possessed the "whole plenitude" of supreme power in the Church. The second demand was for inclusion in the definition of infallibility of a statement that the pope relied on the consent of the Church in making infallible pronouncements. Russell added that in the event that these requests were refused, the opposition would vote *non placet* at the public session.[20]

[17] Mansi, LII, 1314–7.
[18] Russell to Manning, Rome, Thursday [July 14, 1870], in Purcell, II, 443. Dupanloup's Roman residence was the Villa Grazioli.
[19] Russell to Manning, Rome, Thursday night [July 14, 1870], in Purcell, II, 442–3.
[20] Russell to Manning, Rome, Friday night [July 15, 1870], in Purcell, II, 446. Six bishops composed the delegation. See Butler, II, 156–7. On July 16, Darboy presented a memorandum of their conversation to the pope (Mansi, LII, 1322; Butler, II, 157).

These activities of the minority had not gone unnoticed, and Bishop Senestréy duly recorded them in his diary. He further recorded that the pope refused to entertain the opposition petitions and referred them back to the council.[21] According to Döllinger, the pontiff had at first seemed disposed to consider the requests, but he was deterred from doing so by the intervention of Senestréy and Manning.[22] The stage was thus set for the eighty-sixth general congregation on July 16. We have already seen the disposition which was made then of the amendments which had been proposed by American bishops on July 13. In point of fact, only two of the two-hundred-odd suggestions submitted were brought to a vote on July 16. One of these was of capital importance, since it reflected the extent of the majority's triumph. The minority had asked as the price of their agreement the inclusion of a declaration that the pope, in making infallible pronouncements, relied on the consent of the Church. Instead of inserting this qualification, the deputation proposed, and the council accepted, a statement to the effect that papal decisions which were irreformable were so of themselves, "but not because of the consent of the Church." The minority viewpoint was thus definitively rejected. The session ended after the fathers had voted to censure two pamphlets which had appeared attacking the council. These were *Ce qui passe au Concile* and *La dernière heure du Concile*. It was then announced that general permission had been granted for any members of the council who wished to leave the city. They were to be permitted to absent themselves until November 11.[23] The implied invitation to the members of the minority who could not reconcile themselves to an affirmative vote in public session was obvious. Although the minutes of the council recorded a unanimous standing vote for the censure of the two pamphlets just mentioned, only forty-two fathers seem to have subscribed the written protests against them which were distributed during the congregation. Among them was

21 Mansi, LIII, 285–6.
22 Döllinger's account of the interview is in Quirinus, pp. 800–803.
23 Mansi, LII, 1317–9.

Dubuis of Galveston.[24] The New York *Tribune* later reported that an unnamed American archbishop had declared that *La dernière heure du Concile* gave a true picture of the situation.[25]

On Sunday, July 17, the day before the fourth public session, at which the constitution *Pastor Aeternus* was to be proclaimed, the international committee held a final meeting. Darboy was ill, and Haynald took the lead in proposing that the opposition attend the public session in force and record a negative vote. He was opposed in this by Dupanloup, who carried the day. By a vote of 36 to 28, the committee resolved to recommend that opponents of the definition absent themselves on the following morning and content themselves with a letter of protest.[26] Two copies of this letter were made. One was addressed to the pope and one to the presidents of the council. They were given to the secretary of the council, Bishop Fessler, at 7 A.M. on the morning of July 18, together with a covering letter from Cardinal Schwarzenberg.[27]

The minority letter simply recalled the fact that they had voted against the constitution on July 13, and that others had voted *placet juxta modum* or absented themselves. Nothing, they continued, had happened since to make them change their opinions, and they would therefore be unable to do other than vote *non placet* at the public session. Since filial piety towards the Holy Father forbade this, they stated that they would leave Rome and return to their flocks. The letter ended with a prayer for the pope and for the Church and the assurance of their faith and obedience. It was signed by fifty-five bishops, including the three Americans Kenrick, Vérot, and Domenec.[28] Bishop Fitzgerald of Little Rock was one of six additional prelates who handed in separate statements to the same effect. He asked that his name not be called at the public session, since he could not

[24] Mansi, LII, 1260–61.

[25] New York *Tribune,* August 11, 1870, in Beiser, p. 87.

[26] Russell to Manning, Rome, Sunday [July 17, 1870], in Purcell, II, 447; Butler, II, 157–8; Mansi, LIII, 286.

[27] Mansi, LII, 1324–5.

[28] Mansi, LII, 1324–8.

vote except negatively.[29] Another opponent, Bishop McQuaid, had obtained permission to leave the council on July 16. He informed Father Early of this on the seventeenth, and added:

> Tomorrow, the public session will be held in which the final voting on the Infallibility will take place. They have ended by making the definition as absolute and strict as it was possible to make it. As a consequence a large non-placet vote will be recorded against it. What will be the consequence in some of these European countries God only knows.[30]

McQuaid's ignorance of the decision reached by the international committee, as well as the absence of his name from the letter of protest which the committee submitted, would seem to indicate that he felt the best course was to dissociate himself completely from further connection with the infallibility debate. He told Early that there was little chance that the council would be able to resume in November, because of the outbreak of the Franco-Prussian War, and he indicated that in any case he did not intend to participate any further in its discussions.

The twin dogmas of papal primacy and infallibility were proclaimed by Pius IX amidst great splendor, and, as is well known, to the accompaniment of thunder and lightning, on the morning of July 18. The fathers of the council and distinguished guests were summoned to appear in the Basilica of St. Peter at 9 A.M. Red vestments were to be worn by all the prelates, and Cardinal Lorenzo Barili opened the ceremonies by celebrating the Mass of the Holy Spirit. After the Mass had been finished, the pope arrived and, after prayers were said, Bishop Antonio Maria Valenziani read the entire text of the constitution *Pastor Aeternus* aloud. A roll-call vote was then taken, the pope gave a short speech, the *Te Deum* was chanted, and the fourth public session of the council was at an end.[31]

Five hundred and thirty-three fathers voted *placet* when their

[29] Fitzgerald to Fessler, Rome, July 17, 1870, in Mansi, LII, 1328.
[30] McQuaid to Early, Rome, July 17, 1870, in Browne, p. 440.
[31] Mansi, LII, 1327–36.

names were called, while only two voted *non placet*. One of these was Luigi Riccio of Cajazzo in southern Italy. The other was Edward Fitzgerald of Little Rock, Arkansas. What prompted Fitzgerald to vote "no" at the public session has never been satisfactorily explained. At least for a time he maintained a separate establishment in Rome, in the Via Rasella, and so he may not have been apprised of the decision of the minority bishops to absent themselves. The fact that he did not sign their letter of protest, but sent in one of his own might lend credence to this theory. In his letter to Fessler on July 17, Fitzgerald had asked only that his name not be called. It would seem that he at least considered the possibility of attending the public session as a passive spectator. However, once he was in the council hall, he sent an usher to Fessler to ask that he be recognized as present.[32] When he was in consequence asked for his vote, he responded with a *non placet*. Immediately after the balloting, he came down from his place and approached the papal throne to make his profession of faith with the words, "Now I believe, Holy Father."[33] One contemporary observer suggested that Fitzgerald had been taken unawares when his name was given out by mistake, but this conflicts with the official version as given in the acts of the council.[34] Another theory—which partakes more of the nature of legend—is that he actually said "*Nunc placet*" but was erroneously thought to have said "*Non placet*."[35] Whatever the reason, the Bishop of Little Rock has gone down in history as one of the two prelates in the council to cast a negative vote at the session of July 18.

Twenty-five Americans were present to vote *placet*. They were Archbishops Spalding, Alemany, Blanchet, and John McCloskey, Bishops Amat, Bayley, Conroy, Dubuis, Elder, Gib-

[32] Mansi, LII, 1328.
[33] *Ibid.*
[34] Henri Ramière, S.J., *Bulletin du Concile,* No. 33 (July 28, 1870), 152.
[35] Robert F. McNamara, *The American College in Rome, 1855–1955* (Rochester: 1956), p. 181.

bons, de Goesbriand, Heiss, Henni, Lootens, Loughlin, William McCloskey, Miége, O'Connell, O'Hara, Persico, Rappe, St.-Palais, Shanahan, Williams, and Abbot Wimmer.[36] The eighteen prelates who had voted *placet* on July 13 all remained to cast their ballot on July 18. They were joined by Archbishop Blanchet, who had never been opposed to the definition, by three bishops who were absent from the eighty-fifth general congregation, namely, Gibbons, O'Connell, and Persico; by Archbishop John McCloskey and Bishop Amat, both of whom had given only a conditional approval on July 13; and by Bishop William McCloskey of Louisville, who had been identified with the minority ever since his arrival in Rome.

Letters from young American ecclesiastics in Rome provide some additional information on the events of July 18. Benjamin Keiley wrote accurately enough to his family that 535 fathers had attended the final session, and he reported that eighty stayed away, among them Kenrick and Vérot. He had gone to the basilica for the ceremonies, and recorded his emotions at seeing Archbishop Manning: "I felt like raising a cheer when I saw glorious Abp Manning come out—the grandest man in the Council—whom all lukewarm Catholics sneer at and infidels and heretics revile—Manning whom I cannot even see without feeling such a sensation of enthusiastic devotion toward him."[37] Peter Geyer and Patrick H. Cusack, two recently ordained priests of the Archdiocese of Cincinnati, reported the day's events to Archbishop Purcell:

His Grace the Mt. Rev. Dr. Kenrick is gone from Rome; he left the evening before the public session of the Council which was held on the 18th. . . . In the voting, which was public and could be heard by the people in the Church particularly by those nearest the door of the Aula, there were but two 'Non Placets.' 'Tis said that a large number of the Opposition were not in attendance. The rumor is pretty true this time.

It is false that Dr. Spalding is very ill; it is doubtful that he has been ill at all since you left. Rt. Rev. Bp. Gibbons had a little fever

[36] Mansi, LII, 1337–1347.

[37] ADC, Keiley Papers, Keiley to "Home Folks," Rome, July 18, 1870.

of three or four days. Rt. Rev. Bp. Ryan came near dying with inflammation of the bowels. He has been sick for two or three weeks, and he may not be yet out of danger, though he is not as bad as he was.

The most of the American prelates are gone from our house. Bp. Vérot went to Naples this morning and will leave when he returns. Bishop Fitzgerald goes this evening; Bishop Loughlin on Saturday next.[38]

There was one last social note to bring that eventful July 18 to a close. On the evening of the definition, thirty-one bishops of the Irish race assembled at the Irish College to present an address to Cardinal Cullen, congratulating him for his able and successful vindication in the council of the rights of the Holy See and of the tradition of the Irish Church in their regard. Bishop Eugene O'Connell of Grass Valley was the only prelate from the United States who was present.[39]

Word of the definition which he awaited so eagerly does not seem to have reached James A. McMaster for some days. However, in the July 30 issue of the *Freeman's Journal* he commented on telegraphic reports concerning the role of Bishop Fitzgerald:

A telegram from Rome perpetrates an abominable outrage on one of our youngest Prelates, in saying he was one of *two* dissidents, in a General Council of five hundred and thirty-eight Prelates. The names are given of the Bishop of Little Rock, Arkansas and of some bishop in Eastern Europe. We denounce it, as the ill-timed pleasantry of some miserably poor wit in Rome. Dr. Fitzgerald is not the man to put himself in so desperately false a position. The Archbishop of Cincinnati is his friend; and the Archbishop of St. Louis is his Metropolitan, but neither of these considerations could ever have so warped the noble intellect of Dr. Fitzgerald as to lead him into a vote *against the Pope with the Oecumenical Council assenting,* as this lying telegram represents him. We insist on denying the truth of so damaging a story.[40]

Two weeks later, McMaster was somewhat better informed, and expressed the pious hope that Fitzgerald would make his sub-

---

[38] AAC, Purcell Papers, Geyer and Cusack to Purcell, Rome, July 20, 1870.

[39] Peadar Mac Suibne, "Ireland at the Vatican Council," *Irish Ecclesiastical Record,* XCIII (May, 1960), 306–307.

[40] *Freeman's Journal,* July 30, 1870.

mission "as soon as he gets out of the fog." The editor had not yet, it would seem, received a complete account of the July 18 session. The names of the bishops who had left Rome to avoid appearing at the session were still unknown to him, but their anonymity was not proof against editorial barbs. McMaster remarked—as so often and so unconcernedly—inaccurately, that they had left two of their number behind "to carry this new phase of *Protestantism* to its utmost limit," and he finished off with the judgment: "Whoever they may be, the Catholic Church has no need of them; but they have great need of the Catholic Church."[41]

Not all the bishops left Rome immediately. John Baptist Miége remained for some weeks to take care of business for his vicariate, and then traveled home to Kansas via his native France and Ireland. He did not reach Leavenworth until November 20.[42] The adventures of Bishop Ignatius Mrak of Sault-Sainte-Marie and Marquette are worth recording. After a visit to his birthplace in Carinthia, he took passage on the Trieste-Glasgow packet. The ship put into a Sicilian port on the eve of the feast of the Assumption to load a cargo of sulphur. Mrak went ashore and was royally welcomed, since no bishop had set foot in the place in years. The villagers organized a parade in his honor, and he is said to have administered confirmation to a number of the inhabitants. These festivities lasted three days, and the ship captain was so annoyed at the delay that for the rest of the voyage he allowed the bishop and a student who was traveling with him only one fork, knife, and spoon between them. Mrak finally arrived home in October, 1870. During his absence from the diocese he had not written even one letter to his administrator.[43]

41 *Ibid.*, August 13, 1870.

42 Peter Beckman, O.S.B., *The Catholic Church on the Kansas Frontier: 1850–1877* (Washington: 1943), p. 122.

43 Antoine Ivan Rezek, *History of the Diocese of Sault Ste. Marie and Marquette* (Houghton, Michigan: 1906), I, 236.

The outbreak of the Franco-Prussian War made travel in Europe difficult. Acton told his friend Lady Blennerhasset: "Among the numerous disappointments which the war brings us, I count this, that the Anglo-Americans, who would have gone by the Brenner, and whom I was hoping to snare at the moment of their release, will take the Mont Cenis route to avoid the armies. I would have liked to present some friends of whom I am proud, like Kenrick and Connolly, to another of whom I am more proud still."[44] By July 28, Bishops Bayley and McQuaid were already in London and preparing to sail on August 13. They had left Rome on the eighteenth. Bayley wrote to Father Corrigan that he had had diphtheria and a bilious attack in Rome, "and was going on from bad to worse when the end came, and we were able to escape from the fiery furnace."[45] One by one, then, the bishops made their way home. For some of them, July 18 ended their active connection with the council. Others continued to be involved with it and with its decrees for some time to come, as will be seen. But it would be fair to say that none of them shared the sentiments of one of McMaster's clerical correspondents, Father Louis Molon of Elyria, Ohio, who had written on July 15: "In the Council of Trent, the Bishops went to the Council as *parish priests* and they came back as *Bishops*. This time many of them went to the Council as *Popes*. I hope they will come back as *Bishops*."[46]

Only three general congregations were held during the summer of 1870. The number in attendance gradually dwindled. On August 13, 136 fathers were present, on August 23 there were 127 on hand, and only 104 attended the final session of the council on September 1.[47] No Americans bishops participated in the desultory debate, although Archbishop Blanchet was named as one of ten new members of the deputation on ecclesiastical

---

[44] Acton Papers, Acton to Blennerhasset, Tegernsee, July, 1870.
[45] AANY, C-2, Bayley to Corrigan, London, July 28, 1870.
[46] UND, McMaster Papers, Molon to McMaster, Elyria, July 15, 1870.
[47] Mansi, LIII, 1–36.

discipline at the August 13 meeting.[48] The only significant United States contribution to the summer's work was a memorandum submitted by Bishop Elder for consideration in connection with the proposed *schema* on apostolic missions. Elder called for the establishment of one universal mission-aid society to collect and distribute alms, so that the amount received by individual missionary areas would not depend on the contacts which bishops of such places were able to make. He further asked that the society be managed by laymen. Besides the obvious advantage that there would be in interesting them in the work of the missions, Elder pointed out that they were better qualified for the task than were priests, and the system would also free priests from temporal cares and give the lie to any possible charges of clerical avarice. Finally, the Bishop of Natchez recommended that the council single out for special praise the Society for the Propagation of the Faith of France which operated along the lines which he would like to see made universal.[49]

Before we discuss the sequel to the council, mention should be made of the activities of Archbishop Spalding as a member of the congregation on proposals, the position to which he had been appointed by Pius IX in December. Since none of the proposals on which Spalding worked ever came before the council, the story of his part in them has not been introduced into the general narrative of its history. A digression on the labors of the congregation will also allow an enumeration of the various petitions submitted to it which carried the names of American bishops.

Spalding attended meetings of the congregation on proposals intermittently from February to April. The minutes of the congregation do not indicate that he made any particular contribution to its discussions, except that at two sessions in late February he joined Archbishop Alessandro Riccardi di Netro of Turin in advocating abrogation of the third degree of consan-

[48] Mansi, LIII, 1–3.
[49] Mansi, LIII, 64–5.

guinity as a matrimonial impediment.[50] Perhaps the most important aspect of his association with the group was the opportunity which it afforded him for contact with some of the leading personalities of the council. On March 3, for example, he was named to a subcommittee headed by Cardinal Constantino Patrizi. Other members were Cardinals Camillo di Pietro and Juan Moreno and Archbishops Dechamps and Manning.[51]

The March 14 meeting of the Patrizi subcommittee was its most significant gathering. The members recommended that the council not attempt to make any decrees touching the law of nations or the nature of war and peace, although they felt that it would be proper to issue an exhortation against unjust wars and to urge that the nations seek to promote peace. They also voted to recommend to the pope the codification of canon law, but they were less enthusiastic about the possibility of defining the dogma of the Assumption of Our Lady. It is curious to note that they made use of arguments in this connection similar to those which were employed by the minority in the council against a definition of papal infallibility, namely, that it was unnecessary since the doctrine was universally accepted in practice by the faithful, that it was inopportune, given the circumstances of the times and of the council, and that the historical difficulties which would be raised only disturb the traditional belief of Catholics.[52] Spalding's last appearance at a session of the congregation was on April 11. He did not attend the subsequent meetings in April, May, and June.[53]

The congregation on proposals received a large number of petitions from individuals or from groups of fathers. Several of these petitions contained the signatures of over half the American hierarchy. A request that the council urge the Jews to accept Christ as the Messias obtained several hundred signers, among

[50] Mansi, LIII, 671.
[51] Mansi, LIII, 677.
[52] Mansi, LIII, 687.
[53] Mansi, LIII, 687–98.

them thirty from the United States.[54] Twenty-eight of the 118 bishops who petitioned that St. Joseph be declared patron and protector of the universal Church were Americans, and the name of the Archbishop of Baltimore headed the list.[55] Twenty-six United States bishops joined eighty-two others in recommending a statement of praise for the work of the St. Vincent de Paul Society.[56] Other *postulata* drew more scattered support from the Americans. Miége was the only one of them to put his name to a request that the feast of the Sacred Heart be raised to the highest liturgical rank and that a solemn act of consecration to the Sacred Heart be made in the council.[57] Among the nearly 200 fathers who asked that the Assumption be defined, only Bishops Martin and Miége added their signatures.[58] O'Connell was the lone American representative among the 108 bishops who wanted the words "immaculate virgin" added to the "Hail Mary."[59] Three bishops who were otherwise frequently at odds in the council joined in a June 20 petition asking for greater liturgical honors for St. Joseph and for a declaration that he was the primary patron of the Church after Our Lady. They were Martin, Domenec, and Amat.[60] Another five co-operated in a plea that the council ask bishops to send men and assistance from their dioceses to the Negro missions of central Africa. American signers of that petition were Spalding, Purcell, Bayley, Elder, and Miége.[61] The proposals on the law of nations and the codification of canon law which came before the Patrizi sub-committee also found supporters from the United States. Alemany, Dubuis, and Gibbons signed the former proposal and Alemany, Domenec, Dubuis, and Quinlan the latter.[62] The

[54] Mansi, LIII, 554–64.
[55] Mansi, LIII, 576–9.
[56] Mansi, LIII, 564–7.
[57] Mansi, LIII, 657–9.
[58] Mansi, LIII, 486.
[59] Mansi, LIII, 592–4.
[60] Mansi, LIII, 581–4.
[61] Mansi, LIII, 634–6.
[62] Mansi, LIII, 477–9.

variety of these petitions not only bore witness to the manifold interests of the Americans, but also pointed up the fact that, while they might disagree on the major issues before the council, they remained ready to co-operate with one another in areas which did not touch upon those disagreements.

There is only one more "European" aspect of the council which must be treated before we can return with the bishops to the United States and post-conciliar developments there. This was the attempt made by Spalding to have the meeting place of the council shifted to Malines in Belgium. The Italian occupation of Rome on September 20, 1870 had made it highly doubtful that the council could reconvene in that city. On September 29, Archbishop Dechamps wrote to Manning: "When will the council meet again? Does Your Grace still agree with Monsignor Spalding that it will have to be continued outside of Rome, in Malines for example?"[63] Early in October, Spalding received official notice from Cardinal Bilio that the pope not only permitted, but desired, his return to Baltimore. The cardinal informed him that the council was not only *de facto* suspended, but that for all practical purposes it was also ended *de jure*.[64] On October 16, the Archbishop of Baltimore was visiting Dechamps at Malines, and he wrote from there to Cardinal Cullen:

Having received official notification from Cards. Antonelli, Bilio & others, that the Council cannot continue for the present, I am en route for home, & shall probably sail from Liverpool next Saturday, 22nd inst. I regret that I cannot do myself the honor to call on yr. Eminence, but I hope to see you again when the Council will be resumed, which I trust will be next Spring.

By the way, I have a great project, which I have been talking over with Mgr. Dechamps, who is perfectly agreed & would be much pleased at its being favorably entertained. It is, to persuade His Holiness to have the Council continued next Spring—say May 1—in this *Old Catholic City;* still calling it the Vatican Council.

[63] AAM, Dechamps Papers, Dechamps to Manning, Malines, September 29, 1870 (copy).

[64] AAB, 35–U–6, Bilio to Spalding, Rome, October 3, 1870

1° All the Bishops can easily be accommodated here; 2° the sessions could continue throughout the Summer, & in fact throughout the Winter; 3° the Bishops would not only not be molested in this truly Catholic old town, where Free Masons *have no* foothold, but the people would honor them & think themselves greatly honored. 4° This being a *free country* (not in name, but in deed), the government could not interfere; 5° The five Card. Presidents could attend as in Rome, & report daily, hourly in fact if needed, by telegraph with Rome, or through some confidential person who could communicate freely with the Holy Father, & send his replies; 6° this step will be a rebuke to that accursed and sacrilegious government which hypocritically pretends to be free & is the greatest tyrant & robber of all the earth, hardly excepting Russia; finally, 7° this place would contribute much better than Rome to the health of the Bishops, who could thus continue in comfort the great work already cut out & most important.

Spalding ended his letter with a request that Cullen study the project, which he said was warmly endorsed by Dechamps, and he asked the Irish cardinal to recommend it to the pope if he approved of it.[65]

On October 20, the council was formally suspended by an apostolic letter.[66] Spalding was by that time in London. Apparently before word of the suspension reached him, he sent Cullen a second letter. He thanked the Archbishop of Dublin for having seconded his Malines scheme and for having written to Rome on its behalf. Manning, he reported, was also in favor of a resumption of the sessions in Malines. As for himself, he would soon sail from Liverpool for Baltimore, but he looked forward to visiting Cullen in Dublin when he returned for the rest of the conciliar meetings.[67] Back in Belgium, Dechamps was becoming more and more enthusiastic about the idea. On October 24, he wrote Spalding that Belgians would welcome the council, and he hoped that the notion of holding it in "a *free* and *neutral* country" would appeal to the Holy Father.[68] Five days

[65] AAD, Cullen Papers, Spalding to Cullen, Malines, October 16, 1870.
[66] Mansi, LIII, 155–8.
[67] AAD, Cullen Papers, Spalding to Cullen, London, October 21, 1870.
[68] AAB, 35–A–7, Dechamps to Spalding, Malines, October 24, 1870.

days later, he wrote Manning in much the same sense, and told him also that there had been serious question of the pope taking up residence at the archiepiscopal palace of Malines, a prospect which he welcomed joyfully.[69]

The first dissonant note in this correspondence was sounded by Bishop Conrad Martin of Paderborn, who had been approached by Dechamps in the name of Cullen, Manning, and Spalding. The German prelate agreed that Malines would be the best spot at which to reconvene the council, but he wondered if it would be practicable to do so in the spring of 1871 in view of the unsettled state of so many European countries.[70] Manning was still optimistic about the possibilities when he wrote to Dechamps on November 11. He told the Belgian archbishop that Spalding had written on the subject to Rome, and that he had himself added a "strong and decisive postscript" to the American's letter. He was particularly anxious that the Holy See adopt the expedient of reassembling the council as a token of its freedom of action and courage, and he thought that Malines was the ideal place for such a manifestation.[71] However, despite the enthusiasm of the four archbishops, the Roman authorities finally decided against their plan. A letter from Dechamps to Spalding in January, 1871, told the story, although it concluded with a slight glimmer of hope. The Archbishop of Malines wrote: "It appears that our Holy Father the pope is not for continuation of the council anywhere but in Rome. At least I hear nothing more said about it. Are you still of the same opinion as Monsignor Manning on the subject?"[72] Whatever reply Spalding made, Dechamps' information was correct, and no more was heard of the Malines plan.

While this activity was going on in Europe, American news-

---

[69] AAM, Dechamps Papers, Dechamps to Spalding, Malines, October 10, 1870 (copy).

[70] *Ibid.,* Martin to Dechamps, Paderborn, November 7, 1870.

[71] *Ibid.,* Manning to Dechamps, London, November 7, 1870.

[72] UND, Spaldings Papers, Dechamps to Spalding, Malines, January 10, 1871.

papers were commenting on the definition. We have already mentioned the attitude of James A. McMaster. Other press reaction was not nearly as violent as that of the *Freeman's Journal.* Nine days before the actual promulgation of the dogma, the Pittsburgh *Catholic* was ready to accept an affirmative decision by the council as a foregone conclusion, but it refused to see the definition as a victory for extremist sheets like the *Journal,* the London *Vatican* and *Tablet,* and the French *L'Univers* and *Le Monde.* Taking its lead editorial from the London *Weekly Register,* the Pennsylvania newspaper criticized those who denounced the opposition bishops as Gallicans, Jansenists, and enemies of the Church of Christ. "No church founded by men," the editorial continued, "could survive the writings of M. Veuillot and of the London *Vatican;* and if, in spite of their advocacy, the dogma of Infallibility is pronounced to be *de fide,* then, indeed, may all men believe that it is protected from on high."[73] The *Western Watchman* of St. Louis greeted the news from Rome in a moderate way. Father David Phelan, the editor, professed his own belief in the dogma, but declared himself sufficiently liberal to appreciate the position of those who might think that the new dogma would lead only to confusion.[74] From the former episcopal see of Augustin Vérot came a calm and sober analysis. The Savannah *Morning News* for August 2 summed up its reaction in the following words:

The doctrine itself, if we understand it properly, compared with what former Popes would have desired, does not carry the great powers the world thinks it does. It evidently bears the impress of the nineteenth century as distinguished from the ideas of the fourteenth. It gives to the Pontiff, it is true, spiritual supremacy, and in a more extended sense, in as far as decisions from the throne of St. Peter's can be given at any time on any religious question, without conclave of Cardinals or future councils; in matters temporal regarding the government of the Papal Dominion, no such supremacy is thought of.[75]

73 The *Catholic,* July 9, 1870.
74 The *Western Watchman,* July 16 and August 2, 1870.
75 Savannah *Morning News,* August 2, 1870.

The Savannah paper also noted that the outbreak of the Franco-Prussian War had relegated the council to a minor place in the news. The return of certain of the opposition bishops to the United States was destined to put it on the front pages again for a brief period, but in general the council had already become history for the American press. Even the Catholic journals would soon be preoccupied with the Italian occupation of Rome, and so, because of the march of events, the definition of infallibility was greeted in the United States by nothing like the furor which had been feared by some of the bishops during the council.

VIII

Return of the Bishops

ARCHBISHOP Spalding was one of the first Americans to address a pastoral letter on the council to the people of his diocese. It was dated from Rome on July 19. The archbishop explained the workings of the council and emphasized that there had been both complete freedom of debate and a thorough consideration of the decrees which were promulgated. He concluded his letter with an exposition and defense of the doctrine of papal infallibility, in which he took particular pains to show how it could be reconciled with true liberty, if not with the doctrinaire liberalism of nineteenth-century Europe.[1]

By the time Spalding returned to the United States in November, 1870, the center of Catholic interest had shifted from the work of the council to the usurpation of Rome by the Italians. The tumultuous receptions accorded the archbishop in both Baltimore and Washington were turned into protest meetings against the Italian action. Several weeks later, Spalding delivered a ringing defense of the papal temporal power at a rally in Philadelphia.[2] He then returned to the round of his episcopal duties, but his health failed rapidly, and he died peacefully at his residence in Baltimore on February 7, 1872.[3]

Other American bishops of what we may style the "moderate"

[1] *Freeman's Journal*, September 3 and 10, 1870. A paraphrase of the pastoral, sprinkled with quotations, is in J. L. Spalding, pp. 416–25.
[2] J. L. Spalding, pp. 430–39.
[3] *Ibid.*, pp. 449–60.

294

party had arrived home while the definition of infallibility still occupied a commanding position in public interest. Bishop Quinlan of Mobile, who had been an ally of Spalding, reached his see city in mid-May, and immediately issued a statement cautioning against inaccurate news reports emanating from Rome.[4] Two weeks later, he defended the right of the opposition bishops to make their views known in another statement, which read, in part:

> In matters open to discussion, there are perhaps mild remonstrances and humble petitions—but no defiant protest or threat of schism among those whom rumor puts upon the imaginary list of prelates. I know them well; none can surpass them in firm faith, loving obedience to authority, chivalrous defense of truth, and live long laborious missionary work in the vineyard of the Lord. No bishop in the hierarchy of the Catholic Church can surpass them.
>
> Let them discuss and humbly demonstrate; they are free to do so. 'In dubiis libertas.' When the discussion is closed, and the voice of authority definitively speaks, then find, if you can, a single voice of the American Episcopate signed in opposition, or the faintest breathing of a voice among them to disturb the harmony of Catholic truth.[5]

Bishop Lynch of Charleston was of much the same mind as the Bishop of Mobile. He preached on the council in his cathedral chapel on Pentecost Sunday, June 5. After explaining exactly what papal infallibility meant, he defended the right of some of the fathers to oppose its definition on the ground of inexpediency and predicted that all would accept the decision of the council as final. For himself, the bishop had always believed that the infallibility of the pope was a logical consequence of of the infallibility of the Church. The definition, he told the congregation, would answer the following question: "Does the guidance and control promised by the Divine Saviour guard

4 *Banner of the South,* May 28, 1870, quoting the Mobile *Register* of May 17.
5 Oscar Hugh Lipscomb, "The Administration of John Quinlan, Second Bishop of Mobile, 1859–1883" (M.A. dissertation, The Catholic University of America, 1959), p. 144, quoting the Mobile *Register,* May 29, 1870.

the Pontiff from error when in virtue of his office he decides and authoritatively announces what has been and is within the Church the true doctrine of Christ on a matter of faith and morals?"[6] One last example of the approach taken by "moderate" bishops is to be found in the sermon which the Vicar Apostolic of North Carolina James Gibbons delivered in the cathedral of Baltimore on October 2. Quinlan and Lynch had spoken before the actual definition; Gibbons, of course, spoke several months after it had been made. He delivered the usual warning about inaccurate newspaper accounts, and then tried to explain the working of the council on the analogy of the United States Supreme Court, which examined both statute and common law before reaching a determination. As for the opposition, Gibbons stressed the fact that the minority bishops had been active in challenging the doctrine before it had been defined, but he declared that their opposition had ceased once the council had spoken.[7]

The small group of American prelates who had from the first espoused the cause of the definition naturally had reason to be gratified by the success of their efforts. Their sentiments were well expressed in a pastoral letter of Archbishop Francis N. Blanchet, "given out of the Flaminian Gates of Rome, July 31, 1870."[8] The first five pages of Blanchet's letter were devoted to the constitution on faith, and he pointed out that it had condemned the errors of rationalism, of semi-rationalism, and of the "pretended reformation" of the sixteenth century. The remaining eight pages of the pastoral discussed the question of infallibility. The Archbishop of Oregon City was unsparing in his criticism of the opposition. He began by setting the record straight:

[6] *Banner of the South,* July 9, 1870.
[7] *Catholic Mirror,* October 8, 1870.
[8] Francis N. Blanchet, *Pastoral Letter and Conciliary Discourse of the Most Rev. F. N. Blanchet, D.D., Archbishop of Oregon City; Also Address to Pope Pius IX of the Clergy and Laity of the Ecclesiastical Province of Oregon* (Portland, Oregon: 1871).

296

Let it be well understood that the Pontifical infallibility is not a novelty or a new doctrine, as some pretend to assert, for it has always been practiced in the Church, though not dogmatically defined. It has always been admitted by all theological schools and the most illustrious doctors, and recognized by the ancient assemblies of the Church before the violent intrusion of Gallicanism, accomplished by the order of Louis XIV. The Church might have continued practicing the Papal infallibility and believing it, as she has done in all past centuries, without defining it, as she has successively defined many other points of doctrine contained in the depository of revelation, had not the sect of Gallicanism boldly come forward and challenged the Church by its opposition and denial of a doctrine she had held from the beginning. It therefore became her imperious duty to defend, prove and define the contested point; and so much so because what was considered by many prelates in the beginning as inopportune, was made by the fierce Gallican opposition, not only opportune, but of the greatest necessity . . . .

The archbishop went on to say that it had been painful to find among the opposition within the council "the names of some of our most respected and loved Fathers and also the names of some illustrious and learned champions of the Church, who, by their writings, had so well deserved of her." However, his main fire was reserved for the "so-called 'liberal Catholic party' " outside the council, and for the "impious and infidel press, pouring daily the filth of their furious rage on the Holy Father and the defenders of his rights." He remarked that these journals had praised the minority bishops, and he associated himself with the sentiments of Bishop Lorenzo Gastaldi of Saluzzo, who had declared, "If I had the misfortune to find my name mentioned by such wicked journals, I would think it was effaced from the Book of Life."

After this introduction, Blanchet gave a short history of the doctrine of infallibility. It had been practically acknowledged, he said, for the first fifteen centuries of the Church's history, and had been called into question only at the time of the great western schism. Gallicanism was all but dead and buried, continued the archbishop, until the appearance of Bishop Henri

297

Maret's book, *Du Concile général et de la Paix religieuse.* Maret had attempted, he charged, to change the constitution of the Church by making its government representative and by claiming for the episcopate a share in papal sovereignty. The consequence of this "anarchical" doctrine had been revolutionary pandemonium and the rousing of public opinion, to which Döllinger had contributed his share. It was, concluded Blanchet, "the formula of so-called liberal Catholicism, which is but a masked transition to Protestantism, or to national churches, under the supremacy of the State." Unfortunately, however, he had found that Maret's teaching was "praised, propagated and supported, not only by the impious and revolutionary, but also by the middle or semi-Catholic press, pretending to conciliate the Catholic affirmation with the humiliation and denial of the Papacy, which they would call the 89 of the Church." This was the situation as the Archbishop of Oregon City saw it at the opening of the Council. He next turned his attention to Bishop Dupanloup, whom he seems to have considered the moving spirit of the opposition.

The Canadian-born prelate's estimate of his French confrere was not a very flattering one. He protested that the Bishop of Orléans had addressed himself "to the popular passions, to the sensibility and anxious suspicions of statesmen," and had "provoked the brutal violence of the masses and the skillful tyranny of the secular arm against the Holy See and the august assembly of the Council." Dupanloup himself he saw as a genuine opponent of the dogma masquerading under the pretense of inopportunism and using specious and fallacious arguments. The French bishop was, he felt, responsible for a spirit of division among the fathers and among the clergy, which had caused great scandal to the faithful, and which left no alternative except a clear definition of the papal prerogative. Blanchet then told of the January petition of the infallibilists and the counter-petition of the minority, and he complained of the "deluge of anonymous pamphlets, full of sophism, threats and slanders," which subsequently "inundated the Fathers." He was of the opinion that those who continued in opposition revealed themselves as genuine Gallicans, and he declared that the historical arguments which they alleged against the dogma were groundless and had been completely refuted.

The final section of Blanchet's pastoral was couched in a more positive vein. The archbishop enumerated the scriptural proofs of the doctrine, and then analyzed the decree of the Council of Florence on papal primacy, which he said demanded recognition of the pope's infallibility. He added arguments from the history of the early Church and finished by citing the letter sent to Pius IX by the Second Plenary Council of Baltimore in 1866. As for the Vatican Council itself, Blanchet asserted that the majority of the most talented fathers supported the definition, and he closed the letter by saying that the *Pastor Aeternus* had given the Church that which it most needed, a reaffirmation of authority.

The pastoral letter just described is valuable as a clear elucidation of the mind of one segment of the American hierarchy, and the sermons and press releases of the "moderate" bishops are interesting as an indication of the way in which they explained the council and its work to their flocks, but the major focus of interest among the returning prelates was bound to be upon Purcell and Kenrick, Vérot, Domenec, McQuaid, and the others who had been most closely identified with the activities of the minority. Some of the American opponents of the definition, like Whelan, seem to have slipped quietly back into their accustomed duties without much fanfare, but most of the rest felt called upon to explain the stand which they had taken. The first to do so was John B. Purcell.

The Archbishop of Cincinnati arrived in New York City on August 10, 1870, and on that same evening gave an interview to a reporter from the *Herald*. The journalist's account of that interview reads as follows:

The Archbishop declared himself an anti-infallibilist, and spoke of Archbishop Manning as a fanatic—in fact as one whom the Anglican party were glad to get rid of on account of the disturbing influence he exercised in their councils.

Archbishop Purcell is a somewhat elderly gentleman, of quiet and courteous manners, and carrying with him much of a reputation for controversial ability. He was satisfied in the belief that the doctrine of Papal infallibility was radically of such an arbitrary character that the final promulgation of the dogma would be almost indefinitely postponed. He spoke of the Archbishop of Paris having declared his disposition to acquiesce in whatever the majority of the Ecumenical Council decided upon, but there was evident in what Archbishop Purcell gave utterance to, that the party of the anti-infallibilists is not of that complexion to be easily disposed of by a vote which places them in a minority. Archbishop Purcell expressed himself to the effect that the Roman Catholic mind in America is not prepared to accept the doctrine of infallibility as applied to the personality of the Pope. That the Church, through the voice of its assembled representative ministers, should lay down certain laws for the government of the entire body, and promulgate final doctrines for its acceptance, receives the endorsement of all Catholics; but the question of personal infallibility is more than it is thought either reasonable or proper to receive. It will take, however, a long time before the dogma of infallibility is officially proclaimed to the world. It will have to be signed by all the Bishops who participated in the Council; and that process, judging by the slow moving machinery of the Papal system, will take years to accomplish.

Archbishop Purcell has no idea what will happen to Rome after the withdrawal of the French troops, but he relies on the devotion of the troops who are enrolled under the Papal standard to repel any Garibaldian or Mazzinian raid on the Holy City.[9]

While newspapers across the country were digesting this rather remarkable statement, Purcell was on his way to Cincinnati. On August 16, Bishop Lynch of Charleston wrote him a long letter which picks up the story and also tells something of the consternation which the *Herald* interview had caused. The southern bishop wrote from Brooklyn, New York:

This afternoon's paper has a long telegraphic statement of a reporter having 'interviewed' you in Cincinnati, and anounces that you are to

[9] New York *Herald,* August 11, 1870.

address the public at Mozart Hall next Sunday evening when *you* will defend *your* course, &c. &c.

Before that, the telegram says, 'He coincided with the Abp of Paris that the decree (on Infallibility) could not be considered binding until the council shall have been closed and the Pope proclaimed (infallible?) under the signatures of the Bishops.' Something to the same effect seemed to be hinted at or implied in the account of his interview with you, which the Herald Reporter gave in N. York.

I do hope this letter will reach your Grace before Sunday. I implore you, the senior bishop of the United States so loved and revered by us all, not to allow yourself to be drawn into any such statement, contrary to sound principles of theology, to the fundamental principles of canon law, and to the facts of the history of the church in councils. Do not, I implore you, allow yourself to be placed in a false position, which is untenable. The Archbishop of Paris has not committed himself to it. Several French Bishops (Dupanloup and others) if the telegraph spoke truly have given in their adhesion to the Decree while you were on the Atlantic. Any how, that is what they will all come to.

Lynch urged the archbishop to consider his position carefully. He was himself satisfied that the adhesion of each and every bishop was not necessary to the validity of a dogmatic decree, and he asked Purcell to admit that the question was at least a doubtful one. He then appealed to the Cincinnati prelate's pastoral sense and reminded him that he would one day have to demand of his people acquiescence in papal infallibility. "Let *us* at least show," he pleaded, "the example of obedient Faith, conquering our own opinions and if need be personal judgments, in subjection to the yoke of Faith." The Bishop of Charleston did his best to impress upon Purcell the extreme caution that had to be used in dealing with the press. Criticism could no longer be kept "within the family," as he pointed out:

We are in times when we must measure every word. It will be caught up and commented on, by good Catholics, by semi-infidels and infidels, and by Protestants. Already the report made in the *N.Y. Herald* has elicited editorials in papers, showing what rich fun it would be to them to be able to ask, why does not the Catholic Church take action in regard to Bishops who reject the decisions of her councils? They will pat a Bishop on the back, and cry out, Liberality, Independence of

301

thought, Freedom of speech, until they think he is committed, and with equal trumpetting call for ecclesiastical censures on him or else jeer the church as imbecile.

Bishop Lynch finished his letter with the plea for preservation of the unity of faith and union with the See of Peter which had always been characteristic of the American Church. He was quite conscious of the problems which had been created by the definition, and he suggested that it would be a good idea for the bishops of the United States to agree on a common policy as to the explanation to be given of it. "Perhaps," he suggested, it would be better "to let those who advocated its introduction, set forth the true meaning of it." The last line of the letter provided a sidelight on the gathering of signatures for the January anti-definition petition, and also indicated Lynch's own views on what had happened in Rome. Earlier in the letter he had said: "I was sorry the subject was brought up in the council." He closed with a final reference to the opportuneness of having done so: "At your request I signed the request to the Holy Father not to allow the subject to be introduced. In the same spirit I now write to your Grace—this time I hope with better success."[10]

Another bishop who was worried about what Purcell might do was Sylvester Rosecrans of Columbus, one of the few Americans who had not attended the Roman meeting. He proceeded by indirection, but in the light of published reports of the archbishop's views his meaning was clear. Rosecrans wrote to Purcell on August 16:

Last Sunday I had the chapters on the Church, solemnly proclaimed by the Holy Father, read in the Church, and along with them some remarks of my own welcoming the end of the long discussion, by a proclamation of the Ancient Faith. The Council was legitimately convened, legitimately conducted, and duly approved. All Christendom prayed for the Holy Ghost to guide its decisions: and hence all the promises of Christ to the Church must have their fulfillment in it.

[10] UND, Purcell Papers, Lynch to Purcell, Brooklyn, August 16, 1870.

After this implied invitation to his metropolitan to accept the definition, Rosecrans added that he had been sorry to read Archbishop Kenrick's *Concio*. He was particularly disturbed by the passage in that pamphlet which contended that the Church could not declare the pope infallible. This, the Bishop of Columbus thought, was "going too far." "However," he concluded on a hopeful note, "I suppose litigation will stop now."[11]

Unfortunately for the sanguine hopes of Lynch and Rosecrans, the aspect of the 'litigation' which concerned Purcell did not end with the New York and Cincinnati newspaper interviews. On Sunday evening, August 21, the archbishop delivered a lecture on the council in his see city's Mozart Hall. Popular exposition of theological niceties is at best a difficult task, and the locale of the talk did not improve the situation. One of the reporters present noted that the room in which it was held was plagued by poor acoustics, and that "its currents of air and peculiar atmosphere operated badly on foreigners."[12] Whatever the full explanation, press reports of the lecture only proved how valid had been Bishop Lynch's forebodings, and in the sequel Archbishop Purcell found himself compelled to issue still one more clarification of his position.

The speaker discussed his views on union of Church and State in a section of the speech which has already been quoted in an earlier chapter. He then went on to the question of papal infallibility. It had first been considered by the Americans, he said, at a meeting held in the American College. As a result of that session, Purcell had been commissioned to draw up the petition which was submitted on January 15, in which the pope was asked not to permit the subject of his infallibility to come before the council. Although they realized that upwards of 530 fathers wanted the definition, the American petitioners felt that they had "discovered inconsistencies in the defense of the dogma" which they thought should be made known to the Holy

11 *Ibid.*, Rosecrans to Purcell, Columbus, August 16, 1870.
12 *Banner of the South*, September 3, 1870.

Father. This, according to Purcell, was the primary motive of their petition.

After he had explained the general position of the American opposition, the archbishop turned to his personal difficulties. He reminded his hearers that Bellarmine had listed some forty popes who taught erroneous doctrines, and he complained that some partisans of the definition—among whom he singled out the Patriarch of Jerusalem Guiseppe Valerga—had not distinguished sufficiently between a personal infallibility of the pope and that which he had as Vicar of Christ. He felt that the council had clarified this point by its insistence that the pontiff was infallible only when he spoke *ex cathedra.* Purcell likewise told the audience that he had been concerned about past papal pronouncements, and had wanted to know how they fitted in with infallibility. As examples of what he meant, he instanced the bull *Unam Sanctam* of Boniface VIII and the power of the pope to depose rulers of nations. However, he declared, all his difficulties had been solved by the council, which had distinguished what popes declared *ex cathedra* from what they might hold as private teachers, and he was therefore prepared to confess his faith in the dogma which had been defined.

There was, however, the further problem of the newspaper interviews. The archbishop was not in a friendly frame of mind toward any journalists. He expressed his anger at the abusive accusations which had been heaped on him by an eastern newspaper which charged that he was obstinately opposed to anything emanating from Rome, especially if it were connected with infallibility. The reference would seem to have been to the *Freeman's Journal.* He also charged that the interviewers in New York and Cincinnati had dishonestly and maliciously misrepresented his words and denied that he had said that promulgation of the dogma must await the signature of all the fathers. Instead, he claimed that he had said the exact opposite, that is, that the public ought not to wait for universal episcopal approval before subscribing to the doctrine of the pope's infallibility.

At this point, Purcell introduced an argument which was to be the source of some confusion. Some years previously he had engaged in a series of debates with the Baptist minister Alexander Campbell. In the course of those debates the archbishop had, as he candidly admitted to the audience in Mozart Hall, made the statement that papal infallibility was not an article of faith. According to the newspaper accounts, he put it this way: "It was not a doctrine of the Church for eighteen hundred years. It never was received as a dogma of the Church till the other day." As those two sentences stand, the first is theologically false, if it implies that the pope's infallibility was an addition to the deposit of Faith. The second sentence is true in the sense that papal infallibility had not been an explicitly defined dogma until July 18, 1870. The archbishop did not help matters by referring his hearers to the text of the Campbell debates and announcing that he stood by what he had said there. In common with most other contemporary American theologians and bishops, Purcell had held before the council that the pope was infallible when speaking—as he put it—"in connection with the Church congregated in Council or dispersed all over the world." This was orthodox doctrine, but it did not hit precisely upon what had, in the final analysis, come to be the crux of the question in the closing days of the Vatican Council, namely, did the pope require some sort of consent of the Church— either prior, concomitant, or subsequent—before he could make an infallible pronouncement? The phrase "personal infallibility of the pope" could have two meanings. It could refer to an infallibility which adhered to declarations made by the pontiff as a private person. This the council did not define, but it did define, in explicit terms, that no consent of the Church was required for infallible papal pronouncements made *ex cathedra* on matters of faith and morals. Neither in his speech at the

305

council itself nor in the Mozart Hall address did Archbishop Purcell demonstrate a clear grasp of these distinctions and therefore, despite the profession of faith which he made during the Mozart Hall lecture, his position remained objectively ambiguous.

Whatever may have been the confusion engendered by Purcell's explanations, he was determined to leave no doubt as to his subjective acceptance of the dogma defined in *Pastor Aeternus*. He read to the assembly the text of the fourth chapter of the constitution and prefaced it by a statement of personal commitment, which was reported as follows:

I come here to proclaim the personal infallibility of the Pope in his own words. I am a true Roman Catholic, as I said in Rome . . . . I have vindicated the rights of the Pope, and the infallibility of the Church in the strongest language I was capable of using in Rome, and I am not now going back on this . . . . I want the editors of newspapers and reporters to send it on the wings of the press, North, South, East and West, that John B. Purcell is one of the most faithful Catholics that ever swore allegiance to the Church. Let them say what they please of me and my course in Rome; for that I have received the thanks of those who do not think exactly as I do. It is by free discussion that truth is elicited, and without such discussion it can not be.[13]

The Mozart Hall speech naturally provoked considerable commotion. Secular papers which had previously lionized the archbishop now accused him of insincerity. The Cincinnati *Daily Gazette*, for example, said that his explanations smacked more of a politician consenting to a platform which he did not fully support than they did to "the saving faith which is necessary to salvation."[14] In New York, McMaster was disturbed by the two press interviews and by first reports of the address. He quoted the Cincinnati *Commoner* as having termed Purcell a "giant among the pigmies," but warned the prelate lest he incur the fate of "those wretched Archbishops Nestorias [*sic*]

[13] *Catholic Telegraph*, August 25, 1870; *Banner of the South*, September 3, 1870.
[14] Cincinnati *Daily Gazette*, August 23, 1870, in Beiser, p. 244.

and Sergius."[15] The St. Louis *Western Watchman* was initially cautious. Phelan noted that he had received by telegram the purported text of the lecture and commented: "If correctly reported His Grace has said some most extraordinary things."[16] One commentator who found the text acceptable was Bishop Rosecrans, who congratulated the archbishop on his effort and told him that he had had the speech read aloud to his priests.[17]

The local controversy stirred up by the Mozart Hall lecture did not last very long, but it was for a time a *cause célèbre* along the banks of the Ohio. One of the last echoes came on September 6, 1870, when the Cincinnati *Inquirer* published a letter from the archbishop in which he protested that in an editorial on August 22 the paper had stated that, although he professed himself a Catholic, he did not believe in the pope's infallibility. Purcell demanded correction of "this false statement," and declared: "Thousands who heard me in Mozart Hall last Sunday, as well as the reports on my remarks in other newspapers, can testify to the injustice which you have thus, no doubt unintentionally, but still most inexcusably done me."[18]

It is difficult, in the absence of a completely reliable transcript of the archbishop's speech, to judge the case completely, but it would seem that a combination of bad acoustics, a certain confusion in Purcell's own thought, and more confusion on the part of reporters untrained in theological terminology conspired to turn the Mozart Hall lecture into something less than the complete vindication of his course of action which the speaker had intended. This was, at any rate, the impression gained by Archbishop Spalding, who heard of the evening's events while he was still in Belgium. He wrote to Cardinal Cullen: "Archbp. Purcell, after a deal of nonsense poured forth in a lecture, has given his adhesion to the definition."[19] Of the last affirmation

---

[15] *Freeman's Journal*, August 27, 1870.

[16] *Western Watchman*, August 27, 1870.

[17] UND, Purcell Papers, Rosecrans to Purcell, Columbus, August 25, 1870.

[18] Cincinnati *Inquirer* of "last Tuesday," quoted in the *Western Watchman*, September 10, 1870.

[19] AAD, Cullen Papers, Spalding to Cullen, Malines, October 16, 1870.

there was no doubt, as the Archbishop of Cincinnati made abundantly clear. His reasoning may have been confused; his faith was not.

Even after the excitement in Cincinnati had died down, Archbishop Purcell had some explaining to do. He sent in a formal adhesion to the decrees of the fourth session of the council which was acknowledged by Cardinal Barnabò on November 11. The cardinal expressed himself as grateful for the letter, especially in light of the opinions which the archbishop had held while in Rome and in view of the newspaper stories which had been reported to him. Although he had shown Purcell's letter to Pius IX, he suggested that a personal submission by the archbishop to the Holy Father would be in order.[20] Purcell complied, in a second letter, sent on December 5 and addressed to the pope. Pius IX responded with a letter of thanks that the false newspaper reports had finally been corrected.[21]

The Archbishop of Cincinnati also maintained a correspondence, for a time at least, with two of the chief European minority bishops. On August 1, 1870, Archbishop Haynald of Kalocsa informed him that the decrees of the fourth session had not yet been published in Hungary, and that nothing would be done about them until the hierarchy of the country had had a chance to meet the following October. He also asked Purcell to explain to him the details of the temporal administration of the Church in the United States, which he said had been recommended as a model by Hungarian émigrés.[22] Purcell sent the required information, and when Haynald wrote to thank him for it in December, he added that the Hungarian hierarchy has as yet done nothing to implement the decrees of the council.[23] Purcell's second correspondent was Félix Dupanloup. On January 7, 1871, the Bishop of Orléans reported that he had heard twice from Bishop Hefele of Rottenburg, who told him that Rome

20 UND, Purcell Papers, Barnabò to Purcell, Rome, November 11, 1870.
21 *Ibid.*, Pius IX to Purcell, Rome, January 11, 1871.
22 AAC, Purcell Papers, Haynald to Purcell, Kalocsa, August 1, 1870.
23 UND, Purcell Papers, Haynald to Purcell, Kalocsa, December 28, 1870.

had not as yet made any demands on him, or on any of the German bishops, relative to the decrees of the council. Dupanloup wanted to know what the situation was in the United States. He told Purcell that he knew of only two French bishops who had been approached. In each case they had been warned by a lay emissary that if they did not give their explicit adhesion to *Pastor Aeternus* they would experience some difficulty in the processing of matrimonial dispensations. The French bishop asked Purcell to send him a report on the American scene.[24] There is no way of knowing if the correspondence continued, and no further reference to the council or to infallibility was found among the Purcell papers, so that his role in the assembly and its problems may be said to have closed with Pius IX's letter to him in January, 1871.

Just before the debates on infallibility began, the New York *Herald* singled out Augustin Vérot as one of the strongest opponents with whom the majority had to contend. The paper's Rome correspondent sent home the following dispatch:

> Rome has never felt such a rebuke as the American Bishops have administered, nor have the ears of the prelates heard such language as fell from the lips of Bishop Vérot of Savannah, and Archbishops Kenrick and Connolly. They uttered sentences that are new to the regions of Rome: it will be wisdom if they are profited by. 'These Americans do not care much about our pomp and splendour,' grimly remarked a 'ring bishop' (one without a diocese) the other day. 'Faith, they do not, nor for your climate and noisome smells either,' responded a bishop *in partibus*.[25]

That Vérot was among the most redoubtable minority fathers in the council has already been amply demonstrated. He was also one of the first opposition bishops to make his formal submission to the will of the majority. On July 25, 1870 he wrote to Bishop Fessler, the secretary of the council: "By this present letter I declare my adherence to the constitution promulgated in the fourth session."[26] Bishop Vérot arrived in Savannah on Oc-

24 *Ibid.*, Dupanloup to Purcell, Orléans, January 7, 1871.
25 New York *Herald*, May 11, 1870, in Beiser, p. 95.
26 Vérot to Fessler, Rome, July 25, 1870, in Mansi, LIII, 1010.

tober 7, enroute to his new Diocese of St. Augustine.[27] Two weeks later he spoke for the first time to the people of his new see. He promised them a series of lectures on the council, but he also wished at that first confrontation to explain his activities in Rome. He felt, he said, that such an explanation was due in justice, not only to himself, but to the faithful of the two dioceses which he had represented at the assembly.

The bishop's first point was similar to the remarks which we have seen were made by Quinlan and Gibbons. He declared that his opinions had been distorted in the press and that he had been made to seem a heretic. The approach taken by the press was, he acknowledged, particularly attributable to the secrecy which had been enforced concerning the council's proceedings, but the calumnies which he had suffered were nonetheless painful. Vérot went on to single out some of the more atrocious falsehoods which had been fastened to his name. He had been pictured as an ultraliberal who denied original sin, and who was hostile to the Church and to the Holy See, when in fact he had done nothing but use his episcopal prerogative to express his own sincere convictions. Infallibility, he continued, was a many-sided question. The pope was not infallible as a private teacher, or when he gave his opinion in matters of history, geography, or grammar. All this had been thrashed out at the council, and Vérot's difficulties had been explained to his satisfaction, so that he now accepted the definition which had been made.[28]

Bishop Vérot subsequently delivered four more lectures on the council, but efforts to find copies of them have been unsuccessful. Some indication of their content and tone can, however, be deduced from the fact that the new Bishop of Savannah, Ignatius Persico, O.F.M.Cap., an infallibilist during the council, congratulated him on the great good that they had accomplished.[29]

A final picture of the much maligned and certainly contro-

[27] Savannah *Republican,* October 7, 1870.
[28] *Catholic Mirror,* November 26, 1870. Vérot spoke in St. Augustine on October 23.
[29] ADSA, Vérot Papers, Persico to Vérot, Savannah, February 23, 1871.

versial French-born southern bishop comes from the pen of Bishop James Wood of Philadelphia, who visited Florida in 1875. He told the then Archbishop of Baltimore, James Roosevelt Bayley, that he had found their colleague of St. Augustine in fine spirits and working hard. His irrepressible sense of humor had not failed him, and he still loved to tell a joke. Apropos of the events of 1870, Wood informed the archbishop: "He [Vérot] did not discuss the infallibility nor allude to his peculiar '*Acta*' at the Vatican Council."[30] And on that note Augustin Vérot passes out of our story.

Bishop McQuaid made at least two public pronouncements on the council after his return to the United States. The first was in the form of a sermon preached in St. Patrick's Cathedral, Rochester, on Sunday, August 28, 1870. The bishop began by stating it as a fact that the pope was infallible when he spoke *ex cathedra* on matters of faith and morals, but he pointed out that the prerogative did not extend to other areas like business and politics. He also expressed his astonishment that those outside the Church should be more upset over this papal infallibility than they were over the infallibility of the Church.

McQuaid next turned to the actual discussions in the council, and his initial effort was to explain the disagreements which had occurred:

Now, you will say, there was a variety of opinions and much disputing among the Bishops with regard to this matter. Well, there was; and what was the point of the dispute, and upon what did they differ? It was whether, in making these definitions, the Holy Father should consult the Bishops, just as in the council he had consulted them.

Having thus established the point at issue, the bishop told his congregation that, while the text of the definition itself spoke of consultation of the bishops in the past, and while he thought that this would doubtless continue to be the procedure for the future, still it was not necessary. That was what had been decided by the fathers. A minority had held the contrary opinion, but their position was explicitly and clearly excluded, and it was

---

[30] AAB, 42–U–51, Wood to Bayley, Jacksonville, April 1, 1875.

now "by no means necessary on the part of the Sovereign Pontiff
to consult the Bishops before rendering an infallible definition
on faith and morals."

Bishop McQuaid's attempt to explain the need for the definition was somewhat less successful than his lucid exposition of
what infallibility meant, but he declared that it had been necessary because the pope had always to be on guard to deal with
assaults on the faith. He finished his sermon with a frank confession of his own opposition during the council and gave the
reason for it when he said: "I have now no difficulty in accepting the dogma, although to the last I opposed it; because somehow or other it was in my head that the Bishops ought to be
consulted." Finally he appealed to the faith of his hearers, and asserted that for the believing Catholic there should be no difficulty in accepting the decision of the Church in the matter.[31]
Two months later, the Bishop of Rochester repeated the closing
remarks of the August sermon in a speech which he delivered
at the laying of the cornerstone of St. Mary's Church in Auburn,
New York. On that occasion he phrased it in the following
words:

A year ago had I spoken to you, standing here, I would have given
you my views, my opinion about infallibility. I would have told you
that I thought the Pope and the Bishops were infallible. Today, I tell
you, on the authority of the Church, that the Pope alone is infallible.[32]

The always forthright Bernard McQuaid had spoken his mind
in Rome; he was equally forthright in his adherence to what
the council defined.

Before coming to the more complicated story of Peter Richard
Kenrick, mention may be made of two of the other principal
American opponents of the definition. Bishop Ignatius Mrak
must have sent his submission to Rome late in 1870 or early

---

[31] Frederick J. Zwierlein, *The Life and Letters of Bishop McQuaid*
(Rochester: 1962), II, 60–63.
[32] *Ibid.*, II, 63–4.

in 1871. On February 4, 1871, Cardinal Barnabò acknowledged its receipt.[33] It was not until eleven months later that Bishop Domenec of Pittsburgh forwarded his formal acceptance of *Pastor Aeternus*. He wrote to Barnabò on December 31, 1871. In his letter Domenec told the cardinal that from the moment of his return to his diocese he had publicly accepted the definition of infallibility and had preached in its defense to both Catholic and non-Catholic audiences. When the clergy of the diocese gathered to celebrate the silver jubilee of Pius IX's pontificate, the bishop had again made a public profession of his belief, and had signed with his own hand a letter to the pope in which explicit acceptance of the decrees of the council was stated. Domenec felt that these actions constituted sufficient proof of his orthodoxy, but he had recently been informed by Archbishop Spalding that the pope required of him a formal document testifying to his belief in infallibility. He therefore sent such an affirmation to Barnabò in the form of a confession of faith which laid special stress on the dogma declared in the fourth chapter of the constitution *de ecclesia*.[34]

Orestes Brownson later reprinted an example of the type of lecture to which Bishop Domenec had referred in his letter to the Prefect of Propaganda. Domenec began by declaring that the primary issue in the council had been the expediency or inexpediency of the definition. He illustrated this by what he said was his own position:

I was one of the prelates who was opposed, most vigorously, to this doctrine being defined. I signed my name to a petition which we addressed to the Holy Father, imploring and begging him not to allow this question to be introduced into the council, and I did all that I could to prevent its definition, but does this prove that I did not believe in the infallible teaching of the Roman Pontiff previous to its definition in the Vatican Council? Not at all. For many years, as professor in the Theological Seminary of Philadelphia, and elsewhere, I

[33] Mansi, LIII, 1053.

[34] Domenec to Barnabò, Pittsburgh, December 31, 1870, in Mansi, LIII, 1017–8.

313

taught the doctrine of infallibility as defined in the Vatican Council. In 1864, in a Pastoral Letter which I wrote to the faithful of my diocese, I taught and explained that doctrine . . . .

Now, the reason why I was so much opposed to the defining of this doctrine of infallibility was, because I feared that many of our dissenting brethren would make use of this definition to oppose the Catholic Church; that many who were favorably disposed towards the Catholic Church might change their views; that the infidel and unbeliever would rather scorn and ridicule, than to bring them to our faith and religion. I was convinced in my very heart and soul, that the definition would be rather detrimental than beneficial; that the enemies of the Church would give a wrong interpretation to its meaning; that through the pulpit and the press false statements would be conveyed to the minds of many, who thereby would be embittered against the Catholic Church, and the breach which separates Protestantism from Catholicity would become deeper and wider, and the chances of conversion, either among Protestants or infidels, would be far less. These being my convictions, I could not act otherwise than I did.[35]

Bishop Domenec's reasoning in the above-quoted paragraphs corresponded closely to the speech which he delivered at the fifty-second general congregation on June 3, in which he spoke of the harm that would result from the definition. However, he did refer to papal infallibility in June, 1870, as a "new dogma," and he candidly confessed at that time that he and many other American bishops had consistently preached that the infallibility of the pope was not an article of faith. This was one of his principal objections to its definition by the council, an objection which, as we have seen, he expressed not only in the council hall, but also, with some vehemence, in private conversation with Father Henri Icard.[36] This evidence casts some doubt on Domenec's later assertion that he had always and consistently upheld the doctrine. There was, however, no doubt about his acceptance of the dogma once it had been defined.

The post-conciliar involvement of Archbishop Kenrick with

[35] Henry F. Brownson (ed.), *The Works of Orestes A. Brownson* (Detroit, 1905), XIII, 413–20. Orestes Brownson originally used Domenec's lecture in an article which appeared in his *Quarterly Review* for July, 1873.

[36] Mansi, LII, 425–7; ASS, Icard Journal, pp. 255–6.

the issues which had been raised by the council was considerably more varied that that of any of his American colleagues. His prominence in the international committee of the minority and the two pamphlets which he had had published at Naples earned him more than the usual attention from the Roman Curia, an attention that does not seem to have perturbed the archbishop unduly, although it was a source of worry for his Vicar-General, Father Patrick J. Ryan.

The first indication that Kenrick's actions in Rome would not be allowed to pass unnoticed came in a letter from a Sulpician priest, Jean-Baptiste Larne, who told Father Icard from Rome on July 20, 1870, that a commission of archbishops had been appointed to examine the writings of the Archbishop of St. Louis. Larne had been unable to find out anything about the meetings of the commission, but he felt sure that Kenrick would be required to accept the definitions of the council in writing and also to disavow certain propositions contained in his pamphlets.[37]

The archbishop was still traveling in Europe when the first Roman communication on the subject reached the United States. It was in the form of a letter, dated October 15, 1870, from Cardinal Filippo de Angelis and was sent, not directly to St. Louis, but to one of the suffragan bishops of the province, who was instructed to pass it on to his metropolitan. De Angelis informed Kenrick that his *Concio* had been reviewed by the Sacred Congregation of the Index and that it had been condemned as containing grave errors. However, out of personal consideration, the condemnation had not been published, and the archbishop was invited to prevent such publication by an explicit acceptance of the decrees of the council.[38]

For unexplained reasons, Cardinal de Angelis' message was

[37] ASS, Icard Papers, Larne to Icard, Rome, July 20, 1870
[38] Kenrick to Acton, St. Louis, March 29, 1871, in Johann Friedrich von Schulte, *Der Altkatholicismus; Geschichte seiner Entwicklung, inneren Gestaltung und rechtlichen Stellung in Deutschland* (Giessen: 1887), p. 267. See also Kenrick to de Angelis, St. Louis, March 28, 1871, in Mansi, LIII, 955.

not given to Kenrick until March 28, 1871.[39] In the meantime, further action had been taken in Rome. A cardinalitial commission had been set up in October, 1870, to look into matters connected with the council. At the third meeting of this commission, which was held on October 26, a resolution was passed to write to Kenrick, "according to the mind of the Sacred Congregation of the Index, to induce him to retract the errors contained in his *Concio habenda et* [*sic*] *non habita*," with the threat that if he did not do so the pertinent decree of condemnation would be published.[40] A copy of this letter, if it was written, has not been found.

While Archbishop Kenrick was making a leisurely journey home, his future was a matter of some speculation in the United States. Father Ryan, the St. Louis vicar-general, wrote to Purcell on September 14:

> I expect our Archbishop home late in October. I think he will find *no difficulty* in getting permission to absent himself from the remaining sessions of the Council! How I wish to speak with Yr. Grace on the history of these months in Rome. I hope however all will now be as calm as before.[41]

Three weeks later, Ryan was no better informed as to his ordinary's plans, although he had heard from him. He told Purcell:

> I had a note from our Archbishop lately. He says little of the dogma, but now that the Church has recd. it, I cannot see that even any defects in the organization of the Council &c. could justify refusal to accept it.[42]

The vicar-general of St. Louis was not the only one who was following with interest the fortunes of Archbishop Kenrick. Bishop William McCloskey of Louisville sent two inquiries on the subject to Rome within a space of nine days in the fall of 1870. On September 23, he wrote his Benedictine friend, Ber-

---

39 Mansi, LIII, 955.
40 Betti, p. 205, quoting from the diary of Cardinal Luigi Bilio.
41 AAC, Purcell Papers, Ryan to Purcell, St. Louis, September 14, 1870.
42 *Ibid.*, Ryan to Purcell, St. Louis, October 5, 1870.

nard Smith: "Is there any likelihood of action being taken in the case of St. Louis—we have disagreeable rumours, but I give them no credit."[43] A week later, the Bishop of Louisville penned another note to Smith, in which he reported: "No news as yet of Dr. Kenrick. Do not fail to let me know if there is any trouble in that quarter."[44] One last interested observer was Archbishop Spalding, who remarked to Cardinal Cullen in mid-October: "I have not yet heard from AB of St. Louis, & I have my apprehensions on the subject, but trust it may all go right & without further scandal."[45]

The object of all this concern was in the meantime traveling in Spain. Acton met him in Brussels in the late fall, and sent the following account to Döllinger:

Kenrick had made a trip to Spain, in order not to spend the first difficult times among his flock, and in consequence lost all contact with inquisitive clerics. He showed me an unlooked for confidence. He has remained unchanged, and gave his consent to the reprinting of his writings with the avowal that he took back not a word of them. I have half committed myself to publish the Concio in England. He is firm in his opinion that the council must first be completed before its decrees can oblige. The decrees of Basle were confirmed and published and then afterwards the council was held to be not ecumenical. It is incorrect, as Hecker reported, that Kenrick protested against the exclusion of the procurators at the very beginning. He had then by anticipation already taken the view that the whole affair was a sad comedy. As for the question of what he will do, he has no plans. He will attempt nothing directly against the ecumenicity of the council. He will most probably keep silent, but will retract nothing, will not teach the dogma and will not believe it. He is prepared to be deposed, but says that this does not save him, since even as a layman he could not submit, and still less as a deposed archbishop.

Kenrick gives the impression of great strength and peace. He was very pleased with my dispatches. Now he has already arrived in America. He wrote me, on passing through London, a very friendly farewell letter.[46]

1870.

[43] AASP, Smith Papers, McCloskey to Smith, Louisville, September 23, 1870.
[44] *Ibid.,* McCloskey to Smith, Louisville, October 1, 1870.
[45] AAD, Cullen Papers, Spalding to Cullen, Malines, October 16, 1870.
[46] Conzemius Transcripts, Acton to Döllinger, Aldenham, December 23,

It is not easy to distinguish in Acton's letter between Kenrick's feelings and what the English lord would have liked him to think, but the fact that the archbishop deliberately delayed his return to St. Louis argues to the possibility that during the summer and fall of 1870 he underwent something of a *crise de conscience* on the subject of infallibility. There is no doubt at all that he was deeply disturbed by what had happened at the council and it is by no means beyond belief that when he met Acton in Brussels he did actually give voice to some of the melancholy thoughts which the Englishman reported to Döllinger. No letters from Kenrick for the period have been found, and in their absence all conclusions about his true state of mind must necessarily be conjectural. The first evidence we have of the line which he intended to take was not forthcoming until after he had returned to his diocese, and it came in the form of his response to an address of welcome by Father Ryan.

A formal reception of the archbishop in St. Louis had been organized for Monday, January 2, and it was held in St. John's Church. The vicar-general spoke for the clergy and faithful of the archdiocese, and then Archbishop Kenrick rose to respond. The pertinent passages of his speech read as follows:

With regard to that portion of the address [of Father Ryan] that refers to my course in the Vatican Council, I will state briefly the motives of my action, and the motive of my entire and unreserved submission to the definition emanating from that authority.

Up until the very period of the assembling of that Council, I held as a theological opinion what that Council has declared to be an article of Christian faith; and yet I was opposed, most strongly opposed, to the definition. I knew that the misconceptions of its real character would be an obstacle in the way of the diffusion of Catholic truth. At least I thought so. I feared in certain parts of Europe, especially, that such a definition might lead to the danger of schism in the Church; and on more closely examining the question itself, in its intrinsic evidence, I was not convinced of the conclusiveness of the arguments by which it was sustained, or of its compatibility with certain well ascertained facts of ecclesiastical history which rose up strongly before my mind. The motive of my submission is simply and singly the authority of the

318

Catholic Church. That submission is a most reasonable obedience, because of the necessity of obeying and following an authority established by God; and having the guaranty of our Divine Saviour's perpetual assistance is in itself evidence, and cannot be gainsayed by anyone who professes to recognize Jesus Christ as his Saviour and his God.

Simply and singly on that authority I yield obedience and full and unreserved submission to the definition concerning the character of which there can be no doubt as emanating from the Council, and subsequently accepted by the greater part even of those who were in the minority on that occasion. In yielding this submission, I say to the Church in the words of Peter and Paul: 'To whom, O, Holy Mother, shall we go but to Thee? Thou hast the words of eternal life; and we have believed and have known that Thou art the Pillar and the Ground of Truth.[47]

Of this statement, the *Western Watchman* commented:

The shortest, simplest, best vindication of the late dogma the people of America have yet heard was uttered by the Archbishop of St. Louis on the occasion of his late canonical reception. His clear, open avowal of his unhesitating belief in the dogma, and his concise and pertinent statement of his reasons for that belief, have the true catholic ring, and breathe the ancient, undying spirit of the catholic faith. 'I believe because the Church has said it.' Here we have said in a few words, what volumes could not say more clearly, more satisfactorily or more forcibly declare.[48]

Archbishop Kenrick had obviously done a great deal of soul-searching during his long sojourn in Europe. His meditations had not solved the historical problem which had perplexed him in the course of the debates, but he had reconciled himself to the dogma on the highest of motives, that of faith. This was something that would not be easily understood by those whose own faith was not of the same caliber as his. He made only the barest mention in the speech of another motive for his submission when he remarked that the definition had been generally accepted by the Church. This was a facet of his thinking which, as will be seen, was to cause further woe. But for the time being

[47] John J. O'Shea, *The Two Kenricks* (Philadelphia: 1904), pp. 333–4; *Western Watchman*, January 7, 1871.
[48] *Western Watchman*, January 14, 1871.

all was serene in St. Louis, and would remain so until the anonymous suffragan bishop brought Kenrick de Angelis' letter in late March.

One of the archbishop's first acts after reaching St. Louis was to write to Cardinal Barnabò. His message was brief: "Having returned home at the end of the past year, I indicated in a public meeting that I adhere to what was done in the fourth session of the Vatican Council."[49] Not until two months later did he express himself again on the subject, but in Europe his name was still prominent in the correspondence of Acton and Döllinger. On February 2, the Englishman told his mentor that Bishop Clifford of Clifton did not believe in the doctrine of infallibility and added that this was also his impression of the attitude of Kenrick. He had consulted his notes on their conversation in Brussels, and summarized that discussion once again for Döllinger's benefit. According to Acton, the archbishop had said that he would not resign because nothing would be accomplished by it. For the sake of peace, he had decided to write nothing against the council. He had, Acton reported, never believed that anything good would come of the council and associated himself with a statement attributed to Bishop Hefele, that the whole affair was a compound of lies. On the other hand, Kenrick was represented as having declared that he would not take back a word of what he had written, not even the statement that the council could never define papal infallibility as a dogma. Instead he had been happy to hear that his conciliar *acta* were to be published. In this connection he had reminded Acton of the observations which he had submitted and had sent him a copy of the *Concio,* with the request that the Englishman correct the typographical errors.

Acton then turned to the statement which Kenrick had made in St. Louis. He interpreted it as a declaration that the archbishop did not intend to attack the council, but not as a declaration that the assembly had been properly run or that its teaching

[49] Kenrick to Barnabò, January 13, 1871, in Mansi, LIII, 955.

was true. The American prelate had simply withdrawn from the struggle, he thought, but this did not imply his belief in the dogma. "I quite see," the letter continued, "that this is very dangerous and not completely honest, that he so inevitably misleads the people, but I do not believe that it is heresy, and make a great distinction between this tune and unqualified acceptance, as at Fulda." Acton concluded by telling Döllinger that but for his inspiration every Catholic in the world would give way as had Kenrick.[50] Rather than try to show how Acton's prejudice against the definition led him to misinterpret Kenrick's intentions, we will shortly let the archbishop speak for himself on the subject. At about the same time as he finally received the letter from de Angelis, he also had a letter from the English lord which asked him to explain his position in the light of the January 2 address. He did so on March 29, 1871, in a letter which will bear extensive quotation.

Archbishop Kenrick began his answer to Acton by admitting that it was only natural that news of his submission had raised questions in his correspondent's mind. He said that he was happy to have the occasion to answer those questions. First he gave his reasons for breaking the silence which he had intended to keep:

On my return from Europe I found it absolutely impossible to remain silent. My opposition in the Council had become a matter of notoriety, and the Archbishop of Cincinnati and myself were made objects of attack on the part of some of our catholic papers. Sufficient time seems to have elapsed to allow the catholic world to decide; whether or not the decrees of the Council were to be accepted. The greater number of Bishops in minority had signified their assent to them. Among other names published in one of the Brussels papers I read with surprise that of Mgr. Maret. Although some still held out, they were so few that hesitancy to declare my submission would have the appearance of rejecting the authority of the Church. This I never

---

[50] Conzemius Transcripts, Acton to Döllinger, Aldenham, February 2, 1871. Acton spoke of Kenrick having expressed himself in a pastoral letter. The archbishop issued no such letter, as he later told his English correspondent.

321

intended to do. I could not defend the Council or its action; but I always professed that the acceptance of either by the Church would supply its deficiency. I accordingly made up my mind to submit to what appeared inevitable, unless I was prepared to separate myself at least in the judgment of most Catholics.

Kenrick then took up the subject of his reply to the address of the clergy on January 2. He sent a text of his speech on that occasion to Acton, and provided him with an exegesis of its most salient feature, the explanation of his reason for accepting the definition:

> You will perceive that I gave as the motive of my submission 'simply and singly' the authority of the Church, by which I was well understood to mean, that the act was one of pure obedience, and was not grounded on the removal of my motives of opposition to the decrees, as referred to in my reply and set forth in my pamphlets. I submitted most reservedly . . . taking the words of the decrees in this strict and literal signification.

The archbishop next told Acton of the letter from Cardinal de Angelis, which he said he had received only on March 28. In answer to the cardinal's demand that he retract what he had said in the Concio, he had simply referred de Angelis to the letter which he had written to Barnabò on January 13. However, he was not sure that this would be sufficient, as he had heard from Rome that when the Rector of the American College told the pope that the Archbishop of St. Louis had made his submission, Pius IX was reported to have replied: "Still he must retract those pamphlets published at Naples." This Kenrick declared he would never do. He also hastened to disabuse Acton of any possible suspicion that his submission had been actuated by a desire to stand well with the Roman authorities. Despite the urging of Cardinal Barnabò, Archbishop Alemany, and of one of his suffragan bishops, he had steadfastly refused to write a pastoral letter on the council. Neither had he acted upon another suggestion of Barnabò, namely that he send a personal letter to the pope. Finally, he informed his English friend: "I have also refused to take part in the demonstrations which have been made generally in the U. States in favour of the Temporal Power; and my name is not found among those, which, in this city, prepared and sent to Rome an address to the Pope on the occasion of the Italian occupation of his territory."

Kenrick then explained the process by which he had arrived at his present state of mind:

> I reconciled myself intellectually to submission by applying Father Newman's theory of development to the case in point. The Pontifical authority as at present exercised is so different from what it appears to have been in the early Church, that it can only be supposed identical in substance by allowing a process of doctrinal development. This principle removed Newman's great difficulty and convinced him that, notwithstanding the difference, he might and should become a Catholic. I thought that it might justify me in remaining one.

But despite the intellectual submission which he had made, Kenrick told Acton that he would never attempt to prove the doctrine of papal infallibility from Scripture or tradition, and that he would leave to others the task of showing its compatibility with the facts of ecclesiastical history.

In the last section of his letter, the archbishop discussed his assertion in the *Concio* to the effect that papal infallibility could not become an article of faith, even by definition of a council:

> My statement . . . resolves itself into two others: namely that what is not already a doctrine of faith cannot be made so by a Conciliar definition; and that Papal Infallibility, anterior to the definition was not a doctrine of faith. The first of those propositions is undeniable. The second, it appears, must be given up.

Kenrick went on to say that he was willing to acknowledge that he had been mistaken in his estimate of the acceptance of the second proposition, even in English-speaking countries. He was obviously not completely happy in his new-found knowledge, and he complained that since the Council of Trent the relationship between pope and Church had become analogous to that which obtained between king and State in the France of Louis

XIV. The fate of the teaching authority of bishops within this framework worried him, and he confessed that Maret's attempted reconciliation of the two had been unsatisfactory. He saw his own situation as a case in point. Because he had had the temerity to criticize what he thought were weak arguments for infallibility and a proof for the primacy drawn from what he considered metaphorical language, he had been convicted by the Congregation of the Index, with the approval of the pope, of having taught grave errors and was liable to have his name "gibbeted before the world as an unsound Divine." "It is evident," he concluded, "that there can be no liberty in future sessions of the Council, with this example to warn Bishops that they must not handle roughly the delicate matters on which they have to decide."[51]

It is not easy to pass judgment on this letter of Kenrick to Acton. George Gordon Coulton, no friend of the Catholic Church, quoted with approval the opinion of an Anglican canon, W. J. Sparrow-Simpson, who declared: "The records of intellectual servitude present few more painful accounts than this." A consideration of Simpson's criticism will perhaps throw Kenrick's positive position into sharper relief. The canon found the letter bristling with "intellectual if not moral inconsistencies," and pointed some of them out:

[Kenrick] thinks acceptance by the Church will redeem the doctrine from conciliar defects: but the essence of the doctrine is Infallibility apart from the Church's consent. As Bishop he is a witness to the Faith: yet he observes in silence and registers one by one the submission of other Bishops. He accepts what he will not proclaim and will not defend. Meanwhile the facts of history continue, as before, demonstrably irreconcilable with the New Decree. The sole virtue by which everything else is supposed to be redeemed is the virtue of submission.[52]

[51] Schulte, pp. 267–70. The letter as printed by Schulte is in somewhat mangled English. It has been quoted as it appears there, except for correction of obvious misspellings. See also Rothensteiner, *History*, II, 313–7.
[52] Coulton, pp. 197–8. The quotation, given without page reference, is from W. J. Sparrow-Simpson, *Roman Catholic Opposition to Papal Infallibility* (London: 1909).

Simpson, of course, refused to accept Kenrick's appeal to the notion of the development of dogma. He also confused issues. The Archbishop of St. Louis did proclaim the dogma, publicly and in his cathedral city, on January 2, 1871. The issuance of a pastoral letter or subsequent preaching on the subject did not pertain to the substantial question of proclamation. Kenrick not only proclaimed the dogma, but he defended it, and gave as his motive for so doing the obedience of faith. Faith is not based on historical evidence. Kenrick saw his act of submission based on faith as a supremely intelligent act; Simpson rejected the very idea of such an act. Kenrick, moreover, never asserted that the facts of history were objectively irreconcilable with the "New Decree." He did declare that he would leave it to others to establish that reconciliation. While this might indicate subjective pique, it did not deny objective possibility. The one serious doubt left by the letter is caused by the archbishop's appeal to acceptance by the Church as a motive for his own adherence to the definition.

As a support to his own faith, Kenrick was certainly entitled to look to the opinions of others, and particularly of the fathers of the council. If this was what he meant when he wrote to Acton, or when he made a similar statement during his St. Louis address, there can be no quarrel with his orthodoxy on that score. But if, as seems more likely, the archbishop meant to appeal to the consent of the Church as a condition of his acceptance of the definition, he was placed in the absurd position of demanding such consent for the dogmatic validity of an infallible decree, promulgated by the pope with the approval of the council, which had as one of its main points the exclusion of the necessity of any such consent. It may be that Kenrick's thought on the point was confused, as was that of Purcell, but in any event he made it otherwise amply clear that he intended to receive the dogma as it was defined on July 18, and therefore his subjective acceptance of the definition was beyond question.

Although the assurances which he had given had satisfied the Roman authorities, so that no further action was taken with regard to the condemnation of his pamphlets, certain strains did develop in the relationship between the Archbishop of St. Louis and the Holy See. On June 25, 1871, the twenty-fifth anniversary of Pius IX's pontificate was celebrated in St. Louis with a four-mile-long procession of Catholic societies and a general illumination of the city. The archbishop was out of town.[53] Three months later, Father Patrick Ryan wrote to explain the incident to Bernard Smith in Rome. The vicar-general claimed that the archbishop had always opposed parades for any occasions other than national events, and that he would have preferred some other means of celebrating the papal jubilee. Ryan had feared to lose his influence with Kenrick by opposing him openly—an influence which he declared had always been employed "for the restoration of cordial feelings with Rome"—and so he had arranged a compromise whereby the affair was not prohibited and was announced in the churches. The archbishop had allowed a collection for the Holy Father, and his vicars-general had signed an address of sympathy over the loss of the temporal power. The ordinary had been absent at the time, but Ryan assured Smith that he and the other vicar-general, Henry Muehlsiepen, would never have put their names to the letter without his approval. Lastly, he commented, Kenrick had "felt sorely some actions of the Propaganda," but he closed with the optimistic hope that such irritations would soon cease, and that "all will yet be, as it should be, in his relation with that Sacred Congregation."[54] With this letter the tale of Peter Richard Kenrick and the First Vatican Council came to a close.

The story of the events of July, of the summer sessions, and of the return of the bishops to the United States completes the narrative of American participation in the council. Other problems—reconstruction in the South and steadily increasing immi-

<hr>

[53] Rothensteiner, *History*, II, 316–7.

[54] AASP, Smith Papers, Ryan to Smith, St. Louis, September 15, 1871.

gration in the North—occupied the attention of the American Church. The bishops of the United States had made their contribution to the twentieth ecumenical council, and it was far from insignificant. It now remains only to summarize and evaluate that contribution.

Epilogue

THE First Vatican Council transported the great majority of the bishops of the United States into a world that was wholly new to them. They were missionary pastors, largely taken up in their home dioceses with problems of day-to-day administration and with the organization of the Church in an environment that was vastly different from anything that their colleagues in ancient European sees knew. It was inevitable that they should at first seem to be inexperienced, perhaps naïve. European commentators judged them by the standards of the Old World and were surprised that the interests and outlook of the Americans did not fit the pattern. When the council was over, that attitude had changed to some extent. Men of the stamp of Kenrick and Vérot and Amat and others were not easily forgotten, even if they were not yet fully understood or appreciated. Spalding emerged from the sessions as the trusted associate of Cullen, Dechamps, and Manning, but the year's events had also revealed that he could not be considered the leader of the American Church as was John Carroll before him or James Gibbons after him. Many of the other bishops made little or no impact in Rome, but all of them brought back to the United States an increased awareness of the Church Universal that was to have an important influence in the crucial years ahead.

The role of their early theological formation in shaping the attitude of certain of the American bishops at the council has been exaggerated. It has been suggested that prelates like Kenrick, Purcell, Domenec, and Vérot imported Gallican leanings into the United States, and that these ideas, learned in the seminaries of France and Ireland, provided sufficient explanation for the American opposition to a definition of papal infallibility.[1] Undoubtedly, there was some such influence, and it tended to make itself manifest as some of the Americans elaborated their reasons for opposition. Vérot freely associated himself with the Gallicans, and it would be hard to deny an equation between Gallicanism and views propounded by Kenrick. The "importation theory" is more difficult to sustain in the case of McQuaid, who felt that the consent of the episcopal college was needed for an infallible proclamation. He had been educated in Canada and in the United States. The point that needs to be made is that it would be a mistake to ignore another—and, in the opinion of this writer—more fundamental reason for the stand of the minority bishops from the United States. It was a reason which they shared with their brethren who followed Spalding, and, according to the testimony of Gibbons, with the majority of their fellow American bishops. They opposed the definition on the very pragmatic grounds that it would worsen relations between Catholics and the dominant Protestant majority of their homeland. Not all the Americans moved from this pragmatic opposition into a theoretical opposition. In the final analysis, only a handful did so. The basic American objection to the definition was a practical one.[2]

Another point is a corollary of the preceding. When the Americans arrived in Europe, they found the Church divided into liberal and conservative factions. Liberalism and conservatism were doctrinaire notions to the European mind. The situation was further confused by accusations that liberal Catholics were

[1] See, for example, the comments of Roger Aubert in M. Nédoncelle et al., *L'Ecclésiologie au XIXe Siècle* (Paris: 1960), p. 375, and Campana, II, 749–61.

[2] See the explanation given of the reasons for opposition to the definition by Bishops Gibbons and Lynch, "The First Oecumenical Council of the Vatican," *Catholic World*, XI (September, 1870), 842. They distinguished between genuine Gallicans, those who believed in the doctrine, but found the evidence of tradition insufficiently clear, and inopportunists. The last category, they declared, was most numerous.

trying to incorporate the principles of the French Revolution into the Church. Americans had had their own revolution and out of it had forged a constitution that granted religious liberty to all. By and large, they were satisfied with what was again a pragmatic solution, and they had very little interest in or comprehension of European theorizing on the subject of Church and State. Unfortunately, they had never evolved a theory from their own adjustment, although, as we have seen, the germ of such a theory was present. The Church in the United States was free to carry on its apostolate. Difficulties might arise from time to time, but on the whole the constitutional guarantees were respected. The almost entirely different circumstances in this regard of the Church in Europe and the Church in America were little appreciated by the European prelates at the council. Most of them would scarcely have understood James Corcoran's comments about the *schema* on Church-State relations and religious toleration if they had known of them.[3] They were treated to a republican oration by Purcell, but the question never came formally before the council, and so what might have been a distinctively American contribution was never made.

There is one last characteristic of American participation that must be mentioned. In almost every speech given by a bishop from the United States, a pronounced pastoral note was present. On occasion they demonstrated a more than casual acquaintance with various branches of theology, both speculative and positive, but they were primarily pastors. Their opposition to the definition of infallibility was prompted by reasons that were basically pastoral. They objected to the tendency to turn dogmatic decrees into theological treatises and called for succinct statements of the faith to be believed. In the discussion on the catechism they showed an acute consciousness of the needs of their people. They represented a young Church, a Church with its own peculiar problems, and they demonstrated their awareness of those problems. No one would claim that the bishops of

[3] Hennesey, "James A. Corcoran's mission to Rome," pp. 176–80.

330

the United States played a decisive role in the First Vatican Council, or even that they played a major role, but they did make their contribution to its discussions, both in and out of the council hall. At the council, the American bishops became aware of Europe's problems and Europe became aware of the American Church. For the first time, representatives of the New World attended an ecumenical council. A new era in the history of the Church had begun.

Index

Ginoulhiac, Jacques, 92, 152, 180, 181
Gladstone, William Ewart, 9, 131
Goesbriand, Louis de, 38, 49, 91, 159, 169, 185, 202, 221, 230, 243, 274, 282
Goold, James, 237, 238, 239
Grace, Thomas L., 24
Granderath, Theodor, 44, 64, 75, 144, 145
Grant, Thomas, 50
Gratry, Auguste-Alphonse, 96, 129, 176, 179
Gregory the Great, St., 222, 258
Guéranger, Prosper, 129
Guibert, Archbishop, 70
Guidi, Filippo, 134, 194
Guierry, Edmond, 190

Hailandière, Celestin de la, 25, 124
Harlay de Champvallon, François de, 241
Haynald, Lajos, 46, 70, 80, 92, 94–95, 114, 176, 180, 181, 243, 279, 308
Healy, Sherwood, 184, 185
Hecker, Isaac, 24, 27, 29, 30, 31, 46, 53, 54, 56, 83, 92, 93, 105, 112, 113, 117, 122, 317
Hefele, Karl Joseph von, 30, 107, 167, 181, 243, 260, 308, 320
Heiss, Michael, 38, 44, 48, 78, 88, 89, 91, 106, 159, 169, 202, 230, 274, 282
Hennessy, John, 38, 101, 159, 169
Henni, John M., 38, 101, 159, 169, 229, 274, 282

Hermes, Georg, 162, 163, 164, 165
Hewit, Augustine F., 117
Hogan, John J., 38, 101, 103, 104, 125, 159, 231
Honorius I, 86, 177, 188, 191, 192, 268
Hughes, John, 84, 242

Icard, Henri, 29, 47, 85, 95, 105, 110, 113, 132, 173, 175, 179, 201, 202, 314, 315
Ireland, John, 24, 28, 54

Jacobini, Angelo, 33
Jacobini, Luigi, 33, 38
Janus, 116; see also Döllinger, Johann
John the Divine, St., 144
John XXII, 192
John XXIII, 12
Jussef, Grégoire, 173

Keiley, Benjamin, 282
Kenrick, Francis P., 205–206, 210–211, 213, 227, 230, 233, 242–243, 244, 245, 246, 263
Kenrick, Peter Richard, 12, 29, 38, 39, 40, 42, 46, 49, 55, 56, 57, 58, 59, 60, 61, 62, 65, 71, 76, 80, 83, 92, 101, 104, 106, 110, 111, 119, 120, 124, 143, 144, 145, 146, 148, 155, 157, 158, 159, 161, 166, 169, 174, 175, 177, 178, 180, 181, 182, 194, 196–200, 205–207, 212, 213, 216, 218, 229, 231–232, 246–250, 256, 261, 274, 279, 282, 285, 299, 303, 309, 312, 314–329

336

339